THE YANKS ARE COMING

THE YANKS ARE COMING

AMERICAN IMMIGRATION TO AUSTRALIA

DENNIS LAURENCE CUDDY

Published by
R & E Research Associates, Incorporated

Published by
R & E Research Associates, Inc.
4843 Mission Street
San Francisco, California 94112

Publishers

Robert D. Reed and Adam S. Eterovich

Dedicated to

JOSEPH L. and PEGGY SHANNON CUDDY

to

AMERICA'S THIRD CENTURY

accent on peace and
the humanities

and to

CAROLINE CHISHOLM, "THE EMIGRANTS' FRIEND"

who did more than any
other person to help
individuals and fami-
lies settle Australia

iii

TABLE OF CONTENTS

vi

LIST OF TABLES

ACKNOWLEDGMENTS

Without the assistance and advice of many individuals, this work would not have been possible. I would first like to thank Drs. Robert Moats Miller, George Mowry, Gillian Cell, Elisha Douglass, Samuel Wells, Frank Klingberg, Shepard Jones and Andrew Scott at the University of North Carolina as well as Dr. William Clifford at North Carolina State University. In addition, invaluable assistance was given by other individuals at the University of North Carolina who assisted in the design or interpretation of this writer's survey questionnaire or the computer programming or analysis of the questionnaire responses, including Dr. Eugene Shaw, Dr. N. Krishnan Namboordiri, Angell Beza, Morse Kalt and the staff at the Computer Center. In Australia, I am grateful to Drs. Charles A. Price and Hector Kinloch of the Australian National University, Dr. Norman Harper of the University of Melbourne and Dr. Herb Qualls of James Cook University, Townsville, Queensland, for their encouragement, help and advice.

This work also would have been quite incomplete, perhaps impossible, without the assistance of those American migrants who responded to my questionnaire and without the extensive help rendered by the many individual Australians and Americans in both countries, including those in the Australian-American Associations and Societies as well as the editors of many Australian newspapers. Sincere appreciation is extended to the officials of the Australian and American Embassies and Consulates, especially to Charles L. Waterman, D. S. Waddell and Bruce McPhail, for their interest and cooperation, in addition to other officers of government agencies in both nations including those in the formerly titled Department of Immigration in Australia as well as those in the Office of the Prime Minister, the Department of Social Security, the Treasury, the Commonwealth Archives Office, the Commissioner of Taxation, the National Library and the Department of Labor in Australia.

Furthermore, I would like to thank the Australian Government for permission to reprint all of the Australian government material included in this work; CBS News for permission to quote from Eric Sevareid's "Commentary" on September 8, 1975; Newsweeks, Inc. for permission to reprint the map and chart in Appendix X; and Sun Books Pty., Ltd. for permission to reprint the material included in Appendixes XII and XIII.

INTRODUCTION

Though this work will deal for the most part with contemporary American immigration to Australia, it is not simply a demographic study but also a critical social commentary on life in both countries today. Sharing in part common historical experiences, yet knowing in part quite different historical experiences, since World War II both the United States and Australia are open to critical social commentary.

In a comparative sense, both nations have followed a parallel course of cultural evolution for approximately two centuries now. Not only have the two nations had historical counterparts such as American Indians and Australian Aborigines, famous explorers, ranchers and squatters, cowboys and jackeroos and the outlaws Jesse James and Ned Kelly, but there have also been significant historical connections. In fact, Australia was first settled in 1788 by convicts from Great Britain, because America could no longer be used as a repository for those who had crowded the British goals. After that point, the two nations would share the common experiences of gold rushes, territorial expansions, the rise of the middle class and unions, economic depressions, the effects of third political parties, two world wars, military alliances, the Vietnam War and inhabitation by a large number of immigrants.

The close ties between the two nations were greatly evidenced throughout the year of the United States bicentennial during which Australia made numerous contributions to foster an enhanced understanding between Americans and Australians. Australia's main contribution to the bicentennial celebrations was the inauguration of a Chair in Australian Studies at Harvard University. Other major contributions during the historic period included the commissioning of Australian author Norman Bartlett to write a book, <u>Australia and America Through 200 Years</u>, to provide an enduring record of the relationships between the two countries; touring historical exhibitions entitled "The Fourth Part of the World" and "The Art of the First Australians"; awarding of special Bicentennial Fellowships; the gift of a colony of koalas to the San Diego Zoo in California; a Radio Exchange Weekend called "Friends Across the Pacific" involving some seventy-five stations in the two countries; a month-long Festival sponsored by the Australian-American Association; and various other exchanges in the areas of culture, entertainment and sports. Today Australia and the United States remain closely united under the ANZUS defense treaty, in trade agreements resulting in billions of dollars of sales and purchases for both nations, in sister city and exchange programs, and in scientific

xi

expeditions and space exploration.

American influence on Australia over the years has been extensive. One may see it today in advertising, brand name products, supermarkets, hotel and motel chains, entertainment, sports, art, clothing, speech, films, television, automobiles and even in quick-eat places in Australia. There is, for example, a Colonel Sanders chicken stand in every major city and in most large towns. At least one American, Perry Crosswhite, who is now an Australian citizen, has played for the Australian Olympic basketball team. Furthermore, many large American firms have become established in the shining antipodean continent, bringing with them tremendous know-how and billions of dollars which have helped make Australia the advanced nation it is.

The influence has not been strictly one way, for Australia has made many new and varied contributions to the United States. In politics, America adopted the "Australian ballot" in the 1890s and in sports we learned the "Australian crawl" swimming stroke in the 1920s. Americans now find popular the green-skinned Granny Smith apple, television shows like "Skippy," Australian beer and Australian beef. The Bonanza chain, for instance, sells Australian steaks almost exclusively.[1]

Each nation has indeed contributed to the other; and because they both have a great deal in common via their culture, traditions, language and urbanized lifestyles, perhaps it should be of little surprise that many Americans, even some of considerable note, have expressed an interest in living "Down Under" in Australia. Former President Lyndon Johnson, for example, remarked that next to being President of the United States he would rather be Ambassador to Australia more than anything else; and a Gallup survey revealed that "more than five million Americans would like to move to Australia"--that would be enough to increase that nations' population by over 35 percent![2]

Regarding the statistics used in analyzing the subject of American immigration to Australia, three primary sources were utilized. First, to form the historical basis from which judgments about the progress of the migration could be made, the Australian Immigration: Consolidated Statistics were very helpful. Also of much assistance was the only major survey previously conducted of American migrants by the Australian government, as far as this writer can determine. In 1969 the Surveys Section of the Australian Department of Immigration interviewed 129 recently arrived settlers, and one year later it reinterviewed 54, as many of the original 129 who then could be reached, concerning matters of employment, accommodation and social

experiences, among other topics.[3] Finally, this writer used
the information obtained from his own original questionnaire
survey conducted via mail in 1974-1975 (Appendix I). To this
person's knowledge, this survey of 200 American migrants to
Australia and the more than 1,100 pages of computer tabulations
and cross-tabulations of their responses are the most extensive
conducted to date by any individual or even by the Australian
or American governments. Survey respondents were contacted by
way of Australian-American Associations and Societies, the
American Embassy and Consulates Australia, American migrants as
well as individual Australians in Australia, though most were
contacted through publication of an open "letter to the editor"
addressed to American migrants in many Australian newspapers.
The survey sample obtained appears to be quite representative
concerning most of the basic categories covered, such as age,
sex, marital status, whether they obtained financial assistance
from the Australian government for their passage, areas of
America from which the migrants departed, occupation in Australia and whether they felt they might resettle in the United
States (Tables 1-7). Years of migration of survey respondents
covered the period from 1950 to 1974 (Table 8).

TABLE 1*

AGE OF MIGRANTS AT THE TIME OF MIGRATION

Age	Absolute Frequency	Relative Frequency (Percentage)	Adjusted Frequency (Percentage)	Cumulative Adj. Freq. (Percentage)
15-19	5	2.5	2.6	2.6
20-24	33	16.5	17.0	19.6
25-29	58	29.0	29.9	49.5
30-34	29	14.5	14.9	64.4
35-39	19	9.5	9.8	74.2
40-44	20	10.0	10.3	84.5
45-49	13	6.5	6.7	91.2
50-54	11	5.5	5.7	96.9
55-59	4	2.0	2.1	99.0
65 and over	2	1.0	1.0	100.0
No answer	6	3.0	. . .	100.0
Total	200	100.0	100.0	100.0

Valid observations - 194

Missing observations - 6

*SOURCE: The source for all tables will be the author's survey unless otherwise indicated.

TABLE 2

SEX OF MIGRANTS

Sex	Absolute Frequency	Relative Frequency (Percentage)	Adjusted Frequency (Percentage)
Male	132	66.0	70.6
Female	55	27.5	29.4
No answer	13	6.5	. . .
Total	200	100.0	100.0

Valid observations - 187

Missing observations -13

TABLE 3

MIGRANTS' MARITAL STATUS AT THE TIME OF MIGRATION

Marital Status	Absolute Frequency	Relative Frequency (Percentage)	Adjusted Frequency (Percentage)
Single	82	41.0	41.4
Married	116	58.0	58.6
No answer	2	1.0	. . .
Total	200	100.0	100.0

Valid observations - 198

Missing observations- 2

TABLE 4

AUSTRALIAN GOVERNMENT FINANCIAL ASSISTANCE
OF MIGRANT PASSAGE TO AUSTRALIA

Assisted Passage	Absolute Frequency	Relative Frequency (Percentage)	Adjusted Frequency (Percentage)
No	95	47.5	47.7
Yes	104	52.0	52.3
No answer	1	0.5	. . .
Total	200	100.0	100.0

Valid observations - 199

Missing observations- 1

TABLE 5

SECTIONS OF THE UNITED STATES FROM WHICH MIGRANTS DEPARTED*

Section from Which Departed	Absolute Frequency	Relative Frequency (Percentage)	Adjusted Frequency (Percentage)
California	56	28.0	29.5
Northeast	30	15.0	15.8
North Central	46	23.0	24.2
West (exclusive of California)	29	14.5	15.3
South	28	14.0	14.7
Puerto Rico	1	0.5	0.5
No answer	10	5.0	. . .
Total	200	100.0	100.0

Valid observations - 190

Missing observations- 10

*Appendix II lists the states included within each section of the United States in survey tabulations and cross-tabulations.

TABLE 6

OCCUPATION OF MIGRANTS IN AUSTRALIA

Occupation in Australia	Absolute Frequency	Relative Frequency (Percentage)	Adjusted Frequency (Percentage)
Student	7	3.5	4.3
Professional, technical or related	90	45.0	54.9
Administrative, executive or managerial	18	9.0	11.0
Clerical	13	6.5	7.9
Other nonmanual	5	2.5	3.0
Manual	20	10.0	12.2
Homemaker	1	0.5	0.6
Other or retired	10	5.0	6.1
Unemployed or no answer	36	18.0	. . .
Total	200	100.0	100.0

Valid observations - 164

Missing observations- 36

TABLE 7

MIGRANT RESETTLEMENT IN THE UNITED STATES

Will Resettle in U.S.	Absolute Frequency	Relative Frequency (Percentage)	Adjusted Frequency (Percentage)
Already back	6	3.0	3.1
Yes	71	35.5	36.8
Probably yes	35	17.5	18.1
No	46	23.0	23.8
Probably not	17	8.5	8.8
Undecided	18	9.0	9.3
No answer	7	3.5	. . .
Total	200	100.0	100.0

Valid observations - 193

Missing observations - 7

TABLE 8

YEAR OF MIGRATION

Year Migrated	Absolute Frequency	Relative Frequency (Percentage)	Adjusted Frequency (Percentage)	Cumulative Adj. Freq. (Percentage)
1950-54	4	2.0	2.0	2.0
1955-59	4	2.0	2.0	4.0
1960-64	8	4.0	4.0	8.1
1965-69	35	17.5	17.7	25.8
1970	13	6.5	6.6	32.3
1971	54	27.0	27.3	59.6
1972	34	17.0	17.2	76.8
1973	34	17.0	17.2	93.9
1974	12	6.0	6.0	100.0
No answer	2	1.0	. . .	100.0
Total	200	100.0	100.0	100.0

Valid observations - 198

Missing observations - 2

Footnotes - Introduction:

1. Ray Aitchison, Americans in Australia (New York: Charles
   Scribner's Sons, 1972), p. 191.

2. U.S. Congress, House, Honorable J. J. Pickle submits to the
   House of Representatives Ambassador Ed Clark's arrival
   speech on his return to the United States on July 23, 1966,
   89th Cong., 2nd sess., February 9, 1966, Congressional
   Record, CXII, Appendix, A642-643.

   John Gunther, Inside Australia, completed and ed. by
   William H. Forbis (New York: Harper & Row, Publishers,
   1972), p. 3.

3. Surveys Section, Department of Immigration, Survey of U.S.
   American Settlers, Phase Two (Canberra: Department of
   Immigration, 1971), pp. 1-2.

1

TWO
IMMIGRANT
NATIONS

It has been stated that "demography abhors a vacuum and culture abhors inefficiency in land use. . . . As long as there is any value to culture in human migration, humans will be made to migrate."[1]

Today the United States has a population of approximately 216,000,000 people. Between the years 1820 and 1976 almost 50,000,000 immigrants, of diverse nationalities, came to the nation's shores or crossed its borders (Table 9). After the earliest immigrants, now known as American Indians, had come to the New World from Asia, and after the primarily British as well as forced black migrants who came later, waves of Irish and Germans came in the middle of the nineteenth century fleeing poverty or political persecution.* They were followed in the late nineteenth and early twentieth centuries by even larger waves of immigrants primarily from southern and eastern Europe, who came to begin a new life in the land of hope and plenty. Prior to 1892, most immigrants were processed through a receiving station at Castle Garden, originally the site of a seventeenth-century Dutch fort, in Manhattan, New York. However, the numbers increased so greatly and so many managed to enter the country without being processed that a larger, more isolated immigrant receiving station at Ellis Island, Upper New York Bay, was selected and used from 1892 to 1943. During the bicentennial year, 1976, this immigrant nation deemed Ellis Island, which was the entry point for at least 12,000,000 immigrants, of such significance that it was reopened permanently, as a historic site.

At the present time, America is becoming less of an

1

TABLE 9

IMMIGRATION TO THE UNITED STATES: 1820 TO 1974

Period	Total Number[a]	Total Rate[b]	Period	Total Number[a]	Total Rate[b]	Year	Total Number[a]	Total Rate[b]
1820-1974	46,713	3.6	1891-1900	3,688	5.3	1965	297	1.5
1820-1830[c]	152	1.2	1901-1910	8,795	10.4	1967	362	1.8
1831-1840[d]	599	3.9	1911-1920	5,736	5.7	1968	454	2.3
1841-1850[e]	1,713	8.4	1921-1930	4,107	3.5	1969	359	1.8
1851-1860[e]	2,598	9.3	1931-1940	528	0.4	1970	373	1.8
1861-1870[f]	2,315	6.4	1941-1950	1,035	0.7	1971	370	1.8
1871-1880	2,812	6.2	1951-1960	2,515	1.5	1972	385	1.8
1881-1890	5,247	9.2	1961-1970	3,322	1.7	1973	400	1.9
						1974	395	1.9

SOURCE: U.S. Department of Commerce, Bureau of the Census, Statistical Abstract of the United States, 1975 (Washington, D.C.: U.S. Government Printing Office, 1975), p. 99.

2

TABLE 9--continued

[For years ending June 30, except as noted. For 1820-1867, alien passengers arriving; 1868-1891 and 1895-1897, immigrants arriving; 1892-1894 and 1898 to the present, immigrants admitted. Rates based on Bureau of the Census estimates as of July for resident population through 1929, and for total population thereafter (excluding Alaska and Hawaii prior to 1959). See also Historical Statistics, Colonial times to 1970, series C 89.]

a In thousands.

b Annual rate per 1,000 U.S. population. 10-year rate computed by dividing sum of annual immigration totals by sum of annual U.S. population totals for same 10 years.

c October 1, 1819-September 30, 1830.

d October 1, 1830-December 31, 1840.

e Calendar years.

f January 1, 1861-June 30, 1870.

3

"immigrant nation" than it was in the nineteenth and early twentieth centuries, as it is more selective in determining who will be admitted and accepted into American society. Regarding admittance, there has been a tendency over the past two decades to look most favorably upon those with special intellectual abilities in various areas, which has given rise to the term, "brain drain," in describing the "luring" of many nations' top professionals and specialists to the United States. Concerning acceptance, though most migrants are still welcomed by the majority of Americans, there have been instances, such as the large influx recently of South Vietnamese, which have tended to concern some Americans in an economic or racial sense. Furthermore, there is a growing ill feeling about the now six to eight million illegal aliens who maintain their residences in the United States and who occupy employment positions which should be held by presently unemployed American citizens or legally admitted aliens.

Most immigrants who came to America did so out of dissatisfaction or desperation, and in the hope that the United States would provide an answer to their discontent. On the other hand, the first immigrants to Australia, after the Aborigines who had come from the north, had little choice in the matter. They were primarily convicts who had been transported by the British government because of the overcrowded conditions of the gaols in England. Transportation, including a number of convicts originally scheduled for America, began in 1787 and ended in 1868.[2] The total number of criminals transported during that period reached approximately 160,000, and it has been calculated that in the early 1970s one in every fifteen Australians was descended from a convict.[3] Some Americans find this fact a great source of amusement when demeaning Australians. Those who demean would do well to recall, however, that well over one hundred years before Australia was first settled by members of the white race, "lewd, disorderly and lawless persons" were transported to the American colonies from England, and propagated here thereby helping make the United States what it is today![4]

From the middle of the nineteenth century to its end, while less than 60 percent of the increase in the Australian population from 400,000 to 3,700,000 during that period was native-born, over 40 percent of the growth during those years consisted of immigrants from Great Britain and Ireland along with some Germans and Chinese in addition to a few Scandinavian, Italian and other migrants.[5] In great part because of the unfavorable experiences with relatively large numbers of Chinese who immigrated to Australia in the mid-nineteenth century, in the early twentieth century almost all non-European migrants were excluded by the Immigration Restriction Act of 1901; and all migrants "deemed unlikely to be readily assimilable" were excluded by the Amending Immigration Act of 1925. World War II temporarily halted immigration to Australia, but in 1945 Prime Minister Joseph Benedict (Ben) Chifley announced the beginning of an immigration program that has greatly altered the nation (Tables 10 and 11).[6] Australians had been shocked by the Japanese attack upon their continent and, as one American serviceman put it, "Australia did not want to be caught again with her population down."[7] The slogan "populate or perish" gained wide acceptance as the government began a determined effort to increase the population through immigration to defend the country. National defense was not the only motive involved in the immigration program, though, as the nation experienced something of a minor "industrial revolution" after the war and there was a shortage of labor. On a single day, one Sydney newspaper alone carried 68 columns of finely printed "situation vacant" advertisements.[8]

All that was required to be subsidized by the Australian government for immigration to Australia was to be of pure European descent, to be "personally suitable" (however the government chose to interpret that vague term) for settlement in Australia and to be classified as an essential worker or readily employable.[9] These "New Australians," as they have been named, have been painlessly assimilated, for the most part, into Australian society. There have been no major riots and little overt hostility.[10]

Between 1950 and 1971, the population of Australia increased from 8,000,000 to 12,700,000 with immigrants and their Australian-born children accounting for 53 percent of the rise.[11] The immigration program was deemed a success throughout the 1960s, and a Special Passage Assistance Program was even instituted in 1966 to help additional migrants come who could not otherwise have afforded it. In the early 1970s, though, the government's program came increasingly under the attack of economists and social scientists. They had become concerned that the massive influx of migrants had placed too much pressure on the school systems and social services, that the immigration program might be racist in its exclusion of nonwhites and that the migrants had been concentrating in enclaves and contributing to the overcrowding of the major cities.[12] In addition, it seemed that the Australian people in general had become disillusioned with the government's program of massive immigration, as a poll showed that 60 percent of the population wanted it terminated.[13] In early 1972, for the first time in Australian history, the government discouraged potential immigrants unless they possessed special

5

TABLE 10

TOTAL RECORDED OVERSEAS ARRIVALS AND DEPARTURES TO AND FROM AUSTRALIA[a]: 1860-1972

Periods	Recorded Arrivals			Recorded Departures			Excess of Recorded Arrivals Over Recorded Departures[b]		
	Males	Females	Persons	Males	Females	Persons	Males	Females	Persons
1860	c	c	c	c	c	c	13,483	10,466	23,949
1 861-1870	c	c	c	c	c	c	79,344	87,221	166,565
1871-1880	c	c	c	c	c	c	124,195	67,609	191,804
1881-1890	c	c	c	c	c	c	244,284	138,457	382,741
1891-1900	c	c	c	c	c	c	14,715	10,164	24,879
1901-1910	448,475	203,719	652,194	358,188	175,763	533,951	90,287	27,956	118,243
1911-1920	861,648	310,657	1,172,305	766,803	183,462	950,265	94,845	127,195	222,040
1921-1930	556,288	392,244	948,532	369,503	274,711	644,214	186,785	117,533	304,318
1931-1940	285,981	274,654	560,635	276,594	253,645	530,239	9,387	21,009	30,396
1941-1950	433,929	331,916	765,845	210,876	194,076	404,952	223,053	137,840	360,893
1951	122,136	91,504	213,640	54,521	47,686	102,207	67,615	43,818	111,433
1952	127,516	88,323	215,839	68,937	52,870	121,807	58,579	35,453	94,032
1953	88,584	74,541	163,125	68,483	51,745	120,228	20,101	22,796	42,897
1954	109,601	88,424	198,025	72,073	57,745	129,818	37,528	30,679	68,207
1955	133,463	103,774	237,237	76,805	63,177	139,982	56,658	40,597	97,255

TABLE 10--continued

Period	Recorded Arrivals			Recorded Departures			Excess of Recorded Arrivals Over Recorded Departures[b]		
	Males	Females	Persons	Males	Females	Persons	Males	Females	Persons
1956	141,408	106,040	247,448	87,013	66,437	153,450	54,395	39,603	93,998
1957	123,487	109,841	233,328	87,081	67,515	154,596	36,406	42,326	78,732
1958	121,030	109,234	230,264	91,367	73,531	164,898	29,663	35,703	65,366
1959	139,941	113,955	253,896	98,917	78,188	177,105	41,024	35,767	76,791
1960	169,579	129,582	299,161	116,857	92,169	209,026	52,722	37,413	90,135
1961	170,404	142,686	313,090	141,349	110,218	251,567	29,055	32,468	61,523
1962	180,732	151,592	332,324	152,112	117,690	269,802	28,620	33,902	62,522
1963	211,430	169,297	380,727	175,211	133,871	309,082	36,219	35,426	71,645
1964	252,669	199,688	452,357	200,611	152,404	353,015	52,058	47,284	99,342
1965	292,184	232,952	525,136	237,673	182,607	420,280	54,511	50,345	104,856
1966	313,219	244,372	557,591	268,313	202,352	470,665	44,906	42,020	86,926
1967	361,345	275,825	637,170	311,727	233,534	545,261	49,618	42,291	91,909
1968	465,232	306,560	771,792	403,748	254,991	658,739	61,484	51,569	113,053
1969	545,559	353,299	898,858	475,840	239,972	769,812	69,719	59,327	129,046
1970	613,899	412,776	1,026,675	548,353	355,448	903,801	65,546	57,328	122,874
1971	625,066	453,732	1,078,798	581,510	412,683	994,193	43,556	41,049	84,605
1972	608,730	501,940	1,110,670	597,765	485,059	1,082,824	10,965	16,881	27,846

TABLE 10--continued

SOURCE: Department of Immigration, Australian Immigration: Consolidated Statistics, No. 7 (Canberra: The Australian Government Publishing Service, 1973), p. 9.

[a]Total arrivals from and departures to places outside Australia. Crew members were included prior to July 1, 1922.

[b]Prior to 1901 figures include an adjustment to make the series of annual increases in population agree with the total intercensal increased revealed by successive censuses.

[c]Not available.

8

TABLE 11

PERMANENT NEW ARRIVALS TO AUSTRALIA FROM 1945 TO 1973

Year	Assisted Settlers	Other Settlers	Total
1945			7,512
1946			18,217
1947			31,765
1948			65,739
1949			167,727
1950			174,540
1951			132,542
1952	N.A.	N.A.	127,824
1953			74,913
1954			104,014
1955			130,795
1956			123,822
1957			118,695
1958			109,857
1959	64,146	33,631	97,777
1960	68,254	41,825	110,079
1961	55,685	39,722	95,407
1962	45,276	45,188	90,464
1963	62,914	45,236	108,150
1964	79,604	54,860	134,464
1965	93,653	53,854	147,507
1966	89,743	51,290	141,033
1967	82,247	52,772	135,019
1968	105,102	54,168	159,270
1969	125,958	57,458	183,416
1970	134,428	50,897	185,325
1971	103,811	51,714	155,525
1972	63,710	48,758	112,468
1973	49,822	55,181	105,003

SOURCE: Australian Bureau of Statistics, Demography (various issues).

N.A. - Not Available.

skills; and with the advent of the following worldwide economic recession, the program was temporarily halted in late 1974
in order to help ease Australia's unemployment problem.[14] A
more prosperous economic outlook has developed recently, however, and the government has stated that it intends increasing
the number of immigrants admitted thus adding to the labor
supply as well as product supply and demand which in turn
should help advance the standard of living. Thus now to be
admitted as a migrant, one must either have employment prearranged in Australia, possess a needed skill or be of a needed profession or be sponsored by a close relative already in
Australia.

There is no doubt that although Australians are still
influenced predominantly by their British heritage, the immigrants from Italy, Greece, Yugoslavia, Germany, the Nether-
lands, New Zealand, the United States, Lebanon, Spain and
other countries who have come since the Second World War have
had a definite impact on Australian society, which at the
present time includes a total of nearly 14,000,000 people.
Cosmopolitan restaurants, boutiques and clubs may be found in
every major city.[15] Australia has rejected a completely
"melting pot" attitude toward migrants and has allowed for a
plurality of ethics instead of an insistence on a single national ethic; and because of this, Australians have lost some
of their insularity and conformity.[16]

Of course not everyone who presently applies for admission as an immigrant is accepted. Members of extremist groups
such as the Ku Klux Klan are screened out.[17] Likewise,
Australia does not desire to have American "hippies" immigrate
because Australian officials are fearful that such undesirable
people would not be a good influence upon Australian youth and
might possibly promote the sale and use of illegal drugs.[18]
Many have strongly criticized, however, the exclusion until
recently of another group of potential migrants, nonwhites, as
an act of racial discrimination. This policy of excluding
nonwhite migrants became known as the "White Australia" policy.

In 1901, the Immigration Restriction Act was passed, excluding nearly all nonwhite migrants from Australia as well as
those of several specified nationalities. According to former
Minister of Immigration, Sir Hubert Opperman, "The experience
of fifty years before 1901 had produced a distrust of minor-
ities, a sharpening of racial differences, a fear of economic
competition and a determination to have a unified society."[19]
The "experiences" to which the Minister referred included the
migration to the southwest Pacific continent of a large number

10

of Chinese laborers who worked for low wages during the Australian gold rush, as well as the later importation of thousands of Pacific Islanders, known as Kanakas, for use as identured plantation workers. Australians were angered by the presence of cheap laborers to such an extent that a leading periodical, the Bulletin, adopted the following motto in the late nineteenth century, "Australia for the Australians--the cheap Chinaman, the cheap nigger and the cheap European pauper to be absolutely excluded."[20]

During the twentieth century, Australia's exclusionary policies were extremely successful as in 1947 fewer than 25,000 Asians could be found on the continent.[21] To a certain degree, racial discrimination was a factor in the formulation and implementation of these immigration policies. Arthur Calwell, Immigration Minister in 1949 and noted for his statement, "Two Wongs don't make a White," defended some discrimination for the sake of maintaining a homogeneous population.[22] He emphasized,

> Australia does not stand alone in this regard. The dominant factor of the U.S. Immigration Law (prior to 1965) is the preservation of the ethnic composition of the population of that country and that principle is inherent in the immigration laws of all countries. Non-Europeans as well as Europeans practice it.[23]

The succeeding Minister of Immigration, Harold E. Holt, justified the discriminatory policy on different grounds in 1951 by proclaiming, "This policy is aimed solely at safeguarding Australia's high standard of living. It is not based on racial prejudice."[24] Clearly, the Australian attitude regarding the admittance of nonwhite migrants changed during the 1950s. When asked their opinion about annually admitting fifty or more nonwhite migrants, a poll revealed that 61 percent of the Australian people wanted to "keep them out" in 1954 but only 34 percent responded in that same manner in 1959 (Table 12). Furthermore, the bars to citizenship for nonwhites were removed in 1956.[25]

Thus it is evident that Australia's exclusionary attitude toward nonwhites was no longer one based purely on racial discrimination. It seemed instead that what Australians actually feared most was the possibly disruptive effect of a "mass" migration of nonwhites to their sparsely populated land. In 1965 a Gallup poll showed that 71 percent of all Australians favored the selective immigration of nonwhites, and by 1966 there were over 100,000 people of Asian extraction in

11

TABLE 12

CHANGE IN AUSTRALIANS' ATTITUDE REGARDING
IMMIGRATION OF NONWHITES

	Keep Out (Percentage)	Let In (Percentage)	No Opinion (Percentage)
1954	61	31	8
1956	51	42	7
1957	55	36	9
1958	45	44	11
1959	34	55	11

SOURCE: Russel Ward, Australia (Englewood Cliffs, N.J.: Prentice-Hall, Inc., 1965), p. 138.

Australia.[26] All the major political parties had dropped "White Australia" from their platforms by that year and the new, liberalized immigration policy permitted the entry of "non-European immigrants" on the basis of possession skills "of a positive value to Australia."[27] Though Australians still did not want the "floodgates" opened to Asian and other nonwhite migrants, the overwhelming majority approved the elimination of the all-white immigration policy.[28] Therefore, in 1973, Immigration Minister Al Grassby announced that the government had barred skin color as a factor in the admission of new settlers.[29]

The admission of American blacks, as opposed to Asians, presented a somewhat different problem. Though there had been a few black Americans in the Australian goldfields in the mid-nineteenth century and some were admitted in the following years prior to the Second World War, black Americans have been quite rare in Australia. Concerning the 1947 recruitment of Americans as migrants, an Australian government spokesman deemed blacks "too foreign" to be easily assimilated.[30] The American organization, the National Association for the Advancement of Colored People, protested this exclusion of blacks, but Immigration Minister Calwell responded that

12

Australia did not want "nations within nations" and that Jews and other minority groups were also being excluded because they could not be easily absorbed.[31] The attitude of the Minister toward the exclusion of black Americans seemed representative of the Australian people, which was revealed in a 1949 questionnaire distributed to a random sample of Melbourne residents by Professor O. A. Oeser and Dr. S. B. Hammond. The survey indicated that 68 percent of the residents wanted to exclude blacks.[32]

Why did Australians develop a negative attitude toward American blacks in general? The primary reason for the development of this attitude has been that outside of news regarding a few black Americans, the only information Australians received about American blacks pertained to racial unrest and violence in the United States.[33] In 1965, the Vice-Chairman of the Immigration Review Committee, Mr. F. M. Daly, pointed across the Pacific to the racial conflict in America and said Australia's freedom from racial hatred and strife should prove the correctness of a polity that excluded blacks.[34]

As far as black Americans themselves are concerned, few want to immigrate to Australia. In the words of former Minister of Immigration Billy Snedden, "The best American Negroes won't come because America is pushing them ahead, and the worst won't because they can't afford it."[35] Though there have been some black Americans who received financial assistance from the Australian government to immigrate, at the beginning of 1972 there were fewer than a dozen blacks living permanently in Australia.[36] Referring to the approximately 150,000 Aborigines (divided about equally between full-bloods and half-castes) living on the continent at present, many Australians ask why they should bring black Americans to Australia when they are having difficulty in assimilating their own nonwhites.[37]

One might easily obtain the impression from reading the aforementioned that Australia is a land inhabited by ardent racists, but such is not the case. Although Australia has its racists, just as other countries have, white Australians seem to get along quite well with nonwhite migrants on a one-to-one basis.[38] One must remember that Australians in general do not fear nonwhite migrants per se, but rather they fear being engulfed by the admission and presence of a large number of nonwhites, who would be difficult to absorb without a cultural upheaval. In fact, Australians are probably less racially discriminatory than Americans and no more so than many Asians! Once nonwhite migrants are admitted to Australia, they are generally treated on an equal basis and accepted into the

13

society.[39] This is true for the American blacks as well as the Vietnamese refugees who have immigrated there, an attitude not completely evident in the United States. Moreover, non-whites have been elected to high government positions such as mayor, senator and governor in Australia. Some Asian nations, on the other hand, are very prejudiced against the admission of black migrants, and even against the admission of migrants from some other Asian nations.[40]

In the final analysis, immigration to Australia has probably worked better than immigration to the United States. Though many of the first generation migrants to both countries have maintained their own national groupings, in Australia there have not been completely closed areas of settlement, separate schools and strong political or church groupings as there have been in America.[41] The vast majority of migrants to both nations, however, have had at least one thing in common. Most moved with a new sense of hope for the future. And in that respect, American immigrants to Australia have been no different.

* * *

The first contact between Americans and Australians occurred on November 1, 1792, when the American brigantine, the Philadelphia, under Captain Thomas Patrickson, sailed into Sydney Harbor with American beef, wine, rum, gin, tobacco, pitch and tar.[42] And probably the first American migrants to Australia were a number of whalers in the 1790s who decided that life in Australia would be more enjoyable than the life they had led on their ships. It would not be until thirty-three years later in 1825, though, that two Americans became the first foreigners admitted to Australian citizenship.[43] In the decade of the 1830s the first American firm established itself and the first American consul, James Hartwell Williams, arrived "Down Under," as a generally amicable relationship between the two nations began to develop.[44] Unfortunately, at the end of the decade in 1839 and 1840, over eighty-five Americans arrived in Van Dieman's Land (later named Tasmania) and Sydney under rather unpleasant circumstances. They were convicts transported from Canada--a most "involuntary" form of immigration!

In 1851 the first large-scale immigration of Americans to Australia began when news arrived in the United States that gold had been discovered in Victoria. Two years later, 10,000 Americans searched for gold in Australia, and their presence was duly noted by local Australians.[45] One Melbourne newspaper branded the diggers from California as "unprincipled idlers who live only on scenes of anarchy and excitement."[46]

14

Some Americans had urged the overthrow of crown rule; and a Captain Brown, who claimed to have lived with the Commanches and to have been a Texas Ranger, vociferated against licensing fees to search for gold to such a degree that he was arrested and removed from the goldfields.[47]

Yet, it would be at Ballarat, Victoria, that a number of Americans would be most remembered as several members of the "Independent Californian Rangers Revolver Brigade," including a black American named John Joseph, became involved in the Battle of Eureka Stockade. This was a battle between police, charging from without, and disgruntled miners, defending from within a small fort they had built. Mark Twain would later compare the conflict to the Battles of Lexington and Concord for American independence.[48]

Not all Americans came in search of gold during the 1850s. George Francis Train, a prominent businessman, arrived in 1853. He frequented the fashionable Criterion Hotel, a famous meeting place for "Yankees" whose proprietor was an American named Sam Moss, and established Melbourne's stock exchange.[49] That same year, Train and another American named Freeman Cobb, as well as others, established perhaps the greatest coach company in the world called Cobb and Company.[50] It was later taken over in 1859 by another American, James Rutherford, who had arrived seven years earlier and who became a goldminer, stockman, horse dealer, stagecoach driver, cattle and sheep rancher, involved in the timber trade and one of the fathers of the Australian steel industry.[51]

Other nineteenth century Americans in Australia also were active in many diverse pursuits. They sold "goldfield's equipment, timber for housing, wagons, coaches, stoves, sewing machines, dried and canned fruits, iced beer, Virginia tobacco and Boston water carts; and they agitated for better roads, railway lines, town-planning and land reform."[52] Furthermore, they were responsible for better mail service and established the Melbourne fire brigade and many new industries.[53]

Although there have been too many other notable Americans in nineteenth century Australia to mention them all, a few additional ones may be cited. Sam McGowan built the first telegraph lines; F. B. Clapp ran Melbourne's bus services; James Marion Matra proposed a colony of American loyalists be founded in Australia; George Washington Lambert became one of Australia's early painters; Dion Boucicault was an actor and director who influenced early theater in the southwest Pacific continent along with actors James Cassius Williamson and his wife Maggie Moore, both of whom "contributed a force to the

Australian theater which was to see out three generations";
George and William Chaffey (Canadian born) who pioneered irri-
gation in Australia; and John Greeley Jenkins who became
Premier of South Australia.[54]

Perhaps the most colorful American in nineteenth century
Australia, as well as in the early twentieth century, was
known as King O'Malley. A man whom newsmen characterized as
a "threefold compromise between a wild-west romantic hero from
the cattle ranches, a spruiker (Australian for spieler) from
Barnum's Circus, and a Western American statesman," he ran for
office from Adelaide, Tasmania and Darwin.[55] He won his first
election on a platform of legitimizing bastards if the parents
later married, lavatories on every train and the abolition of
barmaids.[56] Other credits belonging to O'Malley include mem-
bership in the first Australian Commonwealth Parliament holding the post of Minister for Home Affairs, co-founder of the
Commonwealth Bank of Australia, and originator of the concept
of a federal capital city for Australia.[57]

There have been, of course, many other Americans who did
not settle permanently in Australia, yet spent considerable
time there in the period of the late nineteenth and early
twentieth centuries. In addition to some of the goldminers,
fishermen and merchants who remained only so long as their
life there seemed purposeful or profitable, Herbert Hoover and
Walter Burley Griffin lived and worked in Australia at this
time. Herbert Hoover came to Australia in 1897 as a twenty-
three-year-old mining engineer and stayed intermittently over
a period of ten years in the goldfields of Kalgoorlie, Western
Australia; supposedly in love with a local girl, he even wrote
a poem of eight stanzas, the first of which is:

Do you ever dream my sweetheart, of a twilight long ago,
Of a park in old Kalgoorlie where the bougainvillaeas
    grow,
Where the moon beams on the pathways trace a shimmering
    brocade
And the overhanging peppers form a lovers' promenade?[58]

Probably of more renown in Australia, however, would be Walter
Burley Griffin. A partner of the famous architect Frank Lloyd
Wright, Griffin is remembered for designing the Australian
Capital City of Canberra.

During the 1930s other noteworthy Americans came to
Australia, including Bob Dyer, "the king of Australian tele-
vision" for many years, as well as Bettina Brown, wife of John
Grey Gorton who later became Prime Minister of Australia.[59]

16

Then occurred the event that would increase dramatically
Americans' awareness of the land "Down Under," as the world
once again enjoined in the holocaust of war.

Before World War II, few Americans knew much about
Australia, and many did not even know where it was located.
According to former Prime Minister Robert Menzies, "A gentle-
man in San Francisco once assured me that he understood quite
plainly it was on the east coast of the United States; a sort
of off-shore island."[60] Then as the "Yanks" began to arrive
to assist in the defense of Australia from attacks by the
Japanese, a bond began to form between the American servicemen
and the Australian people. Though there were strains in the
relationship at times, causing some Australians to decry later
that the "Yanks" were "overpaid, oversexed and over here,"
most Australians and American servicemen got along extremely
well.[61] During the war, 500,000 United States servicemen
either were stationed in or visited Australia, and after the
war, 1,000 applied for discharge there.[62]

Contacts between the two nations forged during wartime
did not abate with the coming of peace. In 1946 when twenty
American or United States financed manufacturing companies
started to open branches in Australia, the Australian government opened a consulate in San Francisco.[63] Likewise, in that
same year, both countries raised their respective legations in
Washington and Canberra to Embassy status; and early the following year, Australia opened a new immigration office, though
it was not entitled that at the time, in the United States.[64]
Australians increasingly believed that Americans were essentially the same type of people as themselves.[65] Therefore, with
a new immigration program underway, what better type of migrant could be desired?

Because many American servicemen had chosen to remain in
Australia at the end of the war, it had already been demonstrated that Australia could attract Americans as migrants.
Even before the war's end, the United States War Department
had printed a pamphlet in which the topic was discussed, "Can
Australia attract immigrants from America after the war?"
Possible reasons indicated why Americans might choose to immigrate included "employment opportunities, living conditions,
Australian government policies to promote the economic welfare
of its people, the 'White Australia' policy, personal ties
developed between Americans and Australians, and the Northern
Territory frontier in Australia."[66] Thus, in May, 1947,
Immigration Minister Calwell suggested that an American veteran program be initiated. This program was adopted promptly
by the Australian Parliament; then in August, Calwell

broadened his scope and announced that Australia would like
"at least one million Americans to immigrate."[67] A brochure
was published for distribution from Australian Consulates in
the United States, and in it American servicemen and other
Americans were enticed by visions of "those high, clear skies,
the rollers at Bondi Beach and the surfers' paradise, and the
hurly burly of King's Cross." The advertisement continued,
"Maybe you're married or maybe you want to marry an Australian
girl--perhaps the one you met over there or one of those
you've heard so much about."[68]

     The first Americans under the Australian financial sub-
sidy plan embarked from the United States aboard the Matson
liner, Marine Phoenix, on September 2, 1947.[69] Not unlike a
number of American servicemen who had been in Australia during
the war, Kurtis Martischewsky, the first individual on the
sailing list and a Signal Corps veteran from Nebraska, had met
a girl in Australia in 1943 and had later become engaged by
mail. He was going to his new land to marry her and work for
the Australian telephone company.[70] Minister Calwell, who was
on hand to greet the migrants, commented that they were
"merely following the example of his own Pennsylvania-born
grandfather who, ninety-four years ago, had sailed from New
York 'in a boat of 750 tons' and reached Australia seven
months later to dig for gold."[71] Inquiries from every state
and territory of the United States regarding passage to
Australia poured in to such an extent that the backlog in
immigration offices increased by a thousand or more each
week.[72]

     Quite a number of the Americans who migrated after the
Second World War regarded themselves as pioneers helping to
shape Australia's future as their ancestors had helped shape
America.[73] Unlike the immigrants to America, however, many of
these Americans who were going to Australia had been there
during the war. Therefore, their "pioneering" was based on
what they considered personal knowledge about their future
home. Another difference between these two sets of migrants
was that the immigrants to the United States carried with them
the feeling that they had left their homelands for good,
whereas these American immigrants to Australia had the feeling
that if things did not work out as planned they would simply
return to America.[74]

     Some idea of the causes for increased or decreased
American immigration to Australia in any given period may be
gained by examining the conditions which existed in both
nations during the period under consideration. Any preponder-
ance of negatively perceived conditions in the United States

18

coupled simultaneously with positively perceived conditions in
Australia, or vice versa, would tend to cause immigration to
increase or decrease respectively for the period in question.

American immigration to Australia generally increased
from 1945 to 1949, and then alternately declined, rose and declined from 1949 to 1952 (Tables 13 and 14 show figures for
American immigration to Australia from 1945 to 1975--over
115,000 have migrated between 1945 and the present). Remarkably coincidental, these same patterns were repeated between
1952 and 1958. From 1952 to 1955 American immigration increased, and again alternately declined, rose and declined
from 1955 to 1958. For both countries these were periods of
general economic prosperity, and a mutual agreement was
reached in 1953 to eliminate double taxation; if an American
were in Australia for no more than 183 days, he would not be
required to pay tax on income there.[75] Both nations, however,
also faced difficulties during this same time concerning the
possible internal activities of communists and the war in
Korea. Moreover, the United States faced problems regarding
Southeast Asia, the Middle East, Formosa, and President Dwight
Eisenhower's health, while Australia had to deal with the
splitting of a major political party.

From 1958 to 1972, the situation became quite different
when conditions in the United States slowly worsened while
Australia's outlook brightened. Immigration to the land "Down
Under" increased steadily as America was beset by a business
slowdown, the longest steel strike in its history, race riots,
difficulties relating to Cuba and Berlin, assassinations, the
Vietnam War, drug abuse, increased pollution and crime, and
political demonstrations and protests, among other problems.
After the Democratic Convention in Chicago in 1968, inquiries
by Americans to the Australian Consulates and Embassy regarding immigration rose from about 5,000 a month to 8,000 per
month, and in 1970 approximately 200,000 such inquiries were
made.[76] In 1972, the Mayor of Philadelphia, Frank Rizzo,
stated that he would move to Australia if the Democratic presidential nominee, Senator George McGovern, were elected.

Meanwhile, life in Australia improved sharply during this
same period. Employment was full, salaries and wages were at
a record level, exports increased and overseas investments
were up. Because of a growing consumer market and the initial
development of vast resources in Australia, major American
enterprises, such as Ford, Coca-Cola, I.B.M., General Foods,
Goodyear, Eastman Kodak, Campbell Soup, Alcoa, Kaiser Steel
and Gulf Oil Corporation among many others, had brought their
"know-how" and dollars to the southwest Pacific continent, so

19

TABLE 13

PERMANENT AND LONG-TERM U.S. AMERICAN
(NATIONALITY) ARRIVALS

Year	Assisted	Other	Total
Oct. June			
1945-1948	912	2,126	3,038
1948-1949	704	249	953
1949-1950	526	404	930
1950-1951	443	701	1,144
1951-1952	222	613	835
1952-1953	108	918	1,026
1953-1954	156	947	1,103
1954-1955	201	1,101	1,302
1955-1956	186	1,067	1,253
1956-1957	183	1,167	1,350
1957-1958	190	1,002	1,192
1958-1959	250	1,304	1,554
1959-1960	472	1,423	1,895
1960-1961	505	1,881	2,386
1961-1962	455	2,412	2,867
1962-1963	439	2,993	3,432
1963-1964	707	2,884	3,591
1964-1965	910	3,867	4,777
1965-1966	1,201	4,462	5,663
1966-1967	1,289	4,800	6,089
1967-1968	1,179	5,505	6,684
1968-1969	1,725	5,478	7,203
1969-1970	1,996	7,045	9,041
1970-1971	3,130	8,611	11,741
1971-1972	3,334	8,981	12,315
1972-1973	1,442	7,879	9,321

SOURCES: Department of Immigration, Australian Immigration: Consolidated Statistics, No. 5 (Canberra: Australian Government Publishing Service, 1971), p. 37.

Department of Immigration, Australian Immigration: Consolidated Statistics, No. 7 (Canberra: Australian Government Publishing Service, 1973), p. 37.

TABLE 14

U.S. AMERICAN (NATIONALITY) SETTLER ARRIVALS,
FORMER SETTLER DEPARTURES AND NET GAIN

Year	Assisted Settlers			Unassisted Settlers		
	Males	Females	Persons	Males	Females	Persons
Jan. June						
1959-1962	903	653	1,556	851	691	1,542
1962-1963	258	181	439	361	309	670
1963-1964	387	320	707	396	297	693
1964-1965	519	391	910	542	353	895
1965-1966	655	546	1,201	664	574	1,238
1966-1967	722	567	1,289	671	512	1,183
1967-1968	643	536	1,179	768	639	1,407
1968-1969	932	793	1,725	790	675	1,465
1969-1970	1,080	916	1,996	835	760	1,595
1970-1971	1,743	1,387	3,130	1,290	1,027	2,317
1971-1972	1,828	1,506	3,334	1,813	1,417	3,230
1972-1973	769	673	1,442	1,311	1,075	2,386
1973-1974	...	...	916	...	...	2,408
1974-1975	...	...	...	...	...	...
Total	10,439	8,469	19,824	10,292	8,329	21,029

21

TABLE 14--continued

Total			Former Settlers Departing			Net Gain		
Males	Females	Persons	Males	Females	Persons	Males	Females	Persons
1,754	1,344	3,098	322	211	533	1,432	1,133	2,565
619	490	1,109	158	122	280	461	368	829
783	617	1,400	228	207	435	555	410	965
1,061	744	1,805	300	225	525	761	519	1,280
1,319	1,120	2,439	306	267	573	1,013	853	1,866
1,393	1,079	2,472	404	318	722	989	761	1,750
1,411	1,175	2,586	506	357	863	905	818	1,723
1,722	1,468	3,190	549	469	1,018	1,173	999	2,172
1,915	1,676	3,591	608	462	1,070	1,307	1,214	2,521
3,033	2,414	5,447	569	471	1,040	2,464	1,943	4,407
3,641	2,923	6,564	730	601	1,331	2,911	2,322	5,233
2,080	1,749	3,828	1,134	996	2,130	946	752	1,698
...	...	3,324	...	...	...	...	...	...
...	...	3,192	...	...	...	...	...	...
20,731	16,798	44,045	5,814	4,706	10,520	14,917	12,092	27.009

22

TABLE 14--continued

SOURCES: Department of Immigration, Australian Immigration: Consolidated Statistics, No. 7, (Canberra: Australian Government Publishing Service, 1973), p. 49.

Department of Labor and Immigration, Australian Immigration: Quarterly Statistical Summary, III, No. 30 (Canberra: Australian Government Publishing Service, June, 1974), p. 19.

Letter from the Department of Immigration and Ethnic Affairs, April 28, 1976.

23

that by 1965, 27 percent of all manufacturing industry in
Australia was fully owned by American companies.[77] In 1950
Australia had a pastoral-agricultural economy, but by 1965 the
nation had a growing industrial economy and was beginning to
boom![78]

During the latter part of the 1960s, the situation improved to an even greater extent. The stock market soared, as
one stock went from $A0.60 to $A214 a share in a single year.
Mineral production in Western Australia alone increased from
$54,000,000 in 1965 to $579,000,000 in 1970. Furthermore, the
rate of growth per capita of the Gross Domestic Product of
Australia outstripped that of the United States by 2.28 percent to 1.97 percent in 1969.[79]

The phenomenal growth of the late 1960s continued into
the first year of the next decade, as personal income increased by 13.7 percent and unemployment remained steady at 1.45
percent during 1970-1971.[80] By mid-1971 American company investment in Australia had reached $US3,200,000,000, which rep-
resented America's fourth largest investment overseas, and 500
subsidiaries of United States firms had located there.[81] In
the words of one American business executive, "Australia has
kinda lit the fuse and it's really gonna go! You've almost
got a revolution in growth here--not evolution!"[82]

The year 1972 brought the beginning of worsening economic
conditions throughout the world. The United States during the
next few years would be beleaguered by galloping inflation as
well as the evolving story of "Watergate." Interestingly, the
first person who supposedly preferred to immigrate to
Australia because of "Watergate" was Bay (Angela) Buchanan,
sister of Pat Buchanan, former President Richard Nixon's top
speech-writer.[83]

But conditions in Australia during this period did not
produce a sense of enthusiasm or well-being either. By the
latter half of 1971 a recession had begun and in 1972, sales
suffered, the labor force became more demanding, the cost of
living rose by 7 percent and a certain degree of political
disunity began to develop.[84] Because of increasing inflation
and unemployment, the Australian government began to restrict
migrant intake somewhat, and in the last half of 1972, American immigration decreased significantly.

In December of the same year, the Labor Party under the
leadership of Gough Whitlam defeated the Liberal-Country coalition which had been in power for twenty-three years. Though
Prime Minister Whitlam attempted to arouse a spirit of

nationalism among Australians, he also was responsible for
enacting inflationary measures which many considered economically harmful to the nation. American immigration declined
through the years of the Whitlam administration and into the
first years of the new Liberal administration which gained
power in late 1975.

Under Liberal Prime Minister Malcolm Fraser's more conservative economic policies, American immigration to Australia
may begin to increase once again. The Australian government
will continue to restrict immigration to a certain extent,
however, until the problems of inflation and unemployment are
sharply reduced. And, in fact, the projection for 1976-1977
is for even a substantial reduction in the number of Americans
admitted to approximately 2,000, though many more Americans
would like to immigrate to Australia.

From looking at the number of inquiries Americans have
made concerning immigration to Australia and the number who
actually migrated, one might wonder why more have not embarked
especially considering the tremendous growth which has occurred in that southwest Pacific nation. One of the main reasons
many would-be migrants do not leave the United States is because personal considerations do not allow them to emigrate.
For example, an individual who is single may marry and the
spouse may feel uncertain about moving; or parents with teenagers may feel their offspring are too old to migrate without
facing adjustment problems in addition to those of adolescence
and too young to be on their own in the United States.[85] A
second important reason is that Australia is so far away from
America. Consider for a moment how many Americans might immigrate to Australia if it were where Mexico is geographically
located. Regardless of how many do not leave and why they do
not, the fact remains that a large number do choose to leave
the United States and live in Australia, a nation some have
termed the new "El Dorado." Specific reasons why many
Americans have chosen to emigrate from the United States and
immigrate to Australia have been determined and will be analyzed next in more detail.

25

Footnotes - Chapter I:

*Harvard scholar Barry Fell, in his book America B.C., offers recently deciphered evidence that Celtic Iberians and Basques had settled in New England possibly earlier than 1000 B.C. and that Egyptians, Libyans and perhaps Celts had settled in Iowa possibly as early as 900 B.C. According to Dr. Fell, there is additional evidence that visitors to North America from across the Atlantic Ocean came even centuries earlier.

1. John Greenway, Australia: The Last Frontier (New York: Dodd, Mead & Company, 1972), p. 132.

2. Thomas McKnight, Australia's Corner of the World (Englewood Cliffs, N.J.: Prentice-Hall, Inc., 1970), p. 57.

3. Ibid. Ray Aitchison, Americans in Australia, p. 5.

4. John Gunther, Inside Australia, p. 20.

5. McKnight, Australia's Corner, pp. 57-58.

6. Ibid., p. 58.

7. H. E. Holt, "The New Face of Australia," The Rotarian, April, 1956, p. 13.

8. "Australia: Situation Vacant," Time, July 7, 1947, p. 31.

9. W. D. Borrie, Immigration: Australia's Problems and Prospects (Sydney: Angus & Robertson, 1949), p. 27.

10. James Jupp, Arrivals and Departures (Melbourne: Lansdowne Press Pty., Ltd., 1966), p. 2.

11. Kenneth Randall, "Immigration," in Australia in the Seventies, ed. by Michael Southern (Ringwood, Victoria: Penguin Books, Ltd., 1973), p. 149.

12. Robert Trumbull, "Australia Has Second Thoughts as Immigrants Swell Population," New York Times, August 2, 1970, p. 1.

13. Greenway, Last Frontier, pp. 280-281.

14. Malcolm Colless, "Decline Down Under: Australia, Once

Held a Land of Opportunity, Sees Its Bubble Burst as Prices Rise and Jobs Vanish," Wall Street Journal, March 7, 1972, p. 38.

15. Craig McGregor, Profile of Australia (Ringwood, Victoria; Penguin Books Ltd., 1968), p. 359.

16. Ibid.

17. Harry Gordon, "Americans are Emigrating to Australia," New York Times Magazine, May 17, 1970, p. 85.

18. Laura Faulk and Odie Faulk, The Australian Alternative (New Rochelle, N.Y.: Arlington House Publishers, 1975), p. 175.

19. Robert Trumbull, "Australia Eases Racial Barriers," New York Times, February 22, 1970, p. 24.

20. Gunther, Australia, p. 45.

21. Trumbull, "Racial Barriers," p. 24.

22. McGregor, Profile, pp. 313-314.

23. Herbert London, Non-White Immigration and the "White Australia" Policy (New York: New York University Press, 1970), pp. 82-83.

24. "Is the 'White Australia' Policy Justified?" Senior Scholastic, December 5, 1951, p. 11.

25. Robert Trumbull, "American Negro to be an Aussie," New York Times, December 13, 1970, p. 19.

26. McGregor, Profile, pp. 314-316.
    Trumbull, "Racial Barriers," p. 24.

27. J. M. van der Kroef, "Back to the Billabong?" Far Eastern Economic Review, LXIII (January 9, 1969):58.

28. Faulk and Faulk, Alternative, p. 140.

29. Sylvia Westerman and Martin A. Bacheller, eds., The CBS News Almanac, 1977 (Maplewood, N.J.: Hammond Almanac, Inc., 1976), p. 472.

30. Era Thompson, "Australia: Its White Policy and the Negro," part II, Ebony, September, 1966, p. 106.

31. "Negro Unit Assails Australia's 'Snub'," <u>New York Times</u>, August 17, 1947, p. 28.

32. The Immigration Reform Group, <u>Immigration: Control or Colour Bar?</u> (Melbourne: Melbourne University Press, 1962), pp. 117-118.

33. John Matthews, "Australian Appeal," letter to the editor, <u>Wall Street Journal</u>, May 10, 1966, p. 18.

34. London, <u>Non-White Immigration,</u> p. 90.

35. Jonathan Aitken, <u>Australia: Land of Fortune</u> (New York: Atheneum Publishers, 1971), p. 112.

36. Aitchison, <u>Americans</u>, p. 185.

37. McKnight, <u>Australia's Corner</u>, p. 60.
London, <u>Non-White Immigration</u>, p. 200.

38. Gunther, <u>Australia</u>, p. 348.

39. Era Thompson, "Australia: Its White Policy and the Negro," part I, <u>Ebony</u>, July, 1966, p. 55.

40. Donald Horne, <u>The Lucky Country: Australia Today</u> (Baltimore: Penguin Books, Inc., 1965), pp. 103,112.

41. Ibid., p. 77.

42. Ian Moffitt, <u>The U-Jack Society</u> (Dee Why West, New South Wales: Ure Smith Pty., Ltd., 1972), pp. 173-174.

43. Ibid., p. 174.

44. Ibid., p. 175.

45. Greenway, <u>Last Frontier</u>, p. 22.

46. Moffitt, <u>U-Jack</u>, p. 175.

47. Robert Goodman and George Johnston, <u>The Australians</u> (Adelaide: Rigby Ltd., 1966), p. 107.
Aitchison, <u>Americans</u>, pp. 23-24.

48. Aitchison, <u>Americans</u>, pp. 25,28.

49. Ibid., pp. 15-16.

50. Ibid., p. 18.

51. Greenway, Last Frontier, p. 170.

52. Moffitt, U-Jack, p. 175.

53. Aitchison, Americans, pp. 7-9.

54. Ibid. Goodman and Johnston, The Australians, p. 130.
    Greenway, Last Frontier, pp. 237-238.

55. Gunther, Australia, p. 146.

56. Ibid.

57. Aitchison, Americans, pp. 36-45 passim.

58. Gunther, Australia, p. 204.

59. Aitchison, Americans, p. 192.

60. U.S. Congress, House, speech by Prime Minister Robert
    Menzies, 84th Cong., 1st sess., March 16, 1955,
    Congressional Record, CI, 3069.

61. Jon Powis, "Americans Find No Easy Way to the Top Down
    Under," National Times (Australia), March 20-25, 1972,
    p. 36.

62. Lawrence Davies, "From Old World (America) to New
    (Australia)," New York Times Magazine, September 14, 1947,
    p. 66.
    Borrie, Immigration, p. 27.

63. "U.S. Firms Expand Down Under," Business Week, November 2,
    1946, p. 101.
    Trevor Reese, Australia, New Zealand, and the United
    States 1941-1968 (Fair Lawn, New Jersey: Oxford Univer-
    sity Press, 1969), pp. 79-80.

64. Reese, Australia, New Zealand, and the United States 1941-
    1968, pp. 79-80.
    Trevor Reese, Australia in the 20th Century (New York:
    Praeger Publishers, 1964), p. 137.

65. S. B. Hammond, "International Attitudes," in Social
    Structure and Personality in a City, ed. by O. A. Oeser
    and S. B. Hammond (New York: The Macmillian Co., 1954),
    p. 47.

66. American Historical Association, *Australia...Our Neighbors Down Under* (Washington, D.C.: American Historical Association, 1944), pp. 57-58.

67. Davies, "Old World to New," p. 13.
"Australia Seeks DP Immigrants," *New York Times*, Aug.15, 1947, p. 8.

68. "Australia: Situation Vacant," p. 31.

69. "First U.S. Emigrants Sail for Australia," *New York Times*, September 3, 1947, p. 12.

70. "1,000 Ex-GI's to Go to Australia Soon," *New York Times*, August 27, 1947, p. 15.

71. Davies, "Old World to New," p. 13.

72. Ibid.

73. Ibid.

74. Ibid.

75. U.S. Congress, Senate, Message by President Dwight D. Eisenhower, 83rd Cong., 1st sess., June 3, 1953, *Congressional Record*, IC, 5943.
D. M. Black, "Establishing a Business in Australia," *Overseas Business Reports*, No. 70-89 (December, 1970): 18.

76. Robert Hopkins, *I've Had It* (New York: Holt, Rinehart & Winston, 1972), p. 8.
Aitken, *Australia: Land of Fortune*, p. 112.

77. Horne, *The Lucky Country*, p. 125.

78. McGregor, *Profile*, p. 16.

79. Gunther, *Australia*, p. 206.
Australian Institute of Political Science, *How Many Australians? Immigration and Growth* (Sydney: Angus & Robertson, 1971), p. 135.

80. United States Embassy, *Foreign Economic Trends* (Canberra: United States Embassy, 1972), p. 2.

81. Aitchison, *Americans*, p. 164.

82. Moffitt, *U-Jack*, p. 180.

83. Peter Costigan, "Refugee from Politics," The Sun (Melbourne), June 17, 1974, p. 8.

84. Colless, "Decline Down Under," p. 38.

85. Hopkins, I've Had It, p. 13.

2

"DOWN UNDER" HO!

As a background for an in-depth analysis of specific reasons why Americans have chosen to emigrate, perhaps a few
general speculations are in order. A common belief is that
all emigrating Americans must have come to greatly dislike
their homeland, but such is not the case. Some leave simply
to travel or for adventure, although they admittedly are perhaps less likely to remain abroad than migrants who leave for
other reasons. One point should be remembered about all of
these migrants, however, and that is regardless of whether
their motives for emigrating seem serious enough to actually
compel them to leave the United States, they all perceive that
something is lacking in their lives in America which might be
obtained elsewhere. The "something lacking" may be anything
from a feeling of physical safety to a sense of adventure, but
something each perceived to be missing causes each one of them
to pack up and leave with the hope of filling his or her void
or voids elsewhere. The word, "perceive," should also be
stressed here; for according to migration specialist, Professor
Everett Lee, "It isn't always the reality of factors at home
and abroad that provokes people to emigrate, but rather what
people 'perceive' these factors to be."[1]

Americans have always been prone to migration, as
72,500,000 moved within the United States during the period
between 1970 and 1974 alone. Historically, Americans have been
a people "on the move," and John Babsone Lane Soule's, and
later Horace Greeley's, advice to "Go west, young man" is part
of the American Dream. Since 1967, however, the United States
has become an "emigrant" country as well.[2] In 1970 a Gallup
poll revealed that 12 percent of the American people, twice as

many as in 1959, wanted to emigrate; and 1,452,157 had currently migrated as of 1971.[3]

Why have so many Americans taken such a drastic step as
immigration to another land, instead of merely moving to a
more suitable location within their own nation? For example,
why would a city resident who desired a slower life pace immigrate to Australia, instead of simply moving to a small town
in the States? There are several possible answers to these
questions. Concerning the city dweller, perhaps he enjoys the
cultural advantages of city life which he would not receive in
a small town. Perhaps he is a computer programmer, and there
is little demand for his profession in a small town, or perhaps he is from the Southwest and could find employment in a
small northeastern town but the climate there would not be
suitable for him. Australian cities, on the other hand, have
the cultural advantages of their American counterparts, as
well as a slower pace, employment opportunities in many fields,
and a warmer climate, in general, than most American cities.
In addition, there are two, more subtle reasons why people
might decide to leave their nation for another rather than
simply migrate within the United States. First, people who
become dissatisfied with one aspect of their part of a country
sometimes tend to transfer that dissatisfaction to the entire
country. Second, when certain individuals think they are compelled to move anyway, they feel they may as well move somewhere that is really different. Two examples of Americans who
emigrated should suffice to demonstrate the unacceptability
for some of merely moving elsewhere in the States. Mrs.
Margaret Valance and her husband, Les, decided to emigrate because they "didn't want to subject their son and daughter to
the rising violence they saw in American cities, . . . and
they didn't feel fitted to rural living." [4] Similarly, Paul
Kahl, a cotton farmer from California, felt "it was easier for
my family to settle here (Wee Waa, New South Wales) than it
would have been in the South or New England," after he became
dissatisfied with his situation in the States.[5]

Some criticize those Americans who emigrate by accusing
them of "running away" and of "not being able to adjust."
Again, there are several possible responses to these arguments.
Many Americans who choose to emigrate may not be running "away"
from something but rather "toward" something, perhaps toward a
land such as Australia which in many ways is like the United
States used to be. For these migrants the reality of their
situation may be that they did not leave America as much as
America had left them. Other migrants may have attempted to
help solve America's problems, but found their efforts had
been wasted and would have been more beneficial helping

eliminate another society's ills. Even if they were "running away," one must question "from what?" And if they "could not adjust," one must ask "to what?" If one runs away from or cannot adjust to ever-increasing crime, violence or pollution, for example, can that be considered a fault or character flaw?

The conclusion many American migrants have reached, that life in the United States is unfortunately deteriorating and that this trend will not reverse itself for a number of years, seems regrettably true. At this point, one might say that "deteriorating" is surely too harsh a word and that all American migrants are not leaving because they perceive America to be deteriorating; after all, don't many move merely for the sake of adventure? This assertion is correct to the extent that every migrant, individually, does not conclude that all aspects of American life are degenerating. Yet, at the same time, it must be recognized that all migrants are not moving because of the same few reasons. Some might leave because they feel there is a growing lack of responsibility on the part of Americans and increased materialism. Others might embark because they feel a loss of freedom and consider the United States too crowded. The fact is that Americans are leaving for a myriad of reasons. And when the different reasons of individual Americans for migrating are taken collectively, it seems to indicate something more than dissatisfaction with a few aspects of life in their homeland. It indicates rather that there is a general deterioration of life in the United States, though it should be added as a final note that America is certainly not on the verge of collapse by any stretch of the imagination.

* * *

Thus having looked briefly at several reasons why Americans might want to emigrate, the types of Americans who choose to immigrate to Australia and some of the specific reasons why they leave the United States hoping to make the southwest Pacific continent their future home will now be described. With respect to race, very few nonwhites have immigrated to Australia. The majority of the white population who have immigrated have been males, but about half of each of the sexes has received financial assistance from the Australian government for their passage (Tables 2, 13, 14 and 15). Regarding age, education and marital status, the majority were young at the time of migration, while approximately the same number of people have attended college as have not attended, and approximately the same number of people had been married at the time of migration as had not been married (Tables 1 and 3).[6]

The occupations of the migrants before immigrating to

TABLE 15

AUSTRALIAN GOVERNMENT FINANCIAL ASSISTANCE
OF MIGRANT PASSAGE TO AUSTRALIA
(BY SEX)

Sex	No	Yes	Row Total
Male	63	69	132 (70.6%)
	47.7%	52.3%	
	70.8%	70.4%	
	33.7%	36.9%	
Female	26	29	55 (29.4%)
	47.3%	52.7%	
	29.2%	29.6%	
	13.9%	15.5%	
Column Total	89 (47.6%)	98 (52.4%)	187 (100.0%)

Missing Observations - 13

Australia have been quite varied, and their incomes in the
United States have not been inordinately high. Among the
group which embarked on September 2, 1947, there were electri-
cians from Nebraska and California along with restaurateurs
from Texas and Wisconsin, while more recently there have been
horse-breeders from Montana and Oklahoma along with oil and
minerals men from Alabama and Pennsylvania.[7] The largest
single occupational category since the early 1970s has been
that of American educators who came when an Australian recruitment program was begun in the United States to eliminate
a teacher-shortage that had developed in Australia. The largest general occupational category has been "professional,

technical and related workers," and only 1 percent of the
Americans who have immigrated to the island continent have
been unskilled (Table 16).[8] Concerning their incomes in the
United States, 63 percent earned $12,000 or less annually, but
one should bear in mind that salaries and wages in the past
were considerably lower than they are today (Table 17). It
would seem that those who have the more substantial incomes in
America are less likely to immigrate unless entrepreneurial
possibilities are great in Australia or they have been given a
business assignment there.

More Americans who immigrate to the land "Down Under" are
from California than from any other state (Table 5). It is
only natural that Californians are the most likely to immigrate to Australia, for people tend to look outward from themselves upon the world, and Australia is closer to being within
a Californian's perspective than within a Virginian's, for
example. Not only is it a matter of geographical perspective,
but it might also be that many Californians still want to
follow Soule's and Greeley's advice to "Go west." One other
point should be mentioned concerning the areas of the country
from which Americans have emigrated, this point being that
most people have come to Australia from the urban areas of the
United States.

Now that the types of Americans who immigrated to
Australia have been described, it is important and of much
interest to look at some of the specific reasons why they
chose to leave the United States and make Australia their future home. There are essentially three characteristics of this
migration. First, Americans have been pulled for the most
part by "ideal" rather than by place. In other words, qualitative factors have been generally more important than the
search for economic gain. Second, there has been a conservative aspect to the migration of many Americans. Unlike a
large number of the immigrants to the United States who were
fleeing persecution, which they obviously did not want to suffer, or the immigrants who were looking for sidewalks paved
with gold, many Americans envisioned Australia as a society
which has to some degree conserved what American life was like
thirty or so years ago. And third, American immigration to
Australia has been most often a personal and very individualistic affair, with each human being migrating for his or her
own reasons, and usually it has been for a number of reasons--
not just one.

In the spring of 1975, over 1,100 pages of computer tabulations and cross-tabulations were performed, using a mail
questionnaire designed by the author, on responses by 200

36

TABLE 16

OCCUPATION OF MIGRANTS IN THE UNITED STATES

Occupation	Absolute Frequency	Relative Frequency (Percentage)	Adjusted Frequency (Percentage)
Student	24	12.0	14.3
Professional, technical or related	80	40.0	47.6
Administrative, executive or managerial	14	7.0	8.3
Clerical	13	6.5	7.7
Other nonmanual	7	3.5	4.2
Manual	14	7.0	8.3
Homemaker	3	1.5	1.8
Armed Service	11	5.5	6.5
Other or retired	2	1.0	1.2
Unemployed or no answer	32	16.0	. . .
Total	200	100.0	100.0

Valid observations - 168

Missing observations -32

American migrants in Australia. The ten motives for emigrating from the United States and immigrating to Australia, responded to most frequently by the migrants, are listed as follows: for adventure, becoming too crowded, pace of life too fast, racial unrest, lack of new frontiers, for better business and

37

TABLE 17

INCOME OF MIGRANTS IN THE UNITED STATES

Income in U.S.	Absolute Frequency	Relative Frequency (Percentage)	Adjusted Frequency (Percentage)	Cumulative Adj. Freq. (Percentage)
None	6	3.0	3.4	3.4
Less than $4,000	28	14.0	16.1	19.5
$4,001-$8,000	56	28.0	32.2	51.7
$8,001-$12,000	36	18.0	20.7	72.4
$12,001-$16,000	28	14.0	16.1	88.5
Over $16,000	20	10.0	11.5	100.0
No answer	26	13.0	. . .	100.0
Total	200	100.0	100.0	100.0

Valid observations - 174

Missing observations - 26

TABLE 18

TEN MOST FREQUENTLY INDICATED MOTIVES
FOR EMIGRATING ON QUESTIONNAIRE

Motives	Percentage of Survey Respondents Who Indicated Particular Motives for Emigrating
for adventure	55.5
becoming too crowded	26.5
pace of life too fast	21.5
racial unrest	20.5
lack of new frontiers	20.0
for better business and investment opportunities	19.5
too much pollution	19.0
increased violence	18.5
rise in crime rate	18.0
felt loss of freedom	16.0

investment opportunities, too much pollution, increased violence, rise in crime rate, felt loss of freedom and other motives (Tables 18-20).

For adventure was the motive for immigrating to Australia specified by the largest number of migrants on their questionnaires. This particular motive is perhaps simultaneously the most difficult and most easy to describe. It is difficult to describe because adventure means different things to almost every individual; yet it is easy to describe in the broadest sense as a desire or quest for something new or different. Therefore, because this most popular motive is practically impossible to describe in any meaningful way other than in a

TABLE 19

ELEVEN MOST FREQUENTLY INDICATED MOTIVES
FOR EMIGRATING BY MALES ON QUESTIONNAIRE

Motives	Percentage of Male Survey Respondents Who Indicated Particular Motives for Emigrating
for adventure	51.5
racial unrest	24.2
becoming too crowded	23.5
for better business and investment opportunities	22.7
lack of new frontiers	21.2
increased violence	20.5
rise in crime rate	19.7
pace of life too fast	18.9
felt loss of freedom	17.4
too much pollution	16.7
unemployment	16.7

travel brochure fashion, it will not be analyzed here except to say that of all the migrants, those who do migrate because of a desire for adventure have a kind of temporary wanderlust and are the most likely to resettle in the United States. Only 29.1 percent of those surveyed who specified they immigrated to Australia "for adventure" said they would not or would probably not resettle in the States. The migrants who specified this motive have predominantly the following characteristics:

Demographic Variables	Predominant Characteristics*
sex	females
age at migration	under 30 years of age
marital status at migration	singles
section from which departed	California or the South
occupation in Australia	professional, technical or related workers

The motive for emigrating indicated most often in the survey after "for adventure" was becoming too crowded. As one American in Australia put it, "there were 23 million people in California and they all seemed to be dead ahead of you when you tried to go somewhere." California is not the only state in which it seems that someone is always "dead ahead of you," as the population of the entire nation has increased by one-sixth in the past fifteen years, and the number of automobiles has increased by an even greater figure. Furthermore, open land approximately equal in area to the state of Delaware is now being taken over annually by housing.[10] Today, roads, schools, occupational fields, prisons, national parks and amusement centers, among other areas, are all overcrowded. There simply seems to be too much of too many things in the United States. Formerly in America, bigger nearly always meant better and progress meant more, but these beliefs are no longer unquestionable. Crowding means tension plus other problems, and with more people generating more conflicts and differing opinions about our problems and their possible solutions, it takes longer and longer to get anything done or corrected. The migrants who indicated the motive "becoming too crowded" have predominantly the following characteristics:

Demographic Variables	Predominant Characteristics
sex	females
age at migration	25 to 29 years of age
marital status at migration	singles
income in U.S.	$8,001 to $12,000
section from which departed	California, North Central, or the West
year of migration	1965 to 1973
final place of settlement in Australia	Tasmania, Western Australia, or Queensland

The next most frequently designated motive for emigrating from the United States was pace of life too fast. After the

41

TABLE 20

TEN MOST FREQUENTLY INDICATED MOTIVES FOR
EMIGRATING BY FEMALES ON QUESTIONNAIRE

Motives	Percentage of Female Survey Respondents Who Indicated Particular Motives for Emigrating
for adventure	65.5
becoming too crowded	36.4
pace of life too fast	27.3
too much pollution	27.3
too much materialism	21.8
personal or family problems	20.00
lack of new frontiers	18.2
increased violence	18.2
rise in crime rate	16.4
impersonalized society	16.4

Second World War, a number of ex-servicemen said that one of
the reasons they were going to Australia was because "America
was in too much of a hurry." Today, automobile speed limits,
for example, are often exceeded by people who have come to
place fewer and fewer restraints upon themselves. In this
decade of the 1970s, the United States is a "now" society,
many of whose people seem compelled to instantaneous reactions
because of their impulses and demand instant gratification of
their desires. In the words of Australian author Henry
Williams, "America is one big rat rate chasing the almighty
dollar, where they burn themselves out to get things they
don't need to keep the advertisers going."[11] Some Americans
long, though, for the slower pace of the nation's past and embark for the land "Down Under." For a number of those

"inhabitants of a culture that's moving too fast for either comfort or beauty," according to anthropologist and author Dr. John Greenway in Australia: The Last Frontier, the journey to some parts of the Australian bush may even be "to where we

> have asked to be
> Where no storms come,
> Where the green swell is in the havens dumb,
> And out of the swing of the sea."[12]

The migrants who designated the motive "pace of life too fast" have predominantly the following characteristics:

Demographic Variables	Predominant Characteristics
sex	females
age at migration	50 or more years of age
marital status at migration	singles
occupation in the U.S.	armed services or homemakers
section from which departed	California or the West
year of migration	1965 to 1970
final place of settlement in Australia	Western Australia or Queensland

Fourth on the list of motives given was racial unrest. If one were to suggest that most white Americans are racists to some degree, the response from the people of the United States would probably be an adamant denial. However, if one were able to obtain a truthful public response from white Americans to the question, "Wouldn't most of you be glad if there were no blacks in the United States?" the answer would in all likelihood be affirmative. In the past, race relations appeared to be generally harmonious because black Americans were kept subservient. Now the pendulum of history has swung, and blacks have become more assertive. For some whites, the situation has become intolerable and they have chosen to immigrate to Australia. The migrants who specified the motive "racial unrest" have predominantly the following characteristics:

Demographic Variables	Predominant Characteristics
sex	males
age at migration	40 or more years of age
marital status at migration	marrieds
occupation in the U.S.	homemakers or armed services
section from which departed	Northeast
year of migration	1965 to 1970
final place of settlement in Australia	Western Australia or Queensland

The fifth most commonly designated motive was lack of new frontiers. Many Americans were shocked to hear of the closing of the western frontier in the 1890s, for the frontier had symbolized the American pioneer spirit. Americans have a psychological need for "space." Furthermore, they seem to have always been in search of frontiers, and according to one Australian Consul-General, Fred Homer, many Americans see Australia as the last of the world's "truly pioneer countries."[13] In most nations, human beings have either already conquered or been conquered by the environment--neither has yet happened in the continent in the antipodes which some have called the last frontier.[14] But Australia is not a frontier in the physical sense alone, but in a psychological or romantic sense as well. Some Americans have even immigrated to Australia "because in the far Outback they could carry a gun" just as many did in the American "Old West."[15] The migrants who designated the motive "lack of new frontiers" have predominantly the following characteristics:

Demographic Variables	Predominant Characteristics
sex	males
age at migration	40 to 49, or 25 to 29 years of age
marital status at migration	singled
occupation in the U.S.	students, or professional, technical or related workers
income in the U.S.	$12,001 to $16,000 or under $4,000
section from which departed	California or North Central
final place of settlement	Tasmania, Northern Territory, Western Australia, or Queensland
occupation in Australia	students, clerical, or manual workers

For better business and investment opportunities was the sixth most often specified motive for immigrating to Australia. By the middle of the 1950s, the prospect of a high rate of return on one's investment, compared to that in the United States as well as tax advantages began to lure a number of Americans to the continent in the southwest Pacific.[16] In 1954, Australian Federal Treasurer Harold Holt enticed Americans with the land, natural resources and stable government of his country. Concerning the land, he claimed that "the soil in the delta near Darwin (Northern Territory) is as rich as the fabled Nile Valley, but ten times greater in size."[17] Regarding minerals in Australia, a flood of American investors began to arrive ever since the 1961 Moonie oil field discovery.[18] In 1962, Tom

Price, Vice-President of Kaiser Steel Corporation, arrived in Australia and was astounded at the amount of iron ore obtainable. With amazement he remarked, "There are mountains of iron ore here. It is just staggering. It is like trying to calculate how much air there is."[19]

By the mid-1960s, American businessmen, farmers, ranchers and investors were all coming to the land "Down Under" in steadily increasing numbers. For the entrepreneur or innovator, many felt Australia might provide a unique opportunity to try a new enterprise, and for the businessman Australia provided a new or expanding market in itself as well as a base for business with the growing markets of Southeast Asia. Moreover, on the average, if an American worked in Australia for a United States firm on an American salary level, he could increase his salary by 10 to 15 percent over what his Australian salary would have been for the same type of employment.

American ranchers and farmers have immigrated looking for space, inexpensive land, limited costs and government regulations, and profit. Regarding the desire for space, Arizona rancher Alfred Stansberry stated, "I felt they were closing in on me. I wanted to get back to the big country."[20] Economically, ranchers have found (1972) that land in Australia with the same carrying capacity as that in American cattle country could be purchased for $70 to $100 an acre, while in the United States it would have cost $500 to $600 an acre.[21] And some farmers believe "there's a fortune to be made in Australia," in the words of one American who is the largest tomato grower in New South Wales.[22]

Likewise, American investors have looked for that same fortune to be made in the new mineral discoveries, because in addition to oil and iron ore finds in Australia, the highest grade of uranium and the largest single occurrence of bauxite in the world have been found there. Australia does, however, now require a minimum 75 percent Australian equity on all new uranium projects and a minimum 50 percent Australian equity on other new projects, if it is available. The migrants who specified the motive "for better business and investment opportunities" have predominantly the following characteristics:

Demographic Variables	Predominant Characteristics
sex	males
age at migration	the higher the age category, the greater the percentage who indicated this motive
marital status at migration	marrieds

45

occupation in the U.S.	administrative, executive or managerial
income in the U.S.	$12,001 to $16,000
section from which departed	California or North Central
year of migration	1950 to 1964
final place of settlement in Australia	New South Wales

Too much pollution was the seventh most often indicated motive. Concerning water pollution, government scientists estimate 90 percent of America's streams and rivers are polluted.[23] Regarding air pollution, Americans were supposed to have clean air by 1975, according to federal regulations set by the Environmental Protection Agency under the Clean Air Act Amendments of 1970; but on August 7, 1975, the Environmental Protection Agency declared that potentially hazardous levels of smog had become so widespread that it might be necessary to apply some urban pollution control measures to rural areas as well. In her book, Australian Adventure, Constance Helmericks describes her year's stay in Australia and relates how she wanted to go and take her daughters so they could "at least be able to remember COLOR." She felt the natural color of America was being destroyed and the sweet fresh air and blue sky were vanishing, even in Arizona where they lived. The authoress continues,

> . . . We searched for a land where the sky so blue
> comes right down to the ground, and the land is
> surrounded by the blue sea. A kind of sky country.
> A kind of sea country. Fantastic, wonderful. . . .
> It was to be Australia. . . .[24]

The migrants who indicated the motive "too much pollution" have predominantly the following characteristics:

Demographic Variables	Predominant Characteristics
sex	females
age at migration	15 to 24, or 40 to 49 years of age
marital status at migration	singles
income in the U.S.	under $8,001
section from which departed	California
final place of settlement in Australia	Victoria or Western Australia

The next most commonly given motive was increased violence. Almost all of the 5,500 letters of inquiry received during one period by a United States firm that gives advice on moving to

Australia mentioned social unrest and violence as reasons for possibly immigrating there from the States.[25] And violence is not confined to American streets and homes, as in our schools 70,000 teachers are seriously injured in a single year from attacks by students. Furthermore, violence effects nearly everyone, even our young, for there are 50,000 cases of battered and abused children in the United States each year. The migrants who gave the motive "increased violence" have predominantly the following characteristics:

Demographic Variables	Predominant Characteristics
sex	males
age at migration	40 to 49 years of age
marital status at migration	singles
occupation in the U.S.	armed services or homemakers
income in the U.S.	$4,001 to $8,000
section from which departed	Northeast or the South
year of migration	1965 to 1969
final place of settlement in Australia	Victoria or Western Australia
occupation in Australia	administrative, executive or managerial

Rise in crime rate was the ninth most often designated motive for emigrating by Americans. On September 26, 1975, President Gerald R. Ford announced that America was suffering from a "crime epidemic"; and in March of the following year, Federal Bureau of Investigation Director Clarence M. Kelley claimed that the nation was "beset by a crime wave of unprecedented dimensions and the public apparently doesn't care." The statistics are alarming! From 1963 to 1973, murders went up 129 percent, aggravated assaults went up 139 percent, violent crime increased 174 percent, forcible rapes increased 192 percent, while robberies rose by 226 percent; and from 1974 to 1975, serious crime rose by 9 percent, with a national trend of rising serious crime continuing into the following year. Even Lady Catherine Shaw, wife of the then Australian Ambassador to the United States, has been mugged!

Some Americans have become sick of crime and the fear of crime and some of these have decided to immigrate to Australia. In Australia, Chicago housepainter Thomas Enright proclaimed he loved his seven unmarried children too much to let them grow up in the United States. He continued,

We've been living in fear and disgust. I'm no racist. My parents raised me never to say "nigger" or "polack," and that's the way I've raised my kids. But fear has

47

been building up. These days my parents are afraid
to go out of the house. My kids are big and strong
and healthy. . . . I had to leave before one of
them had a leg blown off at school.[27]

The migrants who designated the motive "rise in crime rate"
have predominantly the following characteristics:

Demographic Variables	Predominant Characteristics
sex	males
age at migration	40 to 49 years of age
marital status at migration	marrieds
occupation in the U.S.	armed services
income in the U.S.	$4,001 to $8,000
section from which departed	Northeast
year of migration	1970 to 1971
final place of settlement in Australia	Victoria or Western Australia

The last of the ten most often indicated motives for emigrating from the United States was felt loss of freedom. This
very personalized motive could include anything from a loss of
freedom to move about in certain areas because of a fear of
possible physical attack by an assailant to a loss of privacy
in one's own personal effects. The migrants who indicated
"felt loss of freedom" have predominantly the following characteristics:

Demographic Variables	Predominant Characteristics
sex	males
age at migration	40 or more years of age
marital status at migration	singles
section from which departed	California
year of migration	1965 to 1969
occupation in Australia	manual workers

After the ten most frequently indicated motives for emigration from America and immigration to Australia designated
by the migrants on the survey questionnaire, the next most
commonly listed motives are the following in rank order of
their specification: personal or family problems (this motive
was probably more important among the migrants though not sta-
tistically demonstrated in this survey); too much materialism;
unemployment; impersonalized society; unstable, fast-changing
society; government ineffectiveness; and poor outlook for the
United States (those who specified these motives have predominantly the characteristics listed for each respective motive

48

in Appendix III). The motive personal or family problems is a highly individualized and variable one which cannot be explained in generalities. The feeling that there is too much materialism in the United States comes from the American emphasis on "things," and because "success" is usually measured by the number and material value of one's possessions. One disenchanted American who left for Australia remarked, "I owned a 1962 Porsche and had all the other amenities in the States, but the society stressed the importance of these things and not of smiling and 'have a good day.'"

Unemployment is still high, after a record high of 8.9 percent in May, 1975, and unemployment figures do not even include almost 5,000,000 "discouraged workers" who could not find jobs and have now stopped looking for work. During the early 1970s, many unemployed American teachers were enticed to Australia by paid transportation there and a starting annual salary of approximately $US10,000, tax-free, for two years.

Concerning the motive impersonalized society, affluence has caused Americans to have less regard or appreciation for things or possessions, and to consider them as only objects to be used. It is not too great a leap then to have less regard for people, especially in a fast-moving society. Therefore, we find the elderly being neglected; a radio or television announcer commenting unconcernedly or even with a lilt in his voice that ten people have just been mangled in an automobile accident; and an acquaintance saying, "How are you?"--when he really doesn't want to hear how you actually feel, or "Come and see me."--when the last thing he expects you to ask is "When?" In a 1970 Report to Congress, President Richard M. Nixon stated that many of America's young people are "skeptical and estranged . . . graduated into the impersonal routine of a bureaucratic, technological society, where many of them see life as a lonely conformity lacking the lift of a driving dream."[28] Many Americans of all ages have come to feel as though they are merely faceless numbers in our modern society, and a recent Harris poll has indicated that the number of Americans who feel "left out of things" has increased from 9 percent to 41 percent in the last nine years!

The United States seems, indeed, to be an unstable, fast-changing society. Years ago, one generation differed slightly from the one which preceded it, but today's generations of Americans are quite different from each other.[29] Now every successive generation demands more and more frequent changes to something new and different, at times even without knowing the exact benefits of giving up something of the past or the consequences of accepting the modern alternative. Some

Americans have refused to accept that type of existence and
have immigrated to Australia.

Many also find it difficult to tolerate government ineffectiveness. Just prior to his death, Senator Wayne Morse
remarked, the "public at grass roots has lost confidence in
government and have every right to--that's what's wrong with
America." In the past, liberal Democratic administrations
have too often attempted to resolve the nation's problems by
merely "tossing" huge quantities of public funds at them.
This expensive habit has helped increase the National Debt to
over $450,000,000,000. Right-wing Republican solutions have
been no better, however, and the following is commentator Eric
Sevareid's definition of their "catechism":

> Disorder is worse than injustice; waste in social pro-
> grams is worse than waste in the military; government
> regulations that bother business are awful; govern-
> ment regulations that aid and abet business are all
> right; quick production has priority over saving the
> environment; inflation is worse than unemployment;
> street crime must be suppressed; white-collar crime
> will cure itself, or something; the free marketplace
> is sacred but so is the power of great corporations
> to freeze it by administered prices.[30]

Governmental leadership has definitely been lacking. Our representatives simply react to problems and events as they arise
instead of planning ahead; and when they do act to alleviate
or solve our national problems, it is too often with little
regard for the full implications and long-term consequences of
their actions.

Comments, such as "We didn't like the idea of subjecting
our young son and daughter to the kind of future we saw taking
shape in the cities," predict a poor outlook for the United
States and have been stated by a number of American immigrants
to Australia.[31] The people of the United States used to have
specific hopes for their future, for an end to hard times, for
new material acquisitions, or for some other desire or aspira-
tion. What do Americans specifically hope for now or for the
future? What are the specific, accessible, tangible and ideal-
istic goals for which the people of America plan and toward
which they strive? These goals are not clear.

Other reasons given by Americans for leaving the United
States and immigrating to Australia have been private or government job assignments; marriage to an Australian; the chance
to find America, the way it used to be, again; "the pursuit of

happiness," as set forth in the American Declaration of Independence; simply to find a better life, with hope for the future; to find a better place in which to rear one's children; high cost of living in the United States (it is disturbing that the number of poor in America increased by 2,500,000 in 1975 and distressing that the projected average annual income for wage earners at the end of 1976 is $4,135, while the official poverty line for a four-person family is $5,500 per year); fear of nuclear fallout or nuclear war; to become removed from the United States so that the nation could be analyzed from an external perspective; and a feeling of political alienation (additional motives are listed in Appendix IV).

Having described some of the specific reasons why many Americans have chosen to emigrate from the United States and immigrate to Australia, it should be stressed that most of those who have migrated have had more than one reason for so doing. John Landis, an entomologist from Riverside, California, for example, left the United States in 1962 because of "the rat race, jammed freeways, crowded beaches, and orange groves and beanfields swamped by subdivisions," and settled in Australia.[32] It is possible, however, for a single event or motive to trigger migration, such as the case of one American surveyed who, upon surviving a near fatal automobile accident, regretted he had not lived his life as he had daydreamed, sold everything, sailed to Western Australia, and drove inland to a small town wherein he has found his "daydream become reality" (Appendix V contains further examples of single events or motives that caused Americans to emigrate from the United States and immigrate to Australia). It is also possible for one to migrate because of a series of occurrences which climaxed in one final, unbearable event--a "last straw."[33] For example, the final "straw" which caused one Nebraska homemaker to migrate to Australia was hearing of Jacqueline Kennedy's marriage to Aristotle Onassis.[34] In some cases, the "straws" which build to an intolerable level may be rather irrational, and it is the contention of Professor Everett Lee that "the decision to migrate is never completely rational, and for some persons the rational component is much less than the irrational."[35]

* * *

A great deal has been said thus far about why Americans have chosen to emigrate from the United States and live in Australia, but what do Americans actually know about Australia? What kind of image do they have of the land "Down Under"; how have they come by their image; and why did those who chose to immigrate there not choose some other country? The image many Americans used to have of Australia was something of a mythological one of kangaroos and koalas, Aborigines and Outback

51

sheep herders.[36] Today, many Americans still have misconceptions regarding Australia. They do not know, for example, that Australia is nearly as large as the mainland United States and that there are tropics in the northern part of the continent and vineyards in the south.[37] Moreover, many Americans have the mistaken impression that they could travel to Australia, easily obtain a good job and salary and immediately purchase all of the material conveniences they were accustomed to having in the States. One should not take too literally the advice offered in Asia Magazine, "If you are looking for the Utopia of the 20th Century, it is there Down Under."[38]

Yet, Americans do have considerably more knowledge about Australia than they once had, and their positive image of a land similar to "the way the United States used to be" is essentially correct. Americans do know, for example, that there are urban centers in Australia and that the population is located primarily along the coasts. Also correct are those who believe that Australia has retained many of the positive aspects which characterized America's past. The antipodean continent does have wide open spaces and a slower life pace than that of the United States; Australia does have a stable social climate where leaders do not get assassinated; and it does offer a healthy outdoor life as well as a school system emphasizing fundamental education.

The image which Americans have of Australia has been obtained for the most part from textbook or magazine material describing such things as the Great Barrier Reef, or from television specials or motion pictures.[39] Others have gained their own impressions by conversing with Australians, or with friends such as the many American servicemen who have been to the island continent, or by corresponding with individuals in Australia. Still others have gained a more concrete impression by actually having had the occasion to visit that country themselves at some time, such as the 284,000 American servicemen who went there from Vietnam for "Rest and Recreation" between 1967 and 1972 and the many servicemen who visited Australia during the Second World War.[40] Those who have contemplated immigration have probably also requested and received a great deal of information from the Australian Consulates or Embassy in the United States or from the individual state governments in Australia.

Most Americans who immigrated have suggested that any American seriously considering moving to Australia should first take a survey trip if that is practicable.[41] This suggestion would be especially helpful "for professional and management people, who have the hardest time of transition."[42] The value of making an investigative exploration of Australia has been and is important for those seriously considering leaving the United States, because no amount of research in America can compensate completely for becoming physically acquainted with a foreign country. However, one should bear in mind also that a brief visit to a nation will not "reveal" that country in its entirety to any prospective immigrant. Some have asserted that it may take at least two years in Australia to know if one really likes it there.[43] Furthermore, one should remember that it costs a great deal to visit a land as far away as Australia, and the expense of a trip prior to immigration may be prohibitive. Most respondents to the questionnaire had not visited Australia before immigrating; those who had visited were predominantly in the armed services or in the administrative executive or managerial field in the States; and those who had visited the potential new homeland prior to immigration had a predominantly greater income level in America (Table 21).

TABLE 21

MIGRANTS' VISIT TO AUSTRALIA BEFORE IMMIGRATION

Visited Before Immigration	Absolute Frequency	Relative Frequency (Percentage)	Adjusted Frequency (Percentage)
No	144	72.0	72.4
Yes	55	27.5	27.6
No answer	1	0.5	. . .
Total	200	100.0	100.0

Valid observations - 199

Missing observations - 1

For the Americans who have decided to emigrate from the United States, there are various reasons taken individually or collectively that tell why each one chose to settle in Australia rather than in some other country. Some chose Australia simply because they had an Australian spouse, and some moved there for the important reasons that Australia was an English-speaking nation or that it was more like the United States than any other country. Still others chose Australia by a process of elimination. In the words of one American businessman, "Switzerland was wiped out because it's almost impossible to become a citizen there, South Africa's apartheid was too much for us. . . . New Zealand is beautiful, but economically naive, so that left Australia."[44] There are, of course, other reasons given by Americans for selecting Australia over all the other nations of the world: Americans are welcome; there is an assisted passage program; the climate is not cold; there is a relatively slow pace of life; and it has both political and social stability. In the eyes of many prospective migrants, Australia is an uncrowded, far away, unique and adventurous land, in which there are greater opportunities for them than in any other foreign country (additional reasons given by the migrants for choosing Australia among the nations of the world are listed in Appendix VI).

In making the decision to migrate, predominantly more of the questionnaire respondents said they took less than five months to finally decide to immigrate from the time they first considered the possibility of moving to Australia, with females deciding more quickly than males. This haste has meant that many Americans have not been well prepared for their migrant status. Emotionally, many have not prepared themselves, for example, for initial periods of loneliness until new friends are met; and professionally, many have not had their technical or professional qualifications reviewed before embarking.[45] Fortunately today, Australian officials conduct more careful interviews of potential migrants, especially of those who request financial assistance to immigrate, and provide them with more accurate information about Australia than in decades past. This is done so that the migrants may make better decisions and preparations regarding immigration, and thus be less likely to become dissatisfied with their new land and want to resettle in the United States should they finally decide to immigrate (Appendix VII). In fact, one high immigration official has stated that Australia might actually discourage potential American migrants a little at times, even though the Australian government wants them, because "we want realists, not dreamers. . . ."[46] The most common waiting period between the time one submits a firm application for migration and the time he or she departs is under three months.[47] Some who have not desired to wait that long have obtained a vistor's visa in approximately one to three weeks and applied for a permanent visa once in Australia.

The physical preparation for immigration to Australia can be a difficult experience. In addition to packing the obvious necessities and documents needed in Australia, the migrant has to decide what to take, such as certain articles of clothing which may be less expensive and made better in the States, and what not to take, such as electrical appliances which will probably need converters to operate in Australia or pets which would have to be quarantined for a period of months after arrival. In addition, there are a number of items, such as certain weapons and some drugs, which are prohibited from importation. The actual trip itself is not so difficult for most, as it is usually either a leisurely three-week ocean cruise or only an eighteen-hour airplane flight from the west coast.

Thus having followed the American migrants through their thoughts, dreams and decisions regarding immigration and having seen them on their way, the next step is to follow them westward--"Down Under" Ho--and describe their "discovery" of Australia, their new home.

Footnotes - Chapter II:

1. Hopkins, *I've Had It*, p. 9.

2. Ibid., p. 3.

3. "Australia: She'll Be Right, Mate--Maybe," *Time*, May 24, 1971, p. 34.
   Hopkins, *I've Had It*, p. 3.

4. Robert Trumbull, "More Americans Go to Australia, Seeking Simpler Life," *New York Times*, August 15, 1969, p. 12.

5. Robert Keatley, "U.S. Migrants Find Australia is Fine--If You have Money," *Wall Street Journal*, March 16, 1966, p. 10.

6. Surveys Section, Department of Immigration, *Survey*, p. 60.

7. Davies, "Old World to New," p. 13.
   Moffitt, *U-Jack*, pp. 179-180.

8. Gordon, "Americans are Emigrating," p. 77.

9. Hopkins, *I've Had It*, p. 12.

* The reader is advised to remember two points regarding these characteristics and all characteristics and other findings mentioned in the following pages. First, the words, "predominant" and "predominantly," do not refer to a greater number of people within a category (e.g., male) compared to the number of people within any other category (e.g., female) who gave the same response (e.g., Yes) to a particular question (e.g., Did you immigrate for adventure?); it rather refers to the percentage of people within a category compared to the percentage of people within any other category who gave the same response to the particular question. Therefore in this case, because a greater number of males than females were surveyed, it might be true that a greater number of males than females indicated one reason they immigrated was "for adventure," but a greater percentage of the total number of females surveyed indicated "for adventure" as a motive for immigration than the percentage of the total number of males surveyed who indicated likewise. Second, the reader is advised to remember that the characteristics should not be considered as forming a composite picture. In other words individuals who indicated one reason they immigrated to

56

Australia was "for adventure," for example, are not necessarily most likely to be females who are under 30 years of age. Instead, each characteristic should be considered separately. Thus, in this case, those who indicated "for adventure" as a motive are more likely to be females regardless of their age, and are more likely to be under 30 years of age regardless of their sex.

10. Newsletter from Planned Parenthood Federation of America, Inc., May, 1976.

11. Henry Williams, Australia--What Is It? (Adelaide: Rigby Ltd., 1971), p. 29.

12. Greenway, Last Frontier, p. 36.

13. U.S. Congress, House, Honorable Jack Brooks referring to speech by Ambassador Ed Clark, 89th Cong., 2nd sess., June 14, 1966, Congressional Record, CXII, Appendix, A3204.

14. McGregor, Profile, p. 181.

15. Faulk and Faulk, Alternative, p. 127.

16. K. F. Ronaldson and K. R. Trimble, The Economic Scene, an Australian Perspective (New York: John Wiley & Sons Australasia Pty., Ltd., 1969), p. 142.

17. Art Linkletter, Linkletter Down Under (Englewood Cliffs, N.J.: Prentice-Hall, Inc., 1968), pp. 1-5 passim.

18. "The Big Rise Down Under," Business Week, December 21, 1963, p. 96.

19. Colin Simpson, The New Australia (Sydney: Angus & Robertson, 1972), p. 475.

20. "What to Expect If You Emigrate to Australia," U.S. News & World Report, July 17, 1967, p. 77.

21. Aitchison, Americans, p. 109.

22. R. T. Appleyard, "Westward the Antipodes," in The California Revolution, ed. by Carey McWilliams (New York: Grossman Publishers, Inc., 1968), p. 226.

23. Natural Resources Defense Council, Your Dollars and Environmental Sense (New York: Natural Resources Defense

Council, Inc., 1975), p. 6.

24. Constance Helmericks, Australian Adventure (Englewood Cliffs, N.J.: Prentice-Hall, Inc., 1971), pp. 1-2.

25. Gunther, Australia, p. 49.

26. "Crime Surge Defies All Efforts, Survey of Cities Shows," U.S. News & World Report, June 10, 1974, pp. 34-35.

27. Gordon, "Americans Are Emigrating," pp. 75, 77, 80.

28. U.S. President, A Report to The Congress by President Richard M. Nixon, U.S. Foreign Policy for the 1970s: A New Strategy for Peace, February 18, 1970, p. 155.

29. McGregor, Profile, p. 287.

30. "Commentary" C.B.S. News, September 8, 1975, Commentator, Eric Sevareid.

31. Gunther, Australia, p. 49.

32. "What to Expect," p. 76.

33. Hopkins, I've Had It, p. 14.

34. Gordin, "Americans Are Emigrating," pp. 75, 77. 80.

35. Hopkins, I've Had It, p. 14.

36. Anne Clark, Australian Adventure (Austin: University of Texas Press, 1969), pp. 4-6.

37. Frank Hopkins, "The American Image of Australia," in Pacific Orbit, ed. by Norman Harper (Melbourne: F. W. Cheshire, 1968), pp. 220-226 passim.

38. Gunther, Australia, p. 346.

39. Reggie Moffat and Peter Tannen, Australia...What's It Really Like? (Orlando, Florida: Southern Cross Publications, 1971), p. 1.

40. David Lamb, "Won't Deport U.S. Deserter, Australia Says," Los Angeles Times, April 8, 1974, sec. 1, p. 10.

41. "What to Expect," p. 76.

42. Moffat and Tannen, What's It Like? p. 18.

43. The Permanent Residents' Group, American Women's Club of Perth, Western Australia, "So--You're Interested in Sunny Western Australia!" Newsletter from Australia, April, 1971, p. 1.

44. Curtis Casewit, Overseas Jobs: The 10 Best Countries (New York: Warner Books, Inc., 1972), p. 38.

45. Martha DuBose, "In Search of the New Frontier," Sydney Morning-Herald, women's supplement, July 1, 1971, p. 1.

46. Gordon, "Americans Are Emigrating," p. 85.

47. Surveys Section, Department of Immigration, Survey, p. 55. (Once one submits an application to an Australian Consulate, for example, he is generally informed within ten days whether he is eligible for processing and is invited for an interview with an immigration officer. The interview is usually about one hour long and conducted at whatever time is suitable for the applicant. If the officer finds from the interview that the applicant is acceptable, the latter is advised what medical documents to obtain; and upon providing such documents to the Consulate, the applicant in all likelihood receives his visa within seven to ten days.)

3

DISCOVERY

Upon arriving in Australia, the migrants' senses become extremely alert as there is a wealth of new information to digest. Most are probably aware immediately that the seasons are reversed from those in the United States. Furthermore, it becomes almost immediately obvious that nearly all of the people are Caucasian with little variation in "dialect, custom and physique."[1] Depending upon where the migrants choose to settle or to travel before settling, they may soon learn that although Australia is physically a large country--sixth largest in the world--it has a relatively small population, less than 14,000,000 people, most of whom are located along the southeast coast (Table 22).[2]

Also, many may discover firsthand that Australia consists mostly of "the bush," which is a descriptive term applicable to all land beyond the cities.[3] There are no great mountain ranges or river systems in Australia; therefore the interior is extremely hot and arid.[4] Oddly enough, the blank interior may be very beneficial, psychologically and otherwise. According to Australian author Henry Williams, it plays "a significant role in the maintenance of sociological stability as a daydream safety valve for harassed city dwellers."[5] Furthermore, because the air over the interior is relatively clean, winds blowing across the center of the continent toward the coasts help push away pollutants hanging over the coastal cities. In the bush, the migrants may see many fascinating sights--from the inanimate Ayers Rock, the world's largest monolith, to the animate marsupials (over 120 species in Australia) and egg-laying mammals like the platypus and spiny anteater, perhaps the most unique animals in existence.[6] Also, it is possible

TABLE 22

POPULATION OF AUSTRALIA JUNE 30, 1945 TO
DECEMBER 31, 1975 (1,000s)

Year	Population of Australia, Year Ended 30 June (1,000s)
1945	7,391.7
1946	7,645.2
1947	7,579.4
1948	7,708.7
1949	7,908.1
1950	8,178.7
1951	8,421.7
1952	8,636.5
1953	8,815.3
1954	8,986.5
1955	9,199.7
1956	9,425.5
1957	9,640.2
1958	9,842.4
1959	10,056.4
1960	10,275.0
1961	10,508.2
1962	10,700.5
1963	10,906.9
1964	11,121.6
1965	11,340.9
1966	11,550.5
1967	11.793.6
1968	11,997.8
1969	12,246.7
1970	12,507.3
1971	12,755.6
1972	12,959.1
1973	13,131.6
1974	13,338.3
1975	13,600.8[a]

SOURCES: Australian Bureau of Statistics' Revised
Inter-Censal Estimates.

Australian Information Service, "News in Brief:
Population." Australia Bulletin, No. 1 (June 1, 1976), p. 6.

aProvisional estimate for December 31, 1975.

for them to admire the magnificent, giant Karri trees (Eucal-
yptus diversicolor) of Western Australia, as well as the abundance of wildflowers since 33 percent of the world's species
of wildflowers grow in Australia.[7]

Australia is an urban nation, however, and most American
migrants choose to settle in the coastal cities. The urban
population of Australia surpassed the rural population in the
1860s, much earlier than the decade before 1920 when the
American urban population became larger than the rural population.[8] Now "Australia is the world's most urban society," with
88.5 percent of the people inhabiting the cities.[9]

The largest city in the nation is Sydney, the capital of
New South Wales. It has a population of approximately
3,000,000 people and has been called "the New York of the
Southern Hemisphere."[10] Though the skyline of Sydney is similar to that of New York, some have compared this largest city
in Australia to San Francisco or Los Angeles.[11] One migrant
characterized it as "San Francisco running at a Los Angeles
tempo."[12] At certain times, the migrant may find that Sydney
has as much pollution as Los Angeles, but it is a city that has
not been torn by violence and it has a sparkling quality about
it which is uplifting for many.

Melbourne is Australia's second largest city and the capital of Victoria. It has almost as many people as Sydney and is
known as the financial capital of the country.[13] Though
Melbourne is similar to Los Angeles in its physical expansive-
ness, it is culturally similar to Boston.[14] Some, such as
Australian columnist Barry Humphries, have been rather sarcas-
tic in their references to the sedateness of the city. He has
remarked, "It's the only place on earth where the visitor from
abroad can close his eyes and wonder if there really is life
before death."[15] Yet others have defended its unperturbed air,
and point with pride to its many beautiful parks and additional
assets.

Other major cities in Australia include Brisbane, Adelaide, Perth, Hobart, Canberra and Darwin. Brisbane is the
capital of Queensland, and with just under 1,000,000 inhabitants is a somewhat humid and easy-going city. Much farther to
the south is Adelaide, which has slightly fewer people than

Brisbane. It is the capital of South Australia and is noted for its churches and cultural activities.[16] Perth, the capital of Western Australia, like Adelaide, is farther from the United States than other Australian cities and is therefore perhaps less susceptible to American influence. With about 800,000 people, Perth--which is Australia's current "boom city" because it is the hub of the mining boom--has been reputed to combine the best qualities of other Australian cities, especially their open-air quality and the friendliness of the people.[17] Hobart, with a population of approximately 175,000, is the capital of the island state of Tasmania and is a modern yet provincial city at the same time.[18] At least 215,000 people inhabit Canberra, the national capital of Australia. It is considerably less pollutted than Washington, D.C., the national capital of the United States, and is a well-planned city with 8,000,000 trees.[19] Unfortunately, Darwin, the capital of the Northern Territory, was destroyed by hurricane Tracy in December, 1974, but it is now being rebuilt and has a population of nearly 45,000.

Although a greater proportion of Australians live in cities than do Americans, Australia also has a greater proportion of farmers, and the opportunities in that occupation as well as in ranching and mining are tremendous if one has the necessary capital and "know-how."[20] Most Americans are unaware of the variety and potential of farming in Australia. For example, most are probably unaware that Australia exports more sugar than any other nation in the world except Cuba.[21] Also, in Wee Waa, New South Wales, near the Namoi River, a variety of crops would have tremendous growth potential. Jack Kitchings from California settled there and has boasted,

> The potential of this place is unlimited. It has the
> fertility of the Mississippi delta with the levelness
> of the San Joaquin Valley in California. The black-
> soil here is up to twenty-five feet deep, and there're
> no extremes of temperature.[22]

With respect to ranching, Australia is primarily sheep and cattle country, and it annually produces 30 percent of the world's supply of wool.[23] In connection with its mining opportunities, Edgar Kaiser of Kaiser Industries has claimed that "Australia's natural resources are possibly the greatest in the world."[24] The richest square mile of rock ever known was purportedly at Kalgoorlie, Western Australia; and now Australia has large and easily accessible deposits of iron ore and bauxite in addition to about one-fifth of the world's known reserves of uranium. Finally, one city alone, Broken Hill, New South Wales, has more minerals in good crystalline quality than any other single place on earth.[25]

Within the cities in which the migrants first arrive, if
no permanent accommodation has been prearranged, they may stay
for a brief period at a motel or a somewhat longer period at a
government hostel. Most of the hostels have improved considerably over the years, but there are still some in which the
living conditions and food leave much to be desired. The majority of these Americans do not remain in either the motels or
hostels for any great length of time though, but display initiative and independence in locating more permanent accommodation.[26] Initially, the accommodation is usually a rented flat,
and later they tend to either rent a flat or house or begin to
make payments on the purchase of a house of their own.[27]

From a somewhat broader perspective, most of the migrants first settle in the states of New South Wales and
Victoria, just as one might suspect. Yet, according to this
writer's study, migrants first settling in either of these two
states are predominantly more likely, than migrants first settling in any other state, to migrate later elsewhere in
Australia. Those first settling in New South Wales were predominantly under thirty years of age and from the Northeast or
California, while those first settling in Victoria were predominantly thirty to thirty-nine years old and from the North
Central part of the United States. Irrespective of place of
initial settlement, the most dramatic shift of people appears
to be predominantly of females to Western Australia and of both
sexes to the Capital Territory. Young, single American migrants also appear to be the most mobile after their initial
settlement.[28] Other relevant characteristics of those first
settling in any particular state in Australia are: predominantly more of those in Queensland, Victoria or New South Wales
visited Australia before immigrating, and predominantly more of
those in Victoria or New South Wales had a job set up "Down
Under" before emigrating from the United States.

From a national perspective, regardless of place of settlement, how do these migrants feel and what do they experience
initially? This is a very difficult query to answer in any
exact sense, for as Thomas Jenkins has judged,

> Migration is a very complex affair. It is, for better
> or for worse, a fundamental experience, a subtle blend
> of stimulus and loss, of exhilaration and desolation,
> of collision and conflict, blood-warming friendship
> and aching loneliness and most other human experiences.[29]

If an attempt were made to generalize about their initial

feelings and experiences, it would probably proceed something in the following manner. First, there might be a feeling of elation at having arrived in their new land, as the senses would become more alive to interpret the new environment.[30] Second, as they begin to participate in everyday affairs of Australian society, they might more fully realize they are "foreigners" in a nation which is not quite the same as the United States. Even though these Americans are indeed foreigners in Australia and may feel like foreigners for some time, this does not mean they will never feel like "Australians." Just as many migrants to the United States have represented American ideals more than have some native-born Americans, it is possible for American migrants in Australia to represent Australian ideals more than do some native-born Australians.

Next, during this initial period, the migrants begin to weigh carefully the positive and negative aspects of life in their new home compared to the life they had known in the States. This weighing process might include everything from major considerations, such as whether there really is less violence or better business and investment opportunities for example in Australia, to minor ones, such as whether they can do without Hershey's chocolate or news commentator Walter Cronkite. If their conclusion is that the positive aspects outweigh the negative aspects, then they might make a tentative decision to remain in Australia for an indefinite period of time, perhaps anywhere from a year or two to permanently.

In describing this initial period more fully, the migrants make numerous observations in addition to the obvious physical ones, such as the sun's path across the nothern sky and automobiles driven on the left side of the road, both opposite from that which occurs in the United States. For example, one of the first things one is certain to notice is the Australian accent. It has a greater nasal quality than the English spoken by Americans and is calmer and more conservative in tone.[31] Certain words and expressions are also different, as in Australia a cookie would be called a "biscuit" and to complain would be to "winge." Humorous incidents sometimes also arise because of differences in words or expressions, such as when an American sits down at a restaurant and asks for a napkin--in Australia a "napkin" means a diaper. In this case one should have asked for a "serviette." Other differences include making a "y" or "o" sound for the ends of words, such as "Tassie" for Tasmania and "Paddo" for Paddington; and in spelling, Australians will sometimes use the letter "y" where Americans use "i," as in the word, "tyre." But perhaps the most unique aspect of the Australian language is "Strine" (the pronounciation of the word "Australian"), which is the habit of running the words of phrases or sentences together when speaking--for instance, "Hazzy gairt non wither mare thorgon?" means "How is he getting on with the mouth organ?"[32]

Another aspect of Australia which the migrants notice immediately is the food. Australian food is excellent and available at reasonable prices.[33] Though some products such as coffee are of inferior quality, others such as grass-fed beef are more palatable than that found in the United States; and Australian fruits and vegetables are fresh, abundant and usually cheaper than those in America.[34] Just as with the Australian language, the "Aussies" have different food preferences and eating habits. Breakfast may include spaghetti on toast, for example, and meat pies are a popular dish for meals later in the day.[35] Furthermore, there are few American-style cafeterias "Down Under," and quick-eat places, like McDonald's, may serve fish and chicken as well as hamburgers.[36] Despite these differences, American migrants are usually glad to find that there are numerous American brand name packaged food products in Australia.

Many of these migrants are also quick to notice news sources, entertainment, housing and schools available in Australia. News of major occurrences in the United States are reported almost daily, and Time and Newsweek are readily available.[37] American motion pictures usually arrive within a few months after their premieres in the States, and a great number of American television programs such as "All in the Family," "Days of Our Lives," "I Love Lucy" and "Streets of San Francisco" are aired in Australia.[38] As to housing, though most migrants said they found it satisfactory, they also found it relatively more expensive than in America and of "generally inferior design and less well-equipped."[39] Australian houses are built to last, but they are small by American standards with smaller rooms, and they usually have only one toilet.[41] School begins in February in Australia, and although students are not legally required to wear school uniforms, many do.

Many Americans do find that Australia is similar to the way the United States used to be. In Perth one of these migrants stated, "I can't get over the feeling that I've seen all this happening before"; and an American executive surveying the Outback said, "It's like America in the 1880s. This is what it must've been like when the railroads opened up the West."[41] One should not infer from the aforementioned that Australia is "behind" the United States in everything, as it had "revenue-sharing" long before America for instance and set a minimum wage at least thirty years before the United States, but life in Australia does move at a comparatively slower pace.[42]

Not only do many migrants find that Australia very much resembles the America of years past, but most Americans find the Australian people quite similar to themselves. One migrant even claimed that the difference between "Aussies" and Americans in general was less than the differences among people from various sections of the United States. Another pleasing discovery made by the majority of the migrants is that, on the whole, Australians are a friendly people. In fact, upon arriving in a country town, a migrant might find that he would be taken immediately to the local pub for a free beer.[43] A number of Australians do display a certain antipathy toward American migrants because they believe all Americans to be rich, but most Australians accept and get along well with the "New Australian Yanks" in their midst. As Australian author and business executive Ray Aitchison has written,

> Australians give Americans a better reception than
> they receive almost anywhere else in the world.
> Australians do not regard American refugees as
> social dropouts who have fled the problems of their
> homeland. As long as Americans can stay out of
> trouble with the law in Australia, can support them-
> selves and do not import America's national problems,
> they are most welcome to stay.[44]

The American migrants do not initially see everything as satisfactory or in a favorable light, of course. Almost immediately the lack of sewerage and roads comparable to those in the States is noted, and the lack of good roads and road surfaces contributes to the 15.5 people killed per 100,000,000 miles driven in Australia compared with 5.5 killed per 100,000,000 miles driven in America.[45] Unfortunately, many Americans arrive in Australia expecting to discover simply a smaller version of the United States. Disappointed, they begin to enumerate those things or amenities that Australia lacks which they had in the States, apparently not realizing that it takes a certain amount of either ignorance or gall to compare the wealth, goods and services available in a nation with less than 14,000,000 inhabitants to those in a nation of approximately 216,000,000 people.

One major problem which many of the migrants do not fully appreciate when immigrating to Australia is the potential difficulty of obtaining desirable employment. According to this writer's survey, most Americans have not had a specific job set up before migrating. Though all new residents have the free services of the Commonwealth Employment Service available to them, the process of being interviewed by prospective employers may take considerable time.[46] Unless a migrant claims to be settling permanently in Australia, an employer is not eager to

hire a "Yank" who he may believe is just on a "working holiday." Other employers are unwilling to hire an American if it
appears that the applicant would not stay at his job for any
length of time either because he was overqualified or because
he would not be satisfied for long with his salary. Additional problems Americans might face in obtaining desirable
employment are that in some professions it is difficult to get
a necessary license; in the nonregistrable professions, such as
engineering or accounting, usually one must belong to a professional organization before employment is possible; in fields
of business or management, employment may be difficult to obtain without knowledge of and experience on the local scene;
and permanent appointment to the national public service is not
allowed for non-Australian citizens or non-British subjects.[47]
To be sure, if a migrant is willing to accept almost any job,
he can certainly find work in Australia. If on the other hand
he wants to search for "the right job," his employment opportunities will be greatly diminished.

A second major problem that many of the migrants begin to
face shortly after their arrival is adjusting to the cost of
living. Before doing nearly anything else after arrival, a
migrant discovers that every $US123 he brought with him
(October, 1976)* is only worth approximately $A100; thus before
he even gets started, he feels as though he is losing money.
Although it is true that the average wage for non-agricultural
labor is not a great deal lower in Australia than it is in the
United States, the purchasing power of that wage in Australia
is not as great in obtaining certain commodities that Americans
seem to think they need. For instance, automobiles, washing
machines and televisions--all of which Americans are quick to
buy--are relatively more expensive in Australia.[48] For some
migrants, toiling for the funds to purchase these "necessities"
seems to take too long, and trying to do without them seems unbearable.

Other problems which the Americans surveyed by this writer
said they had to face during their first few months in Australia include adjusting to the "she'll be right" (meaning "everything will work out just fine, so don't worry about it") philosophy of Australians, the slower pace, the lower standard of
living, forming friendships, dealing with inefficiency and adjusting to school procedures and teaching techniques (Appendix
VIII contains additional problems indicated).

Despite these initial problems, it seems that the vast
majority of Americans who have immigrated to Australia experienced "no difficulty of any significance at any stage of migration. . . ."[49] Those who may have had problems finding

suitable accommodation or adjusting to local conditions, for example, could receive ready assistance from a number of organizations or associations in Australia, such as "Welcome Wagon of Australia," which was founded by an American, Mrs. Mary Suplee, from Coral Gables, Florida, who immigrated to Brisbane in 1965.[50] In general, Americans who have immigrated to their new home under the Southern Cross have found that their expectations have been met and that life in Australia is indeed healthy, wholesome and happy.[51] Most of these "New Australians" from the United States have tended to blend into the Australian society very smoothly; and before a great deal of time expired, many could hardly be distinguished from Australians themselves, except perhaps for not completely adopting the Australian accent or assuming the Australian habit or custom of holding one's fork in the left hand.[52]

Some predominant characteristics of the Americans surveyed by this writer regarding their initial feelings about Australia may be of interest to the reader at this point. Over 42 percent stated they were pleased with Australia compared with only 16 percent who felt disappointed approximately one month after their arrival (39.5 percent indicated they had "mixed feelings" and 2 percent gave no answer). Predominantly more of those who specified the following motives for emigrating from the United States and immigrating to Australia, rather than other motives listed, indicated they were pleased initially.

Motives	Percentage Pleased
felt loss of freedom	75.0
government ineffectiveness	74.0
too much materialism	70.0
poor outlook for the United States	64.0
high cost of living	62.5
unstable, fast-changing society	62.1
increased violence	59.4
pace of life too fast	58.1
impersonalized society	56.7
racial unrest	56.1

And predominantly more of those with the following characteristics, than with other characteristics, indicated they were pleased initially.

Predominant Characteristics	Percentage Pleased
sex - males	44.6
age at migration - 30 to 39 years of age	48.9
or 40 to 49 years of age	48.4
marital status at migration - singles	46.9
income in the U.S. - $12,001 to $16,000,	53.6
or over $16,000	52.6
section from which departed - California	48.0
had visited Australia prior to migration	50.0
year of migration - 1950 to 1964	66.6
initial place of settlement in Australia -	
Queensland,	48.6
or Western Australia	46.9

In contrast, predominantly more of those who specified the following motives for emigrating from the United States and immigrating to Australia, rather than other motives listed, indicated they were disappointed initially.

Motives	Percentage Pleased
personal or family problems	25.0
for adventure	19.1
too much pollution	18.4
unemployment	16.7
becoming too crowded	15.1
unstable, fast-changing society	13.7
lack of new frontiers	12.5
poor outlook for United States	12.0
rise in crime rate	11.2
impersonalized society	10.0

And predominantly more of those with the following characteristics, than with other characteristics, indicated they were disappointed initially.

Predominant Characteristics	Percentage Disappointed
sex - females	18.5
age at migration - 25 to 29 years of age	20.7
marital status at migration - marrieds	19.2
occupation in the U.S. - manual workers	35.7
income in the U.S. - less than $4,000	19.2
had not visited Australia prior to migration	19.1
year of migration - 1974	36.4
initial place of settlement in Australia -	
New South Wales	19.8

Footnotes - Chapter III:

1. Herald & Weekly Times, Wonderful Australia in Pictures (Melbourne: Cologravure, 1953), p. 222.

2. McKnight, Australia's Corner, p. 59.

3. McGregor, Profile, p. 157.

4. Hopkins, I've Had It, p. 158.

5. Williams, What Is It? p. 36.

6. Vincent Serventy, "Wildlife: Wonder and Delight," in Hammond Innes Introduces Australia, ed. by Clive Turnbull (New York: McGraw-Hill Company, 1971), p. 95.

7. There are indications (based on calculations made from stumps found) that some eucalypts, of which there are more than 500 species, in Australia may have been more than 400 feet tall many years ago, or the tallest trees in the world surpassing even the coastal redwoods of California. "Eucalypts in Florida," editorial, American Forests, October, 1976, p. 15.

8. Gunther, Australia, p. 36.

9. Moffitt, U-Jack, pp. 225, 227.

10. Gunther, Australia, p. 127.

11. Kenneth Schubert, "Yank's-Eye View of Australia," Senior Scholastic, November 5, 1945, p. 14.

12. Aitken, Land of Fortune, pp. 57-58.

13. Ibid., p. 64.

14. Faulk and Faulk, Alternative, pp. 77-78. Gunther, Australia, p. 158.

15. Gunther, Australia, p. 157.

16. Aitken, Land of Fortune, p. 75.

17. Ibid., pp. 78-79.

18. Gunther, Australia, p. 179.

19. Ibid., pp. 147, 151.

20. Hopkins, I've Had It, p. 158.

21. Gunther, Australia, p. 237.

22. Gordon, "Americans Are Emigrating," p. 80.

23. Gunther, Australia, p. 120.

24. Linkletter, Down Under, p. 207.

25. Gunther, Australia, p. 199.

26. Department of Immigration, Survey, p. 61.

27. Ibid., p. 32.

28. Ibid., p. 18.

29. Thomas Jenkins, We Came to Australia (London: Constable and Company Ltd., 1972), p. 235.

30. Hopkins, I've Had It, pp. 44-45.

31. McGregor, Profile, pp. 32, 36-37.

32. Gunther, Australia, pp. 39-40.

33. Faulk and Faulk, Alternative, p. 180.

34. Ibid.
    Moffat and Tannen, What's It Like? pp. 28-29.

35. Faulk and Faulk, Alternative, p. 49.

36. Ibid., p. 153.

37. Moffat and Tannen, What's It Like? p. 56.

38. Faulk and Faulk, Alternative, p. 93.

39. Department of Immigration, Survey, p. 5.

40. The Permanent Residents' Group, American Women's Club of Perth, Western Australia, "Housing," Newsletter from Australia, April, 1971, p. 3.

41. "Australia as a Place to Live: the Way It Strikes

Americans," U.S. News & World Report, July 1, 1968, p. 80.
"The American 'Invasion' of Australia," Newsweek, Aug. 10,
1964, p. 54.

42. Gunther, Australia, pp. 91, 93.

43. Aitchison, Americans, p. 199.

44. Ibid., p. x.

45. Moffitt, U-Jack, p. 180.
    Ibid., p. 118.

46. Moffat and Tannen, What's It Like?, pp. 38-39.

 * Varied between $US112 in December, 1966 (when Australia
    converted from pounds to dollars) and $US148 in September,
    1973; a dramatic devaluation to $US102 occurred November
    28, 1976.

47. Faulk and Faulk, Alternative, pp. 88-89.
    Hopkins, I've Had It, p. 169.
    Ibid., p. 170.

48. Department of Immigration, Survey, p. 35.

49. Ibid., p. 62.

50. Letter on living conditions in and general information
    about Queensland from American Families' Association of
    Queensland, September, 1971.
    Aitchison, Americans, p. 195.

51. Department of Immigration, Survey, p. 63.
    Hopkins, "Image of Australia," p. 232.

52. Gunther, Australia, p. 50.

4

A REALISTIC ASSESSMENT
—THEN FEELIN'
AT HOME

After an initial period of discovery, most migrants surveyed by this writer chose to finally settle in the same state
in which they first settled. The majority also decided to
place their roots in the cities of their new land rather than
in the rural areas, and the following reasons for choosing to
settle finally where they did were the most descriptive offered.

Sydney   - "more like the lifestyle I had previously
known"

Melbourne - "provincial, beautiful and five minutes out,
one's in the country"

Brisbane - "a growing city with plenty of work"

Adelaide - "large enough to have good schools and entertainment, but small enough to be quiet and
slow-moving"

Perth   - "perhaps the best climate and the most pleasant pace and atmosphere of all Australian
cities"

Hobart   - "mountains and sea at your front door, and
only a few minutes away from both the symphony
and big trout fishing and hunting"

Canberra - "clean, planned and a crime-free environment"

Darwin   - "a chance to live in a tropical environment"

The most common general reasons given for finally settling in
their last location included job placement, opportunity or location; climate and weather; to go to school; to live near the
beach; and, if not in an urban area, to get out of the city

74

(Appendix IX contains additional reasons specified for the location of final settlement).

Although most Americans have chosen to live in the suburban parts of Australian cities, they have not tended to settle together in "American communities."[1] Instead, according to a government survey, most have not sought to establish contact with other Americans, but rather "seek to allow friendships to develop naturally as the opportunity arises."[2] Yet there are some groups of Americans, such as company executives and their wives, who do tend to establish themselves in rather small communities in the exclusive suburbs of the major cities.[3] There are also other groups such as the American cotton farmers at Wee Waa and the American community at Surfer's Paradise (south of Brisbane), which some older Australians call "Little America" and where one can find aquacades, fruit juice bars, hot dogs and ice cream.[4]

In reference to the professions which Americans enter in Australia, these are extremely varied. Americans have become everything from charter boat fishermen and banana planters to plumbers and schoolteachers.[5] Unfortunately, there have been recently several protests against recruited American teachers by some Australian teachers who claim the Americans have been taking potential jobs away from them.

Occupationally, more Americans entered a professional, technical or related field than any other area, and individuals working in one of these fields were predominantly more likely to have had a job set up before immigrating and to have been from the North Central or Western part of the United States, according to this writer's survey. Regarding salary level, many Americans experienced a decline in the level of income they made in Australia from that which they received in the States, and according to the immediately aforementioned survey, 45 percent were earning $A8,000 or less at the time they completed the questionnaire.

* * *

Having thus briefly described where the American migrants are and what they do for a living, the next section of this chapter will deal with the reasons Americans left the United States for Australia and will look to see if the situation in their new home regarding those reasons warranted their earlier hopes and expectations. As for adventure, there seems to be little question that the expectations of many migrants were fulfilled in most instances, just as one might have easily predicted. The untamed Outback, spectacular Great Barrier Reef, unique marsupials, 33 percent of all the species of wildflowers

75

in the world and a pleasantly different lifestyle among other
attractions are, in fact, all there. Naturally, complications
might have arisen over expenses or the planning of schedules
for excursions, but there is little dispute that at least some
"adventure" was indeed to be found in Australia.

Concerning the problem of crowding, as remarked previously Australia has a relatively small population compared with
that of the United States. There are several benefits resulting from this small population, such as the odds are greater
that one can reach the pinnacle in his profession, or it is
easier to discuss problems and arrive at a consensus on their
solutions. American author John Gunther discerned that because
of its small population, a man can still reach his political
representative. In his book, Inside Australia, which was completed and edited by William H. Forbis, he concluded that "the
average Aussie doesn't delude himself that he can effect the
course of the world, but in the operation of his own country,
he still feels that he has at least a slender grip on the han-
dle of his own fate."[6] Some people, however, have noted that
because most Australians live in the major cities, Australia
must also be considered crowded. The response to this claim is
that even though most Australians do inhabit the capital cities, most urban areas are expansive and there is still a sense
of spaciousness and an open-air freshness to be found. As one
migrant in Adelaide put it, "There is still an emptiness that
absorbs you and ties you to this place." One might ask at this
point how far someone in an American city must travel before he
can be completely alone, beyond any sounds or signs of civilization, and walk freely unconcerned that he is on someone
else's property? In Australia, it is not far.

Those who came to Australia seeking a slower pace have
also not been disappointed. Unlike the rat race in the United
States where life is geared toward work, life in the island
continent is geared toward leisure.[7] The difference is primarily due to the climate and environment of Australia which
invite a more relaxed life pace.[8] The sea, near which most
Aussies live, usually makes one feel more at ease, and Australian cities emphasize parks more than American cities do. This
is important because parks have a psychological effect on individuals. They act as a break from the concrete and asphalt,
which nearly cover many American cities; and too, they are
places where one may enjoy nature, a moment of quietness, shade
from the hot sun and refuge from a cold wind. Some Americans
have been irritated by the slower tempo of life "Down Under,"
but an Australian government survey determined that many American migrants had a positive attitude toward the leisurely pace
which, according to the survey, "provided more opportunities

for enjoying one's family, friends, and the 'simple things' of life."[9]

Because Australia is generally considered a "white country," those Americans who emigrated to escape racial unrest have obviously found their desire fulfilled. Of course, one reason that Australia is largely "white" is that a number of Australians are racists.[10] For example, it is not uncommon to hear slurs against people of various nationalities; similarly, many parents become concerned if their daughter goes out with an Asian. However, most of the Australian people should not be considered racists, because for years polls have shown that the majority have approved of nonwhite immigration. For that majority it has only been a question of limiting the volume of nonwhites admitted so as not to interject great cultural differences into the Australian society which might strain its fabric.

The Americans who immigrated in search of a new frontier have been fortunate enough to find it existing on three levels: historical, intellectual and physical. Historically, many American migrants view Australia as the frontier that the United States once was for their European forefathers. And in an intellectual manner, many also view it as a frontier, just as their ancestors did who came from the continent of Europe and the British Isles in search of liberty, justice and freedom.[11] As one migrant, retired United States Colonel David Hackworth, stated in a moving article in The New York Times, "I have found these qualities in Australia, a young vigorous country that holds these principles high and is very much like you were, America, before you shrugged."[12] Physically, the Outback most certainly must be considered a frontier as well, which provides an area of release for individualistic energies similar to those which provided power for the national growth in the United States.

Regarding the hopes and expectations of Americans in the areas of better business and investment opportunities, perhaps in no other areas have the desires of as many migrants been as "measurably" fulfilled. By 1964, approximately 1,400 United States firms had already established in Australia, and early in the decade of the 1970s more than eighty American companies had regional headquarters there (Appendix X).[13] There have been a few difficulties over the years because of a desire by many of these companies to have 100 percent ownership in Australian interests; but despite the outcries by some Australians that their land has become a "quarry," most of these American firms have played a generally healthy role in the development of the Australian nation.[14] Many individual businessmen also have

found Australia profitable because of the relatively lower
wages paid and pricing practices which do not usually result
in keen competition.[15] Unfortunately, there have been some
who discovered only too late that energy and optimism were not
the sole ingredients for success, as one also usually needs
substantial capital on hand and "know-how" to build and maintain a profitable enterprise in Australia (Appendix XI speci-
fies the requirements for establishing a business in Australia).[16]

Those engaging in agricultural pursuits have found fulfillment to a great extent as well. "Some northern and western regions of Australia almost seem to have become provinces
of the United States," avers Australian author Ray Aitchison.
He claims,

> They are areas of American accents, American manners
> and working methods, American women and kids, Ameri-
> can quarter horses and lariats and white sombreros.
> They have become areas of American determination to
> stay put and build an economic stronghold in
> Australia.[17]

Americans control about 17.1 percent of the Northern Territory's "Top End" and hold long-term leases on 60 to 70 percent,
"which is roughly comparable to holding title to two-thirds of
Ohio, Indiana, and Illinois."[18] Moreover, they control about
11,000,000 acres of cattle land in the far northern part of
Western Australia alone.[19] Of course, not all land controlled
by Americans has been constantly occupied by those who are in
control, although there often have been Americans on the land
for a period of time (Appendix XII shows map and key to Northern Territory American owners, and Appendix XIII shows some of
the bigger American-owned and part-owned stations in Western
Australia).

Concerning investment, little was made prior to the Second
World War, but by 1968 over $2,000,000,000 had been directly
invested in Australia, which by then had become the fifth most
important area of the world as measured by the amount of
American money invested.[20] Currently the level of American investment in Australian industry, primarily in mining, has reached almost $5,000,000,000.[21] There are, though, certain sec-
tors of the Australian economy, such as branch banking, radio
and television stations, public utilities and domestic air-
lines, in which foreign investments might not be made.[22] Those
individuals who invested in businesses or other enterprises and
who experienced the greatest success perhaps followed the advice of other Americans previously in similar circumstances,

78

which was to study closely the situation in the desired field
of investment and not to be impatient in making any major com-
mitment of resources.[23]

Possibly the best characterization of those who emigrated
from America and immigrated to Australia "for better business
and investment opportunities" has been by Australian writer
Ian Moffitt, who said,

> Their dreams flower in steel and concrete, in the gush
> of oil and the glittering pile of minerals. But they
> are prepared to wait, and to take risks. And they con-
> fess their aims with an instant, brave naiveté.[24]

Similar words might be used to characterize ranchers and farmers, who also work hard and are determined to succeed.

Americans who emigrated because of too much pollution
have also found some pollution in Australia's major and industrial cities. Sydney, for example, at times has almost as much
air pollution as Los Angeles; however, it usually only hangs
above the city during the mornings of some days and is swept
away by the wind within a few hours. Other cities, such as
Brisbane with its industrial plants, also have some difficulty
with air pollution especially during the cooler months, May to
September. Generally speaking though, the sky over Australia
is relatively clear compared to that over the United States.
Likewise, Australia's rivers are relatively clean and the water
is safe to consume in most areas without boiling first; but
again, Australia is not free of water pollution.[25] For instance
it has been claimed that sewage disposal was so primitive that
human feces fringed the beaches at Bondi and South Steyne in
Sydney.[26] In Melbourne, it appears that runoffs from the
city's garbage dumps are leaking nearly 9,000,000 gallons of
water containing lead, cadmium and detergents into Port Phillip
Bay each day. And in Hobart, chemistry professor Harry Bloom
has attested that lead, cadmium and mercury pollution is so
severe in the Derwent estuary that the inhabitants may face
serious damage to the nervous system, kidney and bones. Australia also has some problems with other forms of pollution,
such as noise around certain airports and litter; but comparatively, the Australian nation is more pollution-free than the
United States. As one English migrant to Perth, author Thomas
Jenkins, has asserted, "Benefitting from America's example, the
Australian people have now become jealously watchful of their
country's air, water, and beauty. . . ."[27]

Pertaining to increased violence, many migrants have found
that Australia has not been violence-free either. Student pro-

testers have thrown stones; fire bombs have been hurled by radicals; and according to some, thugs have been employed by the building trade unions to gain their ends.[28] Australian youth have also been affected as one American teacher in a Melbourne suburb has claimed he breaks up four or five fights a day at school.[29] On the other hand, violence in Australian schools has not been as acute as in their American counterparts, for disinterested students tend to leave school at an earlier age in Australia; whereas in the United States, the more serious problems have been caused by older students who had rather not be in school, or by dropouts who visit school grounds to cause trouble or for disruptive purposes. From a wider perspective, violence in the island continent has been mostly in the form of fights and almost entirely among the members of lower income groups in addition to youth. Furthermore, these fights do not occur with the degree of vengeance known in the States. In the words of one American migrant:

> When two Americans fight, they seem to do it to prove who is the better man or who is right. ("I'm right, you bastard, and I'll prove it by kicking your face in.") And the loser licks his wounds and plots darkly how he's going to "get even." But in Australia, neither fighter would think of beating the other fellow into a bloody pulp to prove a point.[30]

Crime also exists in Australia, but it is not as serious as in the United States. Some do cheat on their tax reports; many do drive over the speed limits; vandals do damage property; gangs have begun to strike homes in the Outback; and "pack rape" has become so serious that an investigation has been conducted by a select committee of the New South Wales State Parliament![31] Yet, there is still little fear of being mugged in Australia, and murders are still so uncommon as to be placed on the front pages of newspapers.[32] In fact, there are "fewer homicides committed in all of Australia in a typical year than in Atlanta alone, or Baltimore, or Dallas. . . ."[33] There are several possible reasons for the relatively low rate of serious crime in Australia. As far as serious crimes by youths are concerned, many of those who do not graduate become apprentices upon leaving school and do not have a great deal of idle time in which to get into trouble. A factor in the comparatively low number of serious crimes among the population as a whole is the fact that essentially all types of firearms must be licensed. One other factor might be simply that the rate of unemployment in Australia is only about half that in the United States; therefore the economic motive for serious crime may be present to a relatively lesser degree.[34]

80

Although a loss of freedom has occurred in some instances, Australians are still one of the most free people on earth. One Liberal Party candidate reportedly found his telephone bugged in an example of possible political espionage. And in Craig McGregor's Profile of Australia, it is suggested that in the case of Professor Sydney Sparkes Orr, it has not been beyond an Australian institution's administrators to frame him for misdeeds, for a Supreme Court not to find correctly in his favor, and for even an assassination attempt to be aimed at him.[36] Still, Australians are an extremely freedom-loving people, as they were perhaps the first to don micro bikinis, for example; and since 1971 there has been a drastic liberalization of censorship in certain areas. In fact, former Australian Foreign Minister H. V. Evatt went so far as to declare that "Australia is perhaps the nation where the four freedoms of which we speak so much in the abstract have been realized in practice to the greatest extent."[37] What Americans should also realize is that there is an additional aspect to the Australians' concept of freedom. According to Professor Russel Ward,

> Freedom, to an American, tends to mean freedom to be independent of others, to be different. To an Australian, the equally unthought-of meaning of the word tends to be freedom to combine with others for the collective good. . . .[38]

As far as fulfillment of hopes and expectations regarding other motives for emigrating from America and immigrating to Australia, the result has also been generally favorable. If one moved because of personal or family problems to leave a specific person or obligation, obviously his condition in Australia would be better in that respect. As remarked earlier, however, if one has an internal attitude which has caused the problem that he has generalized to include people or obligations in general, then the individual often takes the seeds of his problem with him and is not likely to find fulfillment in the new land.

Over the past several years both materialism and unemployment have increased. According to one Australian author, Aussies devote most of their energies "to the contest for wealth and status"; and after remaining between 1 and 1.5 percent for years, the unemployment rate reached a thirty-year high of 5.1 percent before declining in 1975 (Table 23).[39] For those migrants who emigrated due to unemployment and who are in occupations which either have a high degree of transferability (e.g., teaching) or have comparatively less competition in Australia (e.g., engineering), the potential for the fulfillment of their hopes and expectations concerning employment

opportunities is quite good.[40] On the other hand, for those
migrants who are in occupations which are not as developed in
Australia (e.g., rehabilitation psychology), in which earning
power is lower (e.g., plumber), or where previous experience is
not recognized in Australia (e.g., panel beating trade), the
potential is not very good.[41]

Regrettably, impersonalization is evident in Australian
society too, as Donald Horne has asserted, "There are still
classes of misery--invalids, needy widows, deserted wives, old
people; and too often there is a general indifference toward
them and a lack of knowledge of their problems."[42] Yet on the
positive side, Australia is not an unstable, fast-changing
society. To be sure, there have been the inevitable conflicts
between various segments of the society, but the Aussies in
general have not been fanatics in these matters.[43] Instead,
Australians unlike Americans, seem to know what they want out
of life--a house, a garden, and the enjoyment of life's simple
pleasures--and they pursue them with purpose.[44]

Government ineffectiveness has been noticed to such an
extent that a number of Americans have been given to comment in
effect that although "the country is young and vibrant, the
government is old and tired." Still, the government has accom-
plished a number of things and instituted a number of very positive and worthwhile programs. Before the beginning of the
twentieth century for example, Australia had instituted a system of compulsory arbitration that has achieved a level of success which the United States has not duplicated to date.[45] Two
additional positive examples are that a special task force has
been established to reduce the number of drunk and careless
drivers, and that hundreds of thousands of dollars in benefits
have been obtained for consumers from industry by government.
The outlook for the future of the island continent seems
slightly better than that of the United States; for even though
Australia has most of the same problems which afflict America,
it now suffers from them only to the degree that the United
States was affected ten to twenty years ago.

In sum then, many migrants have found for various reasons
that the Australian nation is a slightly better place in which
to live. From the older migrants seeking an America that once
was, one hears remarks such as, "We feel so young here."[46]
From those who have sought a better land in which to rear their
children, the words of Gerald Stone are typical: "Young people
grow up here under less pressure of permissiveness, of drugs
and pornography. Growing up here in the 1970s is like growing
up in America in the 1950s."[47] But on the broadest scale, Dr.
Eric Matthews who emigrated in 1967 from Manhattan, New York

TABLE 23

UNEMPLOYMENT RATE IN AUSTRALIA AS A
PERCENTAGE OF THE LABOR FORCE
FROM 1945 to 1974

Year	Unemployment Rate
1945	N.A.
1946	0.95
1947	0.77
1948	0.50
1949	0.50
1950	0.33
1951	0.31
1952	1.22
1953	1.39
1954	0.62
1955	0.49
1956	0.86
1957	1.29
1958	1.62
1959	1.56
1960	1.17
1961	2.31
1962	2.17
1963	1.74
1964	1.12
1965	0.97
1966	1.25
1967	1.35
1968	1.31
1969	1.12
1970	1.04
1971	1.34
1972	1.85
1973	1.46
1974	2.07

SOURCE: Australian Department of Labor
and Immigration calculations based on the
number of unemployed persons registered
with the Commonwealth Employment Service.

City, speaks for those migrants who simply had become tired of living where deterioration of the quality of life seemed to prevail when he stated, "In a world that is becoming horribly overcrowded and polluted, Australia may be one of the last lands left where things are still in balance."[48] And lastly, Ron Kaye, an American journalist who immigrated to Australia, offers perhaps the most pithy judgment rendered regarding his new land as he proclaims that "to a war, assassination and injustice-weary Yank, Australia seems like the most advanced society on earth: a sort of Garden of Eden, with plenty for all, a gentle climate, gentle society."[49]

* * *

Although the migrants' fulfillment of hopes and expectations regarding their new land is extremely important, it is the Australian people with whom these Americans must live and deal. Just as it is difficult to generalize about Americans, it is likewise the case with the Aussies; and the images one receives of the Australian people from the American migrants are often contradictory, because different Americans simply see different Australians in different lights. Therefore, one has to know the Aussies quite well before making any thorough analysis of their character. For example, one's first impression of the Australian people may be that they are a rough lot, but often their roughness is merely a facade covering a deeper kindheartedness and a generous nature.[50]

Perhaps the first type of Australian to be mentioned should be "the first Australians," the Aborigines. Recent archeological discoveries reveal that Aboriginals reached southeast Australia at least 40,000 years ago; and anthropologist Andrew Abbie has suggested that the ancestors of the Australian Aborigines were probably "'Proto-Caucasoids' who lived in central Asia . . . and sent out migrations that became the genetically related Ainus of Japan, Veddas of India and Ceylon, and the 'Aryan' Europeans."[51] He suggests further that the now extinct Tasmanian Aborigines probably drifted to the island from somewhere in Melanesia.[52] Regardless from where they might have originated, the Aborigines today are distinct by blood group type from Caucasoids, Negroids and Mongoloids.[53] They are an exceptionally self-sufficient and comparatively noncompetitive people. For instance, to survive in the "Dead Heart" of the Australian continent, all an Aborigine would need is approximately seven instruments including two rubbing sticks and two knife-shaped stones. Whites, however, would have to have everything from a four-wheel-drive vehicle to a radio to request assistance.[54] And regarding the comparative lack of a competitive urge, tennis star Evonne Goolagong at least once offered the surprising comment over television that she "really didn't mind losing!"

It has often been remarked that Australia is a male-dom-
inated society and this is true, although females are becoming
somewhat more assertive. There are still distinct male and
female roles in Australia, which probably originated with the
emphasis on agriculture as the backbone of the economy, before
the mineral boom, and the attendant attitudes regarding male
and female roles typical of such agricultural societies. Today if a male had a choice, which he usually does, he would
rather spend a majority of his time with his "mates" (male
friends, in this case) than with his wife, or girlfriend if he
is not married.[55] In fact, though the habit is changing
slightly, at parties it has not been uncommon to find all of
the males gathered at one end of the room around a keg of beer
while all of the females are at the other end conversing about
their own separate interests.[56] The role of women in Australia
has been rather subservient and apologetic in the past, unfortunately; but some progress has been made recently and women
are now entitled to equal pay for equal work. For those who
choose to work at jobs outside the home, the way is becoming
easier, as it should be. This does not mean, however, that
Australian women have now become obsessed with running out to
seek a job in order to find self-fulfillment. To the contrary,
as one author has perceptively noted, the Australian woman "has
created a much more subtle world than the man's world, not so
dependent on money, a world of multiple difference."[57]

The word, "reserved," might be used to characterize the
Australian people. Their reserve probably comes from their
British heritage and, in fact, until a few years ago many
Aussies referred to Britain as "home." One migrant surveyed
who has travelled considerably to various nations of the world
feels that Australians may be one of the most reserved people
of all, even more so than the British. She comments, "They may
slap you on the back and shout (buy) you a beer, but they will
never tell you what they are really thinking at the time." The
Aussies are relatively undemonstrative in their outward signs
of affection, as they rather disdain public emotionalism.[58]

Yet it might simultaneously be said that Australians are
"a fun-loving people" who do not take life or themselves too
seriously. According to Craig McGregor, this is because
"classical culture has had such a brief history in Australia
that popular culture tends to dominate."[59] "Not to worry" is
a favorite expression of these people who receive tremendous
enjoyment from their weekends, clubs, gambling, sports, as well
as beer--and not necessarily in that order. Viewing a game of
Aussie Rules football, having weekend barbecues, enjoying a

night at the club, playing the "pokeys" (slot machines) or
betting on a lottery ticket, and "shouting" beers with the
"mates" all make life seem worthwhile to a large number of
Australians. Along with having fun, many of these Aussies also
have a sardonic sense of humor and a fast and biting wit, all
of which have on more than one occasion contributed to earn
them the wrath of another type of Australian, the "wowser" (a
straight-laced killjoy)--one who is "supposed to hate everything pretty or jolly," in the words of a verse first published
in The Bulletin in 1912.[60]

Regrettably, many have seen the Australians' delight in
simple pleasures and their casual manner as signs that they are
"nonthinkers." Some Americans have described the Aussies as
"unimaginative and uninspired," while even a number of Australians themselves have offered criticisms. Dr. Ross Terrill, an
Australian political scientist teaching at Harvard University,
has stated for example that outside of a few intellectuals, Australians are "a bronzed, back-slapping, amiable mass, for whom .
. . the world of ideas might as well not exist."[61] What should
be remembered, though, is that Australians are optimists, and
like most optimists everywhere they are simplifiers.[62] This
definitely cannot be taken to mean they are stupid. Nor can it
be taken to mean that Australians are necessarily lazy, even
when many do live by a type of "she'll do" or "near enough is
good enough" philosophy when repairing something or performing
a task. It is somewhat ironical to hear Americans complaining
about lazy Australians when some migrants say they cannot tolerate life "Down Under" without the labor-saving, gasoline-
powered lawnmowers or automatic dishwashers they relied upon
"back home." Australians are merely easy-going, patient and
fatalistic--not lazy. In the coastal cities there has always
been a historical need for patience, for example, whether one
were a pastoralist or a merchant waiting for a ship, or a typical digger, swagman or urbanite set upon by misfortune. This
helps to explain their acceptance of life's vicissitudes and
their fatalistic attitude. The same is true of Australian country people, who have adapted well to their environment.[63]

Another complaint by some Americans has been that Australians are "crude." While this charge is true of some to a certain degree as is nearly every other charge, and even members
of Parliament have indeed scuffled openly during session, it
should be remembered that many Aussies are sensitive people
although they do not openly demonstrate their sensitivity.[64]
An American migrant noted in this regard that "Australians are
people who really seem to care if another person lived well or
is happy or not."[65] And one American author has asserted that
"although many Aussies are crude, there still can be found a

86

genteel social life, which has disappeared from America."[66]

"Conformists" is the next word that might be used to describe the Australian people. Actually, one might be able to sense the power of conformity in the very air one breathes, and anyone who attempts to be too individualistic runs the risk of being called a "ratbag" (one who professes contrary opinions).[67] Aussies want to like people and be liked in return; they want to feel as though they "belong."[68] At times the pressure to conform can cause problems, such as a complacent or apathetic attitude toward facing life's challenges, yet it also can provide a spirit of public cooperativeness in meeting difficulties as well.

Either way, conformity of action goes hand in hand with the image of Australians as egalitarian, which is a "basically" accurate image. For instance, there are proportionately neither a great many rich nor poor people; and an additional matter of evidence is the fact that lone passengers will most often sit in the front seat of a taxi and not in the rear, so as not to imply a socially superior position.[69] Moreover, there seems to be a definite dislike of intellectuals throughout the nation, which in turn has led to a prevailing attitude against intellectually-oriented education.[70] The reason for this attitude is perhaps best summarized by one Australian who defined it as a "we don't need those sorts of things to run the farm or factory" philosophy. There are, of course, sacrifices in terms of creativity and excellence with such an attitude; but as hinted at earlier with the use of the word, "basically," in referring to Australians as egalitarian, they are not completely egalitarian.[71] For example, those who have a good deal of money are considered to be quite important, even if they are not considered to be "better" as human beings.[72] Thus, Australians can in no sense of the term be considered a completely "classless people," as there is a distinct working class which is separate from the middle and upper classes, each of which in turn is socially generally exclusive.

Previously it has been mentioned that the images one receives of the Australian people from the American migrants are often contradictory. This happens to be the case with the view that Australians are conformists and egalitarians, for a number of migrants view the Aussies as independent and skeptical with a distinct dislike of authority, especially the police. It was not too many years ago, for example, that a young Yugoslav migrant saved a policeman in Melbourne from death at the hands of a certified lunatic while a gathering of Australians cheered for the lunatic.[73] They can be an extremely independent-minded people, as one American gladly noted and remarked, "You can't

buy an Aussie; you can't even rent one."[74] The reason for
this apparent independence may be the uncrowded nature of the
continent, for with room one is better able to develop confidence in one's own personality and view of matters unlike
Americans who inhabit a crowded environment and have had to
develop a sense of tact and compromise in their daily lives.

Many migrants consider the Aussies as being a skeptical
people as well. Consistently, they have resisted high pressure salesmanship of the American variety, and have repeatedly
rejected the use of trading stamps.[75] They have been called
"knockers" and are even somewhat cynical by nature.[76] This
cynicism is not all bad, however, as it has prevented them from
becoming individually egocentric or self-deluded.[77] And according to an Australian author, it means "they are more likely
to achieve change" as a people "organically than by cata-
clysm."[78] Unfortunately for some migrants, a few Australians
extend their skepticism and cynicism to criticism of the United
States in an all too vocal manner. One American has even con-
tended in this respect that "Australians all seem to have some
complaint about the United States which they have to tell you
as soon as they meet you."[79] It should be added in all fair-
ness here though that it is only a small minority of Australians who are really anti-American.[80]

Having thus described the Aussies as a critical "mob" (a
group with similar characteristics or interests), it may seem
slightly surprising to learn that they generally do not appreciate criticism pertaining either to themselves or to their
country.[81] Perhaps one reason many Australians are very defensive toward this type of criticism is because they firmly believe that they and their lifestyle are superior.[82] James
McCausland, an American journalist who immigrated to Australia,
offers another interpretation for this defensive attitude, however, when he states that Australians "seem to suffer from a
tremendous inferiority complex which they sublimate with an
aggressive superiority attitude."[83] One might pause here for a
moment and ask in regard to the Australians' defensive reaction
toward criticism "what is the reaction of Americans to criticisms of the United States by foreigners?" The answer, of
course, is that the reactions of both Australians and Americans
are quite similar--and understandable.

Despite any faults the Australians have, they are, as a
whole, a friendly, helpful, generous and honest people. Although some have challenged that the "friendliness" of
Australians is only superficial, a government survey showed
that 79 percent of the American migrants interviewed found
their Aussie neighbors "either quite friendly or very

friendly."[84] An American summarized the situation best in his
comment that "Aussies don't make friends fast. . . . . But
once you're accepted as one of them . . . they'll loan you
their car or their house or even money faster than the so-
called friends I had back home."[85] Regarding Australians'
helpfulness, they are not usually voluntarily helpful, but if
their assistance is requested in some endeavor, they are quite
willing to lend a hand. And one question should suffice to
demonstrate Australian generosity--where in the United States
or anywhere else for that matter will one find a cab driver
who turns off his meter before reaching one's destination,
round the charge down in one's favor, and who does not expect
a tip, as in Australia?[86] Lastly, the Aussies, even their
politicians, seem to be a basically honest people (Appendix
XIV includes additional opinions regarding the Australian people given by the American migrants surveyed to this writer).[87]

* * *

Thus far only one side of the picture has been presented,
and it would be most unjust not to consider the Australians'
opinions of Americans. Actually, most Australians do not personally know any American migrants to their land. Most of
their knowledge of Americans comes rather from Hollywood films,
television shows, news stories and encounters with American
tourists. This obviously gives most Australians an unrealistic
view of Americans. First of all the Yanks are supposed to be
rich, in the Hollywood image.[88] Second, all Americans must be
arrogant, thanks to the impression given by loud-mouthed, know-
it-all tourists who demand to be served; and the Australians do
not like the idea of serving anyone.[89] An American visitor in
Australia at one point tried to distinguish visually between
the Americans and the Aussies he saw and he differentiated,
"there was a look about Americans, a look that said they owned
the earth."[90]

Still, the truth of the matter is that most Australians
generally like individual Americans. One reason for this, perhaps, is a kindred feeling toward Americans because of the
similar development of both nations from a wilderness and their
alliances during four wars.[91] After the Second World War a
Yank in Australia almost surely would have found that he was
welcomed nearly everywhere, and today the situation is essentially the same.[92] This is only true, of course, if the American
comes in a genuine spirit of friendship, for Australians have
developed a definite dislike for those who have come to their
land for the sole reason of exploiting it for financial gain.
The "ambitious" Yank who is determined to be "a success at any
cost" might find that he is not very welcome "Down Under."[93]
In a caustically insinuatory passage from his book, Australia--

What Is It?, Henry Williams asserts,

> The self-made-man of business has nothing like the
> shining-example-of-what-can-be-done aura that he
> carries in the U.S.A. Success in most fields, ex-
> cept sport, is automatically suspect. It is not
> absolutely certain that a man who has made a million
> is a ruthless, scheming two-timing con man, but that
> is the way to lay the odds unless there are strong
> indications to the contrary. Honest work does not
> pay rates like that.[94]

Therefore, it is the American who finally convinces the Aussies
that he is not rich and that he has come to join their society,
who will probably be best received.[95] And apparently most of
the migrants have succeeded in not offending their Australian
acquaintances, associates and neighbors, as a government survey
revealed that 85 percent of the American migrants interviewed
found the Aussies' attitude toward them "either favorable or
very favorable."[96]

* * *

After residing in Australia for a period of time, the migrants are better able to discern what they really "like" about
the nation and its people, and the "likes" are numerous. The
"variety" of the place seems to be a most attractive feature--
there is not only the hustle and bustle of Sydney and the excitement of speculation in and exploration of minerals; but
Australia also offers an individual time to explore his own
nature and his environment should he so wish, as there is a
slower life pace and a sense of timelessness that arises from
the land, especially from the interior. Unlike the United
States, there is "no sense of perpetual crisis," in the words
on one author.[97]

Furthermore, many migrants like the physical aspects, food,
opportunities available, vacations, health programs, sports,
schools, Aussie women, and the activities for senior citizens.
The environment, the wide open spaces, unspoiled physical beauty, wildlife, climate and weather, as well as the outdoor life
all have been specified by Americans in Australia as some of
the most positive attributes of the nation. In addition they
have noted the fresh foods available most of the year; the
tasty fruits, "veggies" and meats; the one hundred varieties of
sausages; and the great beer, good wines and chocolate.[98]

There is also the opportunity for advancement in one's
profession; for according to one migrant, "though initial salaries in Australia may not be high, Australian companies

recognize and appreciate ability and reward it with salary
increases." Moreover, workers receive at least four weeks vacation a year from the time they commence their jobs, and are
entitled to bonuses, which amount to anywhere from 17.5 to 25
percent of their total base pay, while they are on vacation.[99]
The migrants enjoy the subsidizing of medical benefits and
Australian sports like soccer as well as the growing popularity
of basketball and baseball; and they appreciate schools which
still offer an academic rather than a social experience.[100]
For the young American male, Australian women seem especially
attractive as one young male migrant remarked ecstatically, "if
you are single, there are women, women, women!" And for the
American senior citizens, particularly welcomed and enjoyed are
the many free activities, such as bowls (lawn bowling), fishing, boating, and activities on Australia's beaches and in
their many beautiful parks. Other aspects which the migrants
surveyed by this writer stated they "liked" include the nation's cultural values, its remoteness and cleanliness, one's
job and working conditions, the lack of snobbery on the part of
the Australian people, and little things--like food served hot
when it is supposed to be hot and served cold when it is supposed to be cold (Appendix XV lists the additional "likes" indicated by the migrants surveyed).[101]

It must be immediately stated, however, that Americans
have also noted a number of negative aspects concerning Australia and its people. Many expressed displeasure with the lower
standard of living; the lack of central heating, air condition-
ing, nighttime and weekend shopping, and personalized service;
and the poor quality of goods and services.[102] American female
migrants noted that despite some gains, Australia was still a
sexist country where men rule. Furthermore, many Americans
disliked the former Labor Government's policies, which some
migrants felt were too socialistic, as well as the seemingly
innumerable strikes of Australia's powerful unions. Although
it is not compulsory to belong to a union in Australia, if one
chooses not to in some places, he may find that the grocer,
butcher, milkman and others will boycott him. Along with this
power to cause services to be withheld from individuals, the
unions are also quite capable of bringing the entire nation
almost to a standstill via strikes, and the situation has not
improved in recent years.[103] At no time between 1946 and 1972
were there more days lost, through industrial disputes per
1,000 people employed, in Australia than in the United States;
but after 1972 the situation became quite different, as in
1973 there were at least five workdays lost through strikes in
Australia for every four workdays lost in the United States per
1,000 people employed (Table 24).

Other complaints expressed by the migrants surveyed by

TABLE 24

DAYS LOST BY INDUSTRIAL DISPUTES
PER 1,000 PEOPLE EMPLOYED

Year	U.S.	Aust.
1945	1,755	1,787
1946	5,482	1,734
1947	1,450	1,050
1948	1,450	1,250
1949	2,290	960
1950	1,670	1,440
1951	920	600
1952	2,400	810
1953	1,070	660
1954	890	540
1955	1,100	580
1956	1,300	630
1957	630	370
1958	1,030	250
1959	2,770	200
1960	750	380
1961	650	330
1962	730	280
1963	630	320
1964	850	480
1965	860	410
1966	880	360
1967	1,430	320
1968	1,590	460
1959	1,390	860
1970	2,210	1,040
1971	1,620	1,300
1972	870	840
1973	770[a]	1,030[a]
1974	N.A.	N.A.

SOURCES: Robert Woodbury, "Industrial Disputes: Rates of Time Loss, 1927-1947," The International Labour Review, LX (November, 1949), pp. 452-66.

"Industrial Disputes 1937-

1954," The International Labour
Review, LXXII (July, 1955), pp.
78-91.

[a]Preliminary figures.

N.A. - Not Available.

TABLE 25

DAILY AVERAGE HOURS OF SUNSHINE IN
SEVEN OF AUSTRALIA'S CAPITAL CITIES

Capitals	Hours
Perth	7.8
Brisbane	7.5
Adelaide	7.0
Sydney	6.8
Canberra	6.8
Hobart	5.9
Melbourne	5.6

SOURCE: Craig McGregor, Profile of Australia (Ringwood, Victoria: Penguin Books, 1968), p. 119.

this writer pertained to the extremely high federal income
tax; the slower pace and "she'll be right" attitude; poor
roads; substandard facilities, teaching aids and syllabi in
the schools; television programming, in general; dull social
life; preference of Australian businessmen for the status quo
instead of for innovation; the widespread presence of large
numbers of small flies during some parts of the year; and the
unfortunate practice of adopting the worst American habits
(Appendix XVI lists additional "dislikes" indicated by the
migrants surveyed).[104]

* * *

Although it has been stated earlier that it seems quite
unfair to compare Australia, which has only about 6.5 percent
of the population of America, to the United States, it appears
inevitable that human beings, especially migrants, will make
such comparisons. Since that is the case, some space will now
be devoted to the various comparisons which the migrants have
made between what Herman Melville in Moby Dick called "that
other great America on the other side of the sphere, Australia," and the United States. In a physical sense, the migrants
have made several comparisons, such as the sun shines more frequently in Australia and the light appears brighter as the air
is cleaner (Tables 25 and 26). Food also received a more favorable rating in Australia, because of its taste and fresher
quality. Yet the migrants were critical of the housing in
Australia, stating that the average house there was smaller and
less comfortable than the average American house. Furthermore,
they judged the average house lots to be smaller in Australia,
and the quality of the average Australian flat to be inferior
to that of the average American apartment. In total, although
a government study showed that the great majority of the migrants were "satisfied" with their accommodations, it also
showed that 45 percent compared their housing in Australia un-
favorably with that which they had in the United States.[105]
With respect to material possessions, they noted that Australians had less, as few people had clothes driers, for example.[106]   As to athletic activities, they found cricket more
prevalent than baseball and they found Australian Rules football, a combination of Rugby and soccer, more popular than the
American variety.[107]   Local participation and interest in
sports also seemed greater in Australia, with the expense of
engaging in athletic activities being less.

Qualitatively, the migrants made a number of comparisons
as well. First, they welcome the smaller sense of urgency in
conducting the day-to-day affairs of life in Australia.[108]   In
the opposite direction, however, they do not like at all the
inferior quality of many goods and services provided. The

TABLE 26

RAINFALL AND TEMPERATURE IN AUSTRALIA'S CAPITAL CITIES

Capitals	Average Rainfall (Inches)	Lowest Mean Temperature (Fahrenheit)	Highest Mean Temperature (Fahrenheit)
Sydney	47.68	56.3	70.5
Melbourne	25.78	49.7	67.4
Brisbane	44.96	59.9	77.8
Adelaide	20.81	53.2	72.3
Perth	34.77	55.4	73.6
Hobart	24.77	46.5	62.0
Canberra	24.78	43.1	66.7
Darwin	60.40	74.1	90.3

SOURCE: Government of Australia, Australia, July, 1971 (Canberra: The Australian Government Publishing Service, 1971), p. 6.

quality of most manufactured items in Australia is low by American standards, as is the quality of plumbing, for example; and customers rarely see waterfountains in stores, are rarely served water with their meals, and rarely have their windshields wiped at gas stations.[109] Concerning welfare and social services, on the other hand, one study found that 45.6 percent of the migrants interviewed thought "provisions in Australia compared either favorably or very favorably with provisions in the United States" and 68.5 percent felt "Australian provisions were either about the same or better."[110] Under the heading of "favorable," they mentioned the general health provisions made under the various medical and hospital benefit funds; and under the heading "unfavorable," they included pension provisions in general, but particularly for the aged, and relief for the unemployed and deserted wives.[111]

In the area of business, Australia seems to be tied to a "credit" economy to the same degree the United States is, as one author has been caused to remark, "In no way has Australia become more Americanized than in the style of 'possess now, pay later.'"[112] And in 1975, Australians finally got their first national credit card, called "Bankcard," from a corporation formed by the nine major banks of the nation. On the positive side, though, business is not conducted as ferociously in Australia. Henry Clark, a salesman from Pomona, California, who emigrated "to escape the business rat race, and who became the Australian national marketing manager for Minnesota Mining and Manufacturing Company, claims, "Business here is not pressure-cooked like it is in the States. People have time for people and are more courteous and honest."[113]

In the broad perspective of industry, the Australian economic system like the American system promotes oligopoly, and the Australian work force is distributed in a manner strikingly similar to that of the United States (Table 27).[114] And on a more personal basis concerning general work and employment conditions, the most common response given by the migrants on one survey was that conditions were about the same as in America with the majority stating that conditions "were either the same or worse in Australia."[115] Those factors which they considered worse in Australia were that "employers offered fewer financial rewards and fringe benefits, used obsolete methods, and were generally too conservative."[116] It might be added, however, that in at least two areas related to work, Australia seems to be ahead, as there are an average of twelve public holidays annually along with regular work holidays; and after ten, twelve, or fifteen years depending on the industry, one is entitled to three months vacation with pay.[117]

The worker also enjoys a wage and a cost of living in Australia which appear to be approximately equal to those in the United States. The average weekly wage announced in October, 1975, in Australia, was $A158 (approximately $US200 as of the same date) compared with the average weekly wage in the United States, for all nonagricultural workers announced in November, 1975, of $US170. And the United Nations Statistical Office figures for that year showed that the cost of living in Sydney was 95 percent of the cost of living in New York. Relatively more expensive in Australia are most manufactured items such as appliances, clothing and paper products, as well as housing, rent, processed foods, gasoline and cigarettes; but relatively less expensive are such things as cultural and athletic activities, prescription drugs, meat, vegetables, dining out, amusements and newspapers. Yet many Americans have complained about what they, at least, consider to be the relatively higher cost

TABLE 27

WORK FORCE DISTRIBUTION IN AUSTRALIA AND THE UNITED STATES
(Work Force in Industry as a Percentage of
Total Work Force)

Industry	Australia (Percentage)	United States (Percentage)
Agriculture (including fishing and forestry)	13.4	12.5
Mining and Quarrying	1.7	1.7
Manufacturing (including electricity, gas, and water supply)	30.0	28.9
Building and Construction	8.9	6.4
Transportation and Communication	9.2	7.2
Commerce	18.5	19.0
Other Industries	18.3	24.3

SOURCE: Australian News & Information Bureau, Australia, an Economic and Investment Reference (Canberra: Australian Government Publishing Service, 1961), p. 15.

Note: Since 1961 the absolute figures in this table obviously have changed, such as the decline in the percentages of workers engaged in "Agriculture" in both countries; the purpose of this table, however, is only to demonstrate the similarity between the two nations in work force distribution.

of living "Down Under," especially when their salaries are not comparable to what they had received in the States. The first point which should be made in this respect is that if one does earn a comparable salary in Australia, then the relative costs of living between the two countries will be equal for the individual. The second point is that even if one were to earn comparatively less in Australia, if he were to "live like an Australian," the cost of living would still be almost equal to that he experienced in America. If, for instance, one were to eat lamb instead of steak, he could save considereably. Many of the Americans who have immigrated felt, though, that they had to have steaks, two large new automobiles, dishwashers, clothes driers and other "necessities" which they enjoyed in the States. For them there is no question that the cost of living in Australia has been, is and probably will be for some time to come definitely higher than in the United States.

According to an Australian government survey, many Americans have also professed that they were worse off under Australian tax provisions than they had been under American provisions.[118] In fact, the vast majority of the migrants felt that way. What is odd about this belief on the part of the migrants is the fact that although the federal income tax burden in Australia is much higher than it is in the States, the overall tax burden does not appear to be all that dissimilar. In this regard, it must be remembered that Australia has no state income tax, no sales or utilities taxes as Americans know them, no separate capital gains taxes and no separate social security deductions from a person's salary as one has in the United States.[119] And even though the total tax burden upon the individual in Australia is indeed higher than it is in America, on a national level taxes as a percent of the Gross National Product appear to be actually higher in the United States (Table 28).

TABLE 28

TAXES AS A PERCENTAGE OF GROSS NATIONAL PRODUCT

Year	Australia (Percentage)	United States (Percentage)
1965	23.9	25.3
1968	25.4	26.3
1972	24.3	28.1

SOURCE: Sylvia Westerman and Martin A. Bacheller, eds., The CBS News Almanac, 1977 (Maplewood, N.J.: Hammond Almanac, Inc., 1976), p. 167.

Because of children in their families, many migrants quite naturally have been interested in comparisons between the education offered in both countries. It appears that Australian schools are slightly more demanding than their American counterparts, as the former have placed more emphasis on formal academic achievement and the fundamentals of learning rather than on the students' social growth.[120] Even so, one survey determined that a majority of the migrants interviewed felt their children "had progressed at about the same rate as they had in the U.S.A."[121] In Australia, as it has never been in American public schools, school uniforms are still worn today; but dress codes regarding the wearing of uniforms are becoming more and more relaxed. Also many schools are still segregated by sex in Australia, unlike in the United States, but that situation is gradually changing too.

Sometimes the old ways seem better, however, as stricter discipline in the schools of Australia has allowed less disruption so that learning could take place more easily with fewer distractions. The only difficulty which may have resulted is that when discipline has been too strict, students have not been allowed to develop self-discipline so that they had to be constantly guided in what and when to study. Although many Americans have preferred the increased discipline and the more studious atmosphere it brought, a large number have also criticized that the stricter discipline and conformity which were emphasized occurred "at the expense of personal development and freedom of expression." Moreover, many felt that Australian educational methods were less advanced than those used in America, that the schools were less well-equipped, and that the curricula were more rigid with "fewer options offered to fulfill individual interests and talents."[122]

Two other negative comparisons regarding education were offered as well. First, Australian schools required a student to choose a future occupation at an earlier age than is customary in America. And second, proportionately more students in Australia than in the United States left school at "leaving age" (the age at which one is no longer required to attend). Concerning this latter point, though, it should be realized that students in Australia who left before graduating did so more than likely because they failed to pass a rigorous examination. Students in America, on the other hand, have come to expect eventual graduation for "social reasons," regardless of their level of academic achievement, if only they are willing to remain in school long enough.

In judging the quality of entertainment in Australia, television programming was considered definitely inferior with the exception of the Australian Broadcasting Commission shows which were described by some migrants surveyed by the Australian government as "superior to what was offered in the U.S.A." [123] In the same survey, the interviewees compared the motion picture facilities and programs in Australia as "about the same as in the U.S."; and regarding live entertainment, the migrants noted that though the quality and selection in Australia were not as good on the average as in the United States, "the standards were improving and the quality of the more important productions was good." [124]

In general, then, depending on the area under consideration, different Americans feel that Australia is the same as, or different from, or better or worse than their homeland of the United States. Both societies are so similar--from many positive aspects, such as their love of freedom, to many negative aspects, such as "that shatteringly unfeminine America-derived phenomenon, the marching girls" in the words of one Australian--that the term, "Austerican," has been coined to express the similarities. [125] Yet both nations are simultaneously different, as physically there are no striking regional differences in Australia as there are in America; historically, Australia has had no Revolutionary War or Civil War nor has it had great responsibilities of power as the United States has had; and in the social context of equality, according to Kurt Mayer, Americans have stressed equality of opportunity unlike Australians who have emphasized equality of lifestyle and enjoyment, and who resent superiority. [126]

Many avow that Australia is simply a better nation than the United States (26.5 per cent of those surveyed by this writer)--better socially in resolving problems of poverty and unemployment while providing social services, and better politically with its parliamentary form of government and compulsory voting. [127] After traveling through America and other countries, journalist, editor and author Thomas Jenkins has written,

> The flavor of life tastes best in Australia--and I mean more than a superbly-barbecued steak, a perfect curling wave of jade or a snow-banked ghost gum tree against an unbelievable blue sky. Of course the climate helps . . . but there is more to it than that. [128]

As one American migrant remarked, "The longer I remain in Australia, the worse the United States looks."

This positive attitude regarding Australia as compared to

100

America was not shared, however, by 30 percent of the migrants surveyed, who felt that Australia was worse than the United States (25 percent indicated both nations were "about the same" and 18.5 percent gave no answer). In many cases the comparison of America as "better" than Australia seems both fair and accurate. For instance, the political system does not appear to be as open in Australia as it is in the States. Though difficult it may be, it is still possible for "the average person" to gain political influence in the United States; but to become a political force in Australia it seems one has to have either attended the "right" schools or committed one's self somewhat to the political policies of the trade unions.

Therefore, in the final analysis it would be safest and probably best not to pass qualitative judgment on which nation is better than the other, but only to say as one migrant said, "Australia is different enough to be stimulating, yet enough like America to be convenient." Some predominant characteristics of the Americans surveyed by this writer regarding their comparisons between the two countries may be of interest to the reader at this point. Predominantly more of those who specified the following motives for emigrating from the United States and immigrating to Australia, rather than other motives listed, felt America was worse.

Motives	Percentage Who Felt the United States Was Worse
impersonalized society	76.0
unstable, fast-changing society	69.5
high cost of living	68.2
felt loss of freedom	66.6
too much materialism	66.6
pace of life too fast	62.9
poor outlook for the United States	59.1
rise in crime rate	58.6
increased violence	58.0
too much pollution	57.1

And predominantly more of those with the following characteristics, than with other characteristics, felt the United States was worse.

101

Predominant Characteristics	Percentage Who Felt America Was Worse
occupation in the U.S.-other nonmanual workers	57.2
or students	47.3
income in the U.S. - less than $4,000	52.1
section from which departed - California,	37.0
or Northeast	37.0
had no job set up before migrating	37.5
year of migration - 1965 to 1969,	53.3
or 1970	50.0
Australian government financially assisted passage	35.7
final place of settlement in Australia - Tasmania,	75.0
or Capital Territory	60.0
occupation in Australia - students	57.2
income in Australia - over $16,000	50.1

In contrast, predominantly more of those who specified the following motives for emigrating from America and immigrating to Australia, rather than other motives listed, felt the United States was better.

Motives	Percentage Who Felt America Was Better
for adventure	40.7
unemployment	35.7
personal or family problems	31.0
too much pollution	28.5
lack of new frontiers	26.7
racial unrest	26.5
for better business and investment opportunities	25.0
becoming too crowded	22.5
rise in crime rate	20.7
pace of life too fast	17.1

And predominantly more of those with the following characteristics, than with other characteristics, felt America was better.

Predominant Characteristics	Percentage Who Felt America Was Better
occupation in the U.S. -	
administrative, executive or managerial,	45.5
or professional, technical or related	
workers	43.3
income in the U.S. - $12,001 to $16,000	45.4
section from which departed - South	44.0
had a job set up before migrating	43.9
year of migration - 1974 (latest year of	
the survey)	81.9
Australian government did not financially	
assist passage	40.5
final place of settlement in Australia -	
New South Wales	47.4
occupation in Australia - manual workers	43.8
income in Australia - $12,001 to $16,000,	54.6
or less than $4,000	52.6

* * *

Once again it must be stressed that merely looking at the two nations is not enough, as it is the Australian people with whom the migrants must live and deal. Therefore, their comparisons of the Australian people with Americans are also of important consideration. Physically the Australians appear to be larger, but not in the obese sense, than Americans. Furthermore, their life expectancy is somewhat longer, though there are approximately 15.2 suicides in Australia for every 10.9 in the United States per 100,000 people.[129] Regarding intelligence, Australians may appear to be less articulate than Americans; however, they read more and have a greater general knowledge in some areas.[130] Moreover, Australians are less naive; and they will also not tolerate political representatives who fail to represent them, unlike many Americans who continue to reelect representatives who do as they please supposedly "for the good of the people or nation" regardless of their constituents' views.[131]

The inhabitants of both nations are a relatively young people for the most part, with nearly 40 percent of all Australians under twenty-one years old and over one-third of the population of the United States under twenty years of age.[132] Activity among very young Australians seems less frenzied than the actions of very young Americans and there is far less crying.[133] One is also less likely to find loud-mouthed teenagers "Down Under" than in the States, and Australian children in

103

general appear to be "more respectful and obedient" according to an American teacher in Miles, Queensland.[134]

Although there is discrimination against women in the United States, the situation is somewhat worse for Australian women in their own country. American women probably control more money, are more articulate in the public expression of their views, and receive more publicity for their ideas than their Australian counterparts. Yet, while this is true, Australian females are just as aware of discrimination as are American women and "frequently get square on their menfolk privately and in ways too numerous or subtle to detail," in the words of one Aussie male.[135]

The family is a stronger entity in Australia than it is in America, and it is also mother-centered, as for the most part the Australian mother is in charge of nearly all major family decisions and activities.[136] In Australia the father may seem to be in control, but one writer has found that hardly any ever "take part in virtually all the main regions of family activity, whereas in the United States 90 percent of all fathers take part."[137]

In general, Americans seem more readily and openly pleasant and courteous, with possibly a smile for even a stranger and a response of "Yes, sir" or "Yes, ma'am," to a query or statement. This is not as true for Aussies, who tend not to be as immediately warm or close to others. Instead, Robert Taft has determined in his opinion studies that "Australians put greater emphasis on observing conventional manners than on expressing one's individuality and preferred superficial but correct social relations to deep and intimate ones," while similar studies on Americans in California revealed that the latter were "less likely to endorse conventional manners."[138] On the positive side, however, this means that an Australian is less likely to be a "phony" in his relationships than are many Americans. So even though Australians might be slightly harder to get to know, once one does get to know them, as a migrant has put it, "there's hardly anything they won't do for you."

By far, the Aussies are also less competitive and more collective in spirit than Americans. Robert Goodman and George Johnston have asserted in their classic work, The Australians, that when Australians do attempt to acquire some of "the better things of life," they are "usually trying to answer an inner rather than a competitive urge."[139] And if Australians do have a national dream, it is, according to journalist David Lamb, "to rise collectively rather than individually."[140] In everyday examples of this collective spirit, one finds that people in Australia exchange and share things to a greater degree than do people in America.[141] Thus there is more of a feeling of neighborly helpfulness and sense of community in Australia--like there used to be in the United States.

Which people are more caring and develop more lasting friendships is also readily observable. Australian employers demonstrate more concern for their employees; teachers seem to show a greater interest in their charges; and doctors make themselves more available to their patients. And regarding lasting friendships, it is true, just as Frank S. Hopkins has stated in Dr. Norman Harper's Pacific Orbit, that

> The Australians' loyalty to old friends is a vast
> improvement over the tendency of restless urbanized
> Americans to be continually changing their friends
> as their circumstances are altered in a country
> where so many people are continually on the move.[142]

In offering any concluding remarks about comparisons between the people of the two nations, it would probably be most accurate to say that Australians are a lot like Americans--but not exactly like Americans!

* * *

Finally, one must ask, what is the ultimate decision of the Americans who have immigrated to that new nation on the other side of the world regarding their life in Australia? After an initial period of adjustment, a consideration of the positive and negative aspects of their new land, and a comparison of their situation there to what it was in the States, are they dissatisfied or satisfied with life in their new home? The answer is that while many are definitely dissatisfied, most are satisfied (and 28.5 percent of those surveyed by this writer indicated "mixed feelings" with no answer given by 2 percent).

Those dissatisfied are often among the following types: "go-getters" who do not find ready approval from their fellow Australian workers for their drive toward success; businessmen who are stifled by red tape; those who do not bring enough capital to succeed in some venture or keep themselves solvent until suitable work has been located; or those with sufficient capital to launch an enterprise but not enough know-how in their chosen area.[143] Also, many women are dissatisfied. For women in rural Australia, life can be extremely dull; and single girls often find that Australian males seem to like their beer, "mates," gambling and football more than members of

the opposite sex. Wives are often dissatisfied for several
reasons, according to one female migrant. First, she described, there is the difficulty of "digging in" in the community,
or making friends as close as one had in the States. Second,
there is a lack of contact with family (parents, grown children and others) left behind in America. And third, there is a
feeling of isolation because husbands often have a built-in
group of friends from work, "mates" and other contacts who do
not become part of the family circle of acquaintances. Lastly,
but not exclusively, there are those who are dissatisfied with
their employment because of low earnings or some other reason;
those who cannot adjust to a lower standard of living; and
those who are simply homesick, who were brought up to enjoy
the typical American pastimes of watching football and baseball, for example, and for whom the viewing of soccer and cricket are no substitute.[144]

In the survey conducted by this writer, 13 percent of the
migrants indicated they were dissatisfied; and predominantly
more of those who specified the following motives for emigrating from the United States and immigrating to Australia, rather
than other motives listed, indicated they felt similarly.

Motives	Percentage Dissatisfied
personal or family problems	18.8
poor outlook for the United States	16.7
pace of life too fast	13.9
for adventure	13.6
impersonalized society	13.3
lack of new frontiers	12.8
felt loss of freedom	12.5
racial unrest	12.2
rise in crime rate	11.1
unemployment	10.3

In addition, predominantly more of those with the following
characteristics, than with other characteristics, indicated
they were dissatisfied.

Predominant Characteristics	Percentage Dissatisfied
sex - males	13.8
income in the U.S. - $12,001 to $16,000	28.6
section from which departed - California	16.3
had not visited Australia before migrating	13.4
year of migration - 1973	20.6

Australian government did not financially
   assist passage   15.0
final place of settlement - Western Australia   23.0
income in Australia - $12,001 to $16,000   38.5

(Appendix XVIII contains information from the government survey
on American migrants about its interviewees who were dissatisfied.)

   The majority who indicated they were satisfied are also of
various types, from businessmen who obtained financial success
or position to those individuals who simply found a better
life. As one author has written on the subject, "American cotton farmers in northern New South Wales, U.S. businessmen in
South Australia, and Texas cattlemen in the Northern Territory
have come to think of Australia as God's own country."[145]

   If one has the money and "know-how," success and satisfaction are almost assured in Australia. Cotton farmer Paul Kahl
from Merced, California, immigrated there because he was "fed
up with American low prices, labor problems, and acreage restrictions"; and in 1961 he and his partner, Frank Hadley,
bought farm land in Wee Waa, New South Wales, for $36 an acre
which within one decade became worth $260 an acre![146] On the
opposite side of the continent, two optimistic migrants stated
their conviction that in time their cotton yield in the Ord
River region of Western Australia would be greater than the
yield of the entire state of Arizona from which they came.
In ranching, many American cattlemen found that financially
they could raise and market cattle in Australia for only one-
third what it would cost in the States.   A rancher from
Florida was so successful that he purchased a station in the
Northern Territory for $12,000 and sold it for $300,000 in ten
years.[149] Other ranchers have expressed satisfaction with the
continent itself--F. Benjamin Dillingham II, managing director
of a 750,000-acre spread in the Northern Territory, exclaimed,
"I like this country (Australia), I don't know why, but it gets
me right in the gut."[150] Businessmen, too, have found success
and satisfaction. When Arthur C. Ross experienced a recession
in his hometown, he decided it might be easier to reestablish
in Western Australia where business was expanding than in some
other place in the United States, and he indeed found success
"Down Under." By one account, "he got a million-dollar contract in Perth to build apartments and commercial buildings,
and found the Western Australia boom like the good old days in
the States."[151] Similarly, Bob Cunningham has built a million-
dollar equipment hire and sales business in Canberra; and Jerry
Lapin of New York City became proprietor of the Caprice, one of

Sydney's most prestigious restaurants.[152]

Those expressing satisfaction who simply found a better life include a variety of people. They might be teachers like Bob Jones who hoped he could get a job in California, could not, moved to Australia, and now says about America, "I'm not going back. I'm here to stay. Australia has retained all the good things of life that the States gave away a long time ago."[153] They may be farmers like former Florida manufacturer Ed Nichols who says about Perth, "You couldn't drag me away from this place. The air is clear, the people are straight-forward and friendly, and there's a kind of peacefulness every-where." His parents were happy in Florida and did not believe they would want to settle elsewhere, but he got them to migrate in 1969 and says, "Now you couldn't get them away from here, either."[154] Satisfied migrants might also be assistant hostel managers like Ken Lunde of Seattle, Washington, who immigrated after hearing of American celebrity Art Linkletter's success in Western Australia, and "who liked to say his only regret was that he had not gone to Australia earlier. He found life a lot easier."[155] Or they might be settlers in Australia's Outback who feel the same as the Reverend David Nurse does when talking about his 100,000-mile parish in the northern part of the nation:

> There's no feeling of loneliness up here like you find in the big city. The degree of interdependence is immense. Ask the question here "Am I my brother's keeper?" and the answer is invariably "Yes." This is a life which gives men back their souls, and it is this that captivates us all, from American billionaires to struggling laborers.[156]

Then there is one other type of American who has expressed satisfaction and about whom little has been said because there are few in Australia--the black American. Choreographer and French instructor Bernard Byers from Philadelphia, Pennsylvania, was accepted for Australian citizenship in December, 1970 and has claimed to be "very pleased" with treatment by white Aus-tralians. He stated, "I haven't found the racial bit here. Once you get a job and a circle of friends, you fit in."[157] Ronne Arnold, also from Philadelphia, came in 1959 and has re-mained in Australia in charge of his own dance team, The Australian Contemporary Dance Company. His remarks--"Man, I love it. I have no problems here."[158] Prominent musical con-ductor Dean Dixon became conductor of the Sydney Symphony. One report has it that "Maestro Dixon's color prevented him from following his profession in the United States, but he's most welcome in Australia."[159] And featherweight boxer Don Johnson from California has lived in Melbourne since 1967. Like Ronne Arnold, Don Johnson stated, "I have no problems here."[160]

American migrants who have found success and satisfaction in Australia have generally accepted Australia and the Australian way of life for what they are.[161] Furthermore, they have probably, in the words of John Lardner, "looked for what's Australian in Australia, rather than waht's American."[162] In other words, they attempt to identify with the land and its people.[163] A good example of this type of migrant is Oklahoman Henry Kelly who immigrated to Kununurra in the northwestern part of the continent. He now makes approximately $30,000 per year growing cotton and has become "a fair dinkum (the real thing) Aussie" by really entering into the life of the community--even playing on the local cricket team. Th exclaims about his life in his new home:

> I am absolutely in love with Australia. It is my home now, and I will apply for Australian citizenship. I've just become the father of the first Australian-born American in Kununurra, and I'm glad for him too, because this is a wonderful country offering a lot better opportunities. There are no class or money barriers here like we have back in the States. People accept you for what you are.[164]

One might justifiably ask if Australia is so wonderful and if most migrants are satisfied, why have so few become naturalized Australians after the two-and-one-half year waiting period required for citizenship (Tables 29 and 30)?[165] Actually, there are several reasons for this lack of action on their part. First, there is no real pressure by the Australian government for these migrants to become citizens.[166] Another reason, however, seems more important and that is although most migrants are satisfied in Australia, most also consider it at least a possibility that they might one day want to resettle in America. If in the meantime they had become Australian citizens, they would be required to go through the same procedure as any other Australian citizen who wished to immigrate to the United States. Other reasons why Americans may not want to become Australian citizens involve practical considerations such as how such a decision would effect their American pension rights.[167] While others offer patriotic rationales such as, "I didn't like the idea of having to swear allegiance to the Queen of England!"

In the survey conducted by this writer, 56.5 percent of the migrants indicated they were satisfied; and predominantly more of those who specified the following motives for

TABLE 29

U.S. AMERICANS (NATIONALITY) GRANTED
AUSTRALIAN CITIZENSHIP

Year	Number
Jan. June 1945-1974[a]	2,436
Jan. Dec. 1945-1947	78
1948	32
1949	43
1950	25
1951	15
1952	26
1953	32
1954	24
1955	39
1956	34
1957	47
1958	56
1959	66
1960	62
1961	55
1962	64
1963	92
1964	110
1965	85
1966	114
1967	159
1968	141
1969	148
1970	191
1971	197
1972	206
1973	217

SOURCES: Department of Immigration, Australian Immigration: Consolidated Statistics, No. 7 (Canberra: The Australian Government Publishing Service, 1973), p. 78, 81.

Department of Immigration,
Australian Immigration: Quarterly
Statistical Summary, Vol. III, No.
29 (Canberra: The Australian Government Publishing Service, December
1973), pp. 30-31.

Department of Immigration,
Australian Immigration: Quarterly
Statistical Summary, Vol. III, No.
30 (Canberra: The Australian Government Publishing Service, June, 1974),
p. 32.

[a]Prior to January 29, 1949,
aliens who were naturalized became
British Subjects. With the introduction of the Naturalization and Citizenship Act 1948, all such persons
automatically became Australian
Citizens.

TABLE 30

U.S. AMERICANS (NATIONALITY) GRANTED
AUSTRALIAN CITIZENSHIP FROM
JULY 1964 TO JUNE 1973
(BY AGE AND SEX)

Age	Males	Females
0-9	41	40
10-14	41	38
15-19	129	115
20-24	163	91
25-29	88	36
30-34	54	21
35-39	53	27
40-44	75	35
45-49	92	31
50-54	60	16
55-59	24	13
60 & Over	72	31
Total	892	494

SOURCE: Department of Immigration, Australian Immigration: Consolidated Statistics, No. 7 (Canberra: The Australian Government Publishing Service, 1973), p. 89.

emigrating from the United States and immigrating to Australia, rather than other motives listed, indicated that they felt similarly.

Motives	Percentage Satisfied
unstable, fast-changing society	82.1
too much materialism	73.3
racial unrest	73.1
increased violence	72.9
felt loss of freedom	71.9
lack of new frontiers	71.8
impersonalized society	70.0
pace of life too fast	69.8
rise in crime rate	69.4
for better business and investment opportunities	69.3

In addition, predominantly more of those with the following characteristics, than with other characteristics, indicated they were satisfied.

Predominant Characteristics	Percentage Satisfied
sex - females	62.9
occupation in the U.S. - clerical workers	83.3
income in the U.S. - less than $4,000, or	68.0
$4,001 to $8,000, or	64.3
above $16,000	65.0
section from which departed - Northeast	70.0
had visited Australia before migrating	60.0
year of migration - 1970	77.0
Australian government financially assisted passage	61.1
final place of settlement - Victoria, or	58.8
Queensland	58.6
occupation in Australia - students	85.7
income in Australia - $4,001 to $8,000	66.2

(Appendix XIX contains information from the government survey on American migrants abouts its interviewees who were satisfied.)

112

Footnotes - Chapter IV:

1. Department of Immigration, Survey, pp. 39, 37.

2. Ibid., p. 6.

3. "'Invasion' of Australia," p. 55.

4. Richard Tregaskis, "Down Under Looks Up," Saturday Review November 12, 1960, p. 53.

5. "What to Expect," p. 76.
   Gunther, Australia, p. 50.

6. Gunther, Australia, p. 350.

7. Bruce Grant, "The American Image in Australia," in Pacific Orbit, ed. by Norman Harper (Melbourne: F. W. Cheshire, 1968), p. 209.

8. Trumbull, "Seeking Simpler Life," p. 12.

9. Don Fabun, Australia 2000! (New York: The Free Press, 1974), p. 27.
   Department of Immigration, Survey, p. 40.

10. Moffitt, U-Jack, pp. 101-102.

11. U.S. Congress, Senate, Senator J. William Fulbright pre-sents article, "Why Hackworth Went to Australia," 93rd Cong., 1st sess., February 22, 1973, Congressional Record, CXIX, 5191.

12. Ibid.

13. Eugene Lang, "Now Is the Time," International Commerce, May 4, 1964, p. 21.
    Moffitt, U-Jack, p. 177.

14. Ibid., p. 190.

15. The Permanent Residents' Group, American Women's Club of Perth, Western Australia, "For the Bread Winner," News-letter from Australia, April, 1971, p. 2.

16. Hopkins, I've Had It, p. 164.

17. Aitchison, Americans, p. 111.

18. Moffitt, U-Jack, p. 172.
    Peter Kann, "Boom Down Under," Wall Street Journal,
    February 9, 1970, p. 1.

19. Moffitt, U-Jack, p. 172.

20. "U.S. Firms," p. 101.
    "Things Stirring 'Down Under': Australia Comes of Age,"
    U.S. News & World Report, June 3, 1968, p. 100.
    Ian Potter, "American Investment in Australia," in Pacific
    Orbit, ed. by Norman Harper (Melbourne: F. W. Cheshire,
    1968), p. 67.

21. "Australia: For Many the Goal Is to Become a 'New
    America'," U.S. News & World Report, October 13, 1975, p.
    65.

22. U.S. Department of Commerce, Economic Trends and Their
    Implications for the United States--Australia (Washington,
    D.C.: Government Printing Office, March 1, 1971), p. 8.

23. The Permanent Residents' Group, American Women's Club of
    Perth, Western Australia, "Money," Newsletter from Austra-
    lia, April, 1971, p. 2.
    Casewit, Overseas Jobs, p. 39.

24. Moffitt, U-Jack, p. 180.

25. Moffat and Tannen, What's It Like? p. 2.

26. Moffitt, U-Jack, pp. 193, 227.

27. Thomas Jenkins, "People--Heart of the Environment,"
    Australia Now, August, 1971, p. 5.

28. Gunther, Australia, p. 159.
    Faulk and Faulk, Alternative, p. 140.

29. David Lamb, "Australia Beckons to U.S. Teachers,"
    Washington Post, August 4, 1974, sec. H, p. 7.

30. Letter to the author from a survey respondent, 1974.

31. Faulk and Faulk, Alternative, p. 142.
    Gunther, Australia, p. 142.

32. "Australia as a Place to Live," p. 80.

33. Gunther, Australia, p. 350.

34. Ibid.

35. Faulk and Faulk, Alternative, p. 165.

36. McGregor, Profile, pp. 82-84.

37. "The Land and Its People," Senior Scholastic, December 5, 1951, p. 27.

38. Russel Ward, Australia (Englewood Cliffs, N.J.: Prentice-Hall, Inc., 1965), p. 16.

39. McGregor, Profile, pp. 291-292.
    Henry Albinski, "Australian Society," Current History, March, 1972, p. 134.

40. Department of Immigration, Survey, p. 30.

41. Ibid., p. 29.

42. Horne, The Lucky Country, p. 79.

43. Ibid., p. 14.

44. Ibid., p. 21.

45. Gunther, Australia, p. 31.

46. Elizabeth Riddell, "Seeking a New West," The Australian, August 3, 1971, p. 11.

47. "She'll Be Right," p. 37.

48. Aitchison, Americans, p. 197.

49. Ron Kaye et al., "The U.S.tralians," The Australian, October 25, 1975, p. 23.

50. Jenkins, "People," pp. 3-5.

51. Commonwealth of Australia, The Fourth Part of the World: An Exhibition Concerning the Discovery, Settlement and Exploration of the Continent of Australia (Canberra: Australian Government Publishing Service, 1976), p. 4.
    Gunther, Australia, pp. 72-73.

52. Gunther, Australia, p. 73.

53. Ibid.

54. Ibid., p. 70.

55. Martha DuBose, "Americans Who Kept on West," Sydney
    Morning-Herald, women's supplement, July 1, 1971, p. 3.
    McGregor, Profile, p. 61.

56. McGregor, Profile, p. 61.

57. Horne, The Lucky Country, p. 75.

58. McGregor, Profile, p. 56.
    Horne, The Lucky Country, p. 37.

59. McGregor, Profile, p. 134.

60. Ibid., p. 39.
    Aitken, Land of Fortune, pp. 246-247.

61. Gunther, Australia, p. 35.

62. Horne, The Lucky Country, p. 40.

63. McGregor, Profile, p. 180.

64. Moffitt, U-Jack, p. 101.

65. Aitchison, Americans, p. 197.

66. Helmericks, Adventure, p. 173.

67. McGregor, Profile, pp. 90-91.

68. Ibid.

69. "How a Yank Reacts to the Aussies," U.S. News & World
    Report, January 1, 1968, p. 5.
    Kurt Mayer, "Social Stratification in Two Equalitarian
    Societies: Australia and the United States," Social
    Research, XXXI, No. 4 (Winter, 1964):455.

70. Fabun, Australia 2000! p. 33.

71. Horne, The Lucky Country, pp. 71-72.

72. Ibid., p. 33.

73. Gunther, Australia, p. 159.

74. McGregor, Profile, p. 350.

Helmericks, Adventure, p. 102.

75. "'Invasion' of Australia," p. 55.

76. Faulk and Faulk, Alternative, p. 47.

77. Horne, The Lucky Country, p. 37.

78. Ibid.

79. DuBose, "Americans Who Kept on West," p. 3.

80. Horne, The Lucky Country, p. 94.

81. Department of Immigration, Survey, p. 37.

82. McGregor, Profile, p. 15.

83. Kaye et al., "The U.S.tralians," p. 23.

84. Donald Horne, "Lucky Australia," Holiday, September, 1966,
    p. 59.
    Department of Immigration, Survey, p. 38.

85. Faulk and Faulk, Alternative, p. 122.

86. Gunther, Australia, p. 158.

87. Moffitt, U-Jack, p. 215.
    Horne, The Lucky Country, p. 170.

88. Faulk and Faulk, Alternative, p. 100.

89. Ibid., p. 130.

90. Ibid., p. 176.

91. Trumbull, Seeking Simpler Life," p. 12.

92. C. Slocombe, "Incredible Australia," Travel, June, 1953,
    p. 7.

93. Aitchison, Americans, p. 200.
    Linkletter, Down Under, p. 215.

94. Williams,What Is It? p. 28.

95. Faulk and Faulk, Alternative, p. 85.
    Helmericks, Adventure, pp. 189-190.

117

96. Department of Immigration, Survey, p. 37.

97. Faulk and Faulk, Alternative, p. 179.

98. Ibid., p. 93.

99. "A 'New America'," p. 66.

100. Faulk and Faulk, Alternative, p. 94.

101. "Australia as a Place to Live," p. 81.

102. Department of Immigration, Survey, p. 69.

103. Faulk and Faulk, Alternative, p. 108.

104. David Lamb, "Australia's Lure for . . . American
     Teachers," Washington Post, July 28, 1974, sec. G, p. 11.
     Department of Immigration, Survey, pp. 39-40.
     Keatley, "Australia Is Fine--If You Have Money," p. 1.
     Moffat and Tannen, What's It Like? p. 2.
     Faulk and Faulk, Alternative, p. 180.

105. Department of Immigration, Survey, p. 33.

106. Faulk and Faulk, Alternative, p. 64.

107. Gunther, Australia, p. 52.

108. Letter on living conditions in and general information
     about Queensland from American Families' Association of
     Queensland, September, 1971.

109. Faulk and Faulk, Alternative, p. 53.

110. Department of Immigration, Survey, p. 46.

111. Ibid.

112. Williams, What Is It? p. 40.

113. Aitchison, Americans, p. 105.

114. McGregor, Profile, p. 326.

115. Department of Immigration, Survey, p. 27.

116. Ibid., p. 28.

117. McGregor, Profile, p. 149.

118. Department of Immigration, Survey, p. 45.

119. Letter on living conditions in and general information about Queensland from American Families' Association of Queensland, September, 1971.
Faulk and Faulk, Alternative, p. 71.
Moffat and Tanne, What's It Like? p. 32.

120. Department of Immigration, Survey, p. 43.
Horne, The Lucky Country, p. 26.

121. Department of Immigration, Survey, p. 43.

122. Ibid., pp. 43-44.

123. Ibid., p. 41.

124. Ibid., pp. 40-42.

125. Williams, What Is It? p. 61.
O. K. Spate, Australia (New York: Praeger Publishers, 1968), p. 252.

126. Ward, Australia, p. 4.
Mayer, "Social Stratification":465.

127. Hopkins, "Image of Australia," p. 233.

128. Jenkins, "People," p. 3.

129. Gunther, Australia, p. 42.

130. Schubert, "Yank's-Eye View," p. 14.

131. Faulk and Faulk, Alternative, p. 133.

132. McGregor, Profile, p. 377.
Westerman and Bacheller, eds., Almanac, p. 220.

133. Helmericks, Adventure, p. 182.

134. Faulk and Faulk, Alternative, pp. 87, 170.

135. Aitchison, Americans, pp. 202-203.

136. McGregor, Profile, pp. 352-353.

137. Ibid., p. 353.

138. Horne, The Lucky Country, p. 28.

139. Goodman and Johnston, The Australians, p. 91.

140. David Lamb, "The Final Children of the Earth, Whom Knowledge Has Not Scarred," Los Angeles Times, February 3, 1975, sec. II, p. 5.

141. Faulk and Faulk, Alternative, p. 113.

142. Hopkins, "Image of Australia," p. 234.

143. Moffat and Tannen, What's It Like? p. 17.
Moffit, U-Jack, p. 180.
Fabun, Australia 2000! pp. 15-16.

144. Department of Immigration, Survey, p. 22.

145. Aitchison, Americans, p. ix.

146. John Yeomans, The Scarce Australians (London: Longmans Publishing Company, 1967), pp. 112-114.
Aitken, Land of Fortune, p. 157.

147. "What to Expect," p. 76.

148. Ibid., p. 77.

149. Casewit, Overseas Jobs, p. 37.

150. Kann, "Boom Down Under," p. 1.

151. Aitchison, Americans, p. 198.

152. Trumbull, "Seeking Simpler Life," p. 12.

153. Lamb, "American Teachers," p. 11.

154. Gordon, "Americans Are Emigrating," p. 77.

155. Aitchison, Americans, pp. 102-103.

156. Aitken, Land of Fortune, p. 163.

157. Gunther, Australia, p. 46.
Trumbull, "American Negro," p. 19.

158. Trumbull, "Racial Barriers," p. 24.

159. Thompson, "White Policy," part II, p. 98.

160. Trumbull, "Racial Barriers," p. 24.

161. Aitchison, Americans, p. 196.

162. J. Lardner, "John Lardner's Australia: Cities, Jimmy-grants . . . ," Newsweek, July 18, 1955, p. 78.

163. S. N. Eisenstadt, "Analysis of Patterns of Immigration and Absorption of Immigrants," Population Studies, VII (1953):167-171.

164. Aitken, Land of Fortune, pp. 158-159.

165. Department of Immigration, Australia and Immigration--A Review of Migration to Australia Especially Since World War II, revised (Canberra: Department of Immigration, January, 1974), p. 35.

166. Letter on living conditions in and general information about Queensland from American Families' Association of Queensland, September, 1971.

167. Department of Immigration, Survey, p. 52.

CHAPTER

5

IN THEIR
OWN WORDS

This chapter consists entirely of autobiographical sketches by some of the two hundred American migrants surveyed by this writer regarding their reasons for immigrating and their life in Australia. Except for occasional alterations for the sake of brevity or clarity, the following texts are in the migrants' exact words. The sketches are arranged by states and territories in the order of their populations, and within each state and territory by alphabetical order of the migrants' last names.

New South Wales

Deborah B

A couple of reasons inspired me to leave the U.S. in 1972, but the stronger inspiration was my engagement to an Australian in Sydney. My job with an airline in Atlanta had provided me with numerous opportunities to travel abroad--these trips continued to whet my appetite for more extensive travel and particularly for the chance to actually live overseas for an indefinite period of time. Ironically, my first trip to Europe took me to Igls, Austria, in January, 1969, where I met my (unsuspected at the time) future husband, who was living in London then. Casual correspondence led to a few trips to Australia after he had returned home and ultimately to my emigration in July, 1972.

My departure from the U.S., then, was not spurred by my disenchantment with the country--in fact, I remain quite patriotic; I even have my American flag hanging in our flat--but instead, by my desire to experience other environemnts and, more immediately, by my plans to marry my Australian fiance.

My three years in Australia have been quite eventful.
Careerwise, I managed to break into a new occupation, under-
going teacher training and spending two eye-opening years enduring the public school system at a girls' high school in
Blacktown (a suburb about twenty-two miles west of Sydney). I
am now contentedly settled in a girls' private Church of
England school in Sydney, and am also in my second year of a
three-year, part-time, M.A. history program at Macquarie University, expecting to finish in December, 1976. My husband is
also at Macquarie University, offering moral support and encouragement during many hours at the library. I consider the
study abroad an invaluable experience. Macquarie is an inno-
vative university, operating more along American lines with the
same credit system and choice of elective subjects to supplement the major field. This program differs from the more
widely practised British system of the other Australian universities, which emphasize in-depth study into the major field, at
the exclusion of elective subjects.

Other experiences have included trips around Australia,
particularly along the east coast, which is quite beautiful.
One trip to the Barrier Reef was aborted by the cyclone
(Australian word for hurricane) season in Queensland. Everyone
must experience a flood sometime during his stay in Australia,
because these floods are such usual occurrences. We were stran-
ded in Rockhampton (a one-time cow town), Queensland, for about
four days, spending Christmas (Chrissy) with a bottle of Moselle
and canned Campbell's Chinese Meal, delectably served over
steaming white rice. As soon as the flood waters subsided to a
level as high as the floorboard of our VW beetle, we joined the
exodus, chanced the crossing and proceeded (like escaped convicts) back south to Sydney. Our other camping trips, however,
have been less eventful, more successful and most enjoyable.

My impressions of Australia and Australians are mixed, although my overall feeling toward the country and people is
affectionate. I found settling into the Australian lifestyle
comfortably easy: Sydney is a beautiful harbor city with an
atmosphere comprising European and American influences. Routine
habits of shopping, catching transport, speaking a faintly resembling tongue (Australian jargon is entertaining), etc., are
much the same as in the States. Even the ubiquitous chain of
Kentucky Fried Chicken and McDonald's Hamburger, along with eating places in Kings Cross (a traditional American G.I. hangout),
such as Texas Tavern, Kentucky Bourbon Steak House and American
Pancakes, are constant reminders of Home. The habit of relaxing in the city's numerous flowered parks during lunch hour and
the cluster of old-world buildings and homes are distinctively
European. Australians are generally good-natured and easygoing-

this charmed me initially--although this casualness inevitably penetrates the businesses and public services that one often has to rely upon. That is when the charm wears off, and the motto, "She'll be right, mate," loses its appeal. I find it difficult to decide which I prefer: the nervous busyness of American working routine, where the beeline from A to B often bypasses the park and leaves no time for leisurely lunch hours, or the Australians' casual, often contemptous, attitude toward work and The Boss. Both are _general_ observations, though.

Another feature my three years' experience has brought to my attention is the omnipresence of government agencies: Australian life is far more government-oriented, so that Government (State or Federal) initiatives replace private services, the most obvious being transportation, state departments of education (vs. regional boards), solely state-administered universities, communication services, health insurance (a current controversy), banking and others. Much of this is true of the U.S. and elsewhere, although this feature seems in grander proportion in Australia. The result is that each personal endeavor becomes a bureaucratic (and sometimes traumatic) procedure, and everyone becomes well-trained in filling out triplicate forms. One develops a fatalistic philosophy of giving in rather than beating his head to death against The Wall.

Quite noticeable is the cosmopolitan air of Australia. Among most Australians I meet, those who have not already been abroad at some time plan to do so. Conversely, there is a large population of those from overseas, staying in Australia either temporarily or permanently. There is a large proportion, then, who have experienced extensive travel and who inject much vitality and variety into the life over here.

Despite minor irritations, my experience here has been happy and memorable. Settlement in Australia, however, does not preclude our spending an indefinite time in Europe and North America--there are other civilizations we have yet to absorb.

Hank D

I'm forty-five, white (otherwise I'd not have been admitted past the pearly gates), have six kids and am an inventor, a fix-it-man, panel and spray, etc., and am a vagabond musician. So I can get by anywhere. But if you come to Australia, you better keep your sense of humor, 'cause these good folk have none. I figure a couple of more generations, and more emphasis on education, and forget the isolationist bit, and lots of luck and influence of migrants and Australia will be part of the

124

world. Not that that is any great goal. A reality though.

I've been thinking ever since I hit this place how misin-
formed I was six years ago. Amazing, as I researched it for
five years, and even invested $500 to subsidize a friend's
trip here. Even with all the talking to Aussies, and Yanks
who had been here, and even after extended conversations with
my friend, after he came back from bugging and spooking the
place for a year, and all the dozen books and articles I read,
I was still unprepared for what I found. I wouldn't have believed it if it hadn't happened to me, and I am hard to shock.
I think the human mind is capable of coloring and shading, and
a person believes what he wants to. The place is just like
the States, and the people are just like "Yanks." Only more
so. More greed, petty, jealous, bigoted, jingoistic, uneducated, etc. Like, I'm a cynic, and also realistic.

I've been here for five years. The honeymoon has been
over for four. I am a citizen of the world, and not patriotic
to any place, but try to contribute to make the place I'm at a
better one. You can find out about the geology and other physical facts of the country, so I won't waste time on them. The
people are the main ingredient of any place and Australians are
----. Note that I'm making vast generalizations. The exceptions are very exceptional, as they are so rare, and the system
is not geared to produce rare individuals.

The family is all OK. Wife settled in quite well after she
got over the first year and the shock of such a low standard of
living (like no heat or hot water in a $20-a-week rented house).
I am getting close to perfecting a fat filter for fish and chips
fat. Seems the merchants change the fat every couple of weeks
at sixty-nine bucks a change plus a lot of messy labor. I think
I'd sell some pumps and beautiful stainless steel tubing and
thereafter a hell of a lot of filters. Capitalist opportunistic
Yanks! Why don't they integrate better and be just like us
"dinkie die" (true) Aussies? I think the answer is that the
average Yank would have to make too many compromises and take
giant steps backward and downward. Back is beautiful!

Met a young Yank schoolteacher from Harrisburg, Pennsylvania. Lasted two months teaching. Refused to use the cane and
pandemonium broke loose and got worse. In my opinion he might
be less than an inspiring teacher under any circumstances,
though that is a quick judgment, as I only talked to him for an
hour, and I wasn't entirely sober; and I suspect he had been
smoking. Photography nut. He'll have a ball. Pretty sights
here. Went on shark patrol from Coff's Harbour (saw one shark,
and radioed the swimmers and surfers). About an hour of some of

125

the prettiest shoreline in the world, and a fine pilot and
hell of a fine guy. Like I hope I hasten to point out, the
good Aussie is 11 feet tall, hearty, smart, hospitable, broad-
minded, interesting, well-educated, etc. He was one. Just
depressing that they are so hard to find. I just don't have
time and am too lazy to haunt the campus or the "better" or
more interesting places and cultivate people. Easier to bitch.

Made a hinged bird feeder that swings over to the living
room window, and gradually seduced the parrots, magpies,
kurrawangs and bower birds to come a couple of feet away from
the house and us. The parrots even came in the house (just
inside the open window) and ate from my hand a couple of times.
Fascinating to watch twenty of them on the feeders at once.
Sunflower seeds for the parrots and bread for the rest. They
feed compatibly on the same feeder, with four bowls.

I've also been custom-painting a few bikes lately and having fun and making a buck. Very conservative bikies, I could
add, if I were trying to sell a point of view. Doing a little
sculpture, too. Built a horse house, cheap and dirty, but it
amazed the neighbors, who all thought a stable should be a few
gum posts and sheets of tin. I should be following the form
that you have carefully and thoughtfully outlined, but after
being in the U.S. Army and from a U.S. background, I have been
a slave to forms too long.

Bar conversation is usually pretty shallow and trite in
the States, but worse here (I support local breweries). I
could add that 84 percent of Australian music is not too good
either. I won't though.

About whether someone should immigrate to Australia, a
quick answer would be, "give the place a go." All you have to
lose is your individuality, which you surely must do if you
stay here for more than five or so years. It is just like the
rest of the world. Nice to visit. There are lots of migrants
here, which makes the place bearable. Money can be earned if
you want to work. If you don't want to work, you can make
money anyway if you join the right union. No one starves here--
except for culture, someone to talk intelligently to and for
good tasting food. The place has improved tremendously since
I hit here. Not because of me, but because of the Japanese.
They are shipping good material here. Anyway, I'm sure you'll
remember this is all just one guy's viewpoint.

Marilyn J

Why would a couple in their thirties with two sons, four

126

and eight, decide to sell the family homestead and leave their
hometown, close family ties and lifelong friends to follow
through with a magazine ad, "Australia Wants You"? Although
we had seen the ad years ago and often daydreamed about foreign travel, our dreams were not realized until a number of
circumstances occurred, providing us with the freedom, reasons
and conviction strong enough to make such a dramatic move. We
were tearing away our roots, the comfortable, small town,
middle-class security we had known all our lives. It was like
leaving the womb! But, on the other hand, we were leaving
behind the establishment and the rat race--an existence that
was becoming stagnant.

My husband, Woody, after having been a city police officer
for six years, made an energetic, but unsuccessful, bid in the
race for county sheriff. After losing the election, he entered
the building trades. Police promotions and pension were no
longer incentives to keep us tied down until retirement. Our
travel thoughts wandered to Florida, California, Canada and
eventually abroad. Europe seemed too settled and crowded,
Africa and South America too politically unstable plus language
barriers. The "Land Down Under" filled all our needs and desires for a new life. A fresh, young country with vast opportunities, lost of "wide open spaces" and freedom.

Soon after answering the ad, we received some interesting
literature including the assisted passage program offered by
the Australian Government and the address of the Australian
Consulate-General where we promptly wrote for particulars. We
found out that the breadwinner must be assured of employment as
one of the prerequisites for acceptance in the assisted passage
program. One of our insurance reps had been asking Woody to
join his firm for quite some time, and when we found out the
company had offices in Australia, Woody became a member of the
firm.

We filled out forms, acquired reference letters, medical
exams and immunizations, and filled out more forms until we
were finally accepted as Australian migrants (close to a year
after our initial correspondence with the Consulate). The last
form was our agreement to maintain residence in Australia for
at least two years as the condition for us to acquire governmental financial passage assistance. We wanted to spend
Christmas at home, so we made plans to start our trip
December 28, 1971, and arrived in Sydney on January 1, 1972,
starting a new year in a new country.

After Customs, we accepted the Immigration Department's
offer of lodging at a government hostel, just for that night.

127

Little did we know at the time that the hostel would be "home" for the next three months. The hostel was a converted army barracks area. Singles and married couples without children were housed in the old barracks with a "path to the bath," but we were lucky to live in a new brick condominium, two rooms and bath. Everyone ate meals in a community cafeteria, and it was there that we became friends with people from the U.S.A., Holland, France, South America, Poland, Ireland, as well as "Pommies" (Aussie slang for English). We spent most of January touring Sydney, taking advantage of its beaches, and dancing and drinking "grog" (beer) at the pub with our new friends. I learned to wash clothes in a copper boiler, and we learned to use our feet, buses and trains for transportation until February 22 when we bought a 1962 VW Konbivan outfitted for camping.

Before leaving the hostel and becoming temporary "Sundowners" we were recruited at the hostel to take part in an Immigration Department film now shown to prospective migrants all over the world. It was great fun being "movie stars" if only for two days. Then we packed our belongings in the van, travelled down the coast and spent a five-day Easter holiday on the beach at Tathra. We wanted to try trout farming, and talked to the owner of one being built at Tumut, New South Wales. He suggested that we find area employment for two years. By then the farm would be in operation and he could probably use our help. So we found employment in the Snowy Mountains ski area, living as caretakers in a lodge, working at a ski hire shop, and I was cook and housekeeper for the staff. The following summer I worked at the mountain riding school and Woody in construction of a new ski lift. The next ski season was spent managing a 30-bed lodge, and summer was spent managing one of the largest 165-bed-motel-pub-restaurants, both owned by our employer.

Our ski scene career ended abruptly when I had an auto accident and was hospitalized for a month. It was then that Woody was phoned by the manager of the trout farm we had previously contacted, and was offered an intensive training position which led within a few months to his becoming manager of all growing trout. We also became caretakers and lived in a new house on the farm. I had started to work in disease control and doing a bit of P.R. with tours. We were so pleased with everything at the trout farm and new friends, and Tumut reminded us of our hometown. In October, 1974 our two sons and I made a trip back to Illinois and broke the proverbial apron strings by selling our stored furnishings. We had a six-week whirlwind visit with relatives and friends, showed Aussie films, and gave talks at schools and libraries. Then we had an

overnight visit with "hostel" friends in San Francisco who had
spent two years teaching in Australia, and spent a few days
with relatives in Los Angeles.

A few months after returning home to the farm, management
changed; we felt no future for us there and decided to leave.
We were reluctant to leave for many reasons. This was the largest commercial trout farm in the Southern Hemisphere and the
knowledge and experience we had gained was rewarding. Our
fifteen months stay in the Tumut area, many new friends, and
our opportunity to see that our hometown of Morris, Illinois,
has officially become Tumut's Sister City--all leaves many fond
memories.

We moved back to the ski country and did seasonal work
till summer arrived, drawing us to the coast. We lived in a
small cabin in the "Man From Snowy River" ranching area where
the movie The Sundowners was filmed. Our neighbors have been
cattle, sheep, 'roos, wombats, emus, foxes and brumbies (wild
horses). The kids have helped with cattle branding, sheep
dipping and such.

Tomorrow, February 16, 1976, will find us on our ninth
move since our arrival four years ago in Australia. We originally came here to enjoy the change in climate and to be able to
lie on the beaches, soaking up the sun. Somehow we remained in
the coldest areas, that is--until tomorrow. We have found an
opportunity to reenter the aquaculture business, an oyster farm
at Tathra, on the coast. We've rented a four-bedroom beach
house, so we'll have plenty of room for visiting friends from
the mountains, Tumut and U.S.A.

This must seem a very unstable way to live, but somehow
our sons feel no lack of security. The oldest just started his
first year of high school at a well-established, century-old
boarding school, where he can get more involved with sports,
and develop good study habits and self-discipline. He wants to
try it for at least a year, by that time we hope to be more
settled in our new area and established in the oyster business
in Australia.

M. S. M

I have been in Australia as a migrant for nearly twenty-
five years having come here to make a home at Christmas time
1951. Since coming here, my Australian wife and I have had an
interesting and rewarding life and have a better than average
home which we built ourselves and which is beautifully cared
for by my wife. We have many friends and although I have

129

retained my U.S. Citizenship, I feel accepted and quite at
home.

Here is how it all happened. I was in the U.S. Military
Service from March, 1941 to August, 1946. During that time I
belonged to many different Army units which served in the
Southwest Pacific area, namely, Melbourne, Sydney, and Brisbane
in Australia; Morotai; New Guinea; and Leyte in the Philippines.
However, most of my service was in Australia and while in Sydney
I met my wife to be at the American Services Club in 1944. Sub-
sequently I was posted on North but kept in touch with her.

Late in 1945 after the termination of the war, I came back
to Sydney in order to take an examination for Warrant Officer.
I had made application for this but had missed the examinations
when they were held in forward areas. While in Sydney for the
examinations, I met officers with whom I had worked in subsis-
tence and supply procurement in earlier days; and since I had a
lot of knowledge of food and supplies obtained from the Australian Government, I was kept in Sydney to do the Lend Lease and
Reverse Lend Lease accounts. At the conclusion of this work I
was assigned to the Surplus Supplies section and the disposal
of supplies which kept me busy till June, 1946. Since the war
was over, these later assignments were almost the same as a
civilian job and during this time in Sydney I renewed my acquaintance with my future wife.

We were not married at this stage although we had made
plans to marry and had obtained the Army's permission; however
I suddenly was given the opportunity of returning to the U.S.
and decided to accept this; and when I was transferred to the
Army Reserve, I planned to return to Australia, but this was
not to be. Upon my return to the U.S., my mother was ill with
arthritis and I felt obligated to stay and look after her.

I kept in contact with my fiancee by mail and as the time
passed on, we eventually decided that she come to the U.S. I
had in the meantime returned to civilian life and into the employ of one of the large food producing companies with which I
was employed prior to Service. Under the conscription laws of
the U.S., those going into the Army and subsequently to War
Service were to be reinstated in their previous employment without loss of seniority, promotion, etc. I felt I was treated
shabbily by this concern. I did get employment but only in the
same capacity as previously, and others in the company who had
at one time been in my charge had moved on to superior positions. When it became evident that I was to continue to be
slighted as a result of having gone to serve my country, the
situation became intolerable and I left their employ and joined

130

the U.S. Employment Service.

In November, 1948, my fiancee came to the U.S. We were
married and my wife, who was Australian, became entitled to
residence in the U.S. During the next few years we often dis-
dussed the possibilities of returning to Australia, the prospects and opportunities it offered. We liked the prospect of
getting into business for ourselves one day, a possibility that
was becoming more and more remote in the U.S. in those times.

I had suffered some back trouble which originated during
my overseas service and approached the Veterans Administration
for help in this regard, only to be told after many examinations and tests that there were no medical records to show that
it was service connected.

Though not actually dissatisfied with things in the U.S.,
the facts of the disillusionments with the food company and the
attitude of the Veterans Administration all helped to swing the
decision to migrate to Australia. When we finally arrived at
this decision, we both worked and saved towards that event. We
then liquidated all our assets, pulled up all our roots so to
speak, and on Christmas Eve, 1951 arrived in Australia to begin
again.

Some factors that helped us were: my wife was Australian;
we had some contacts; we had some assets; and we had help with
housing from my wife's relatives, as well as a lot of moral
support.

There are a lot of adjustments to be made in a new country,
and they are not all easy, nor as simple as one might surmise
from a previous visit. Acclimatization is one, and it may take
several years--somehow Xmas is not the same in midsummer and
spent under a beach umbrella. Wintertime in July in houses not
centrally heated is not exactly what one has been used to
either.

In the early 1950s Saturdays were great sports days, but
Sundays were relatively quiet--no large sporting functions--no
Sunday theatre. One had to content oneself with a Sunday
drive, visiting, going to the beaches or perhaps a picnic.
There was a lot of sailing in the harbour, but that is a parti-
cipant sport rather than a spectator sport.

Our first business venture turned out to be short but not
unrewarding. We bought the Lease on a public house, which is
a hotel with bars, lounges and parlors, the main purpose being
dispensing beer and spirituous liquors. Rooms and meals were

131

incidental, and were required to be available to satisfy the laws governing the sale of beer and spirits.

Having been raised the son of a minister, I was not particularly suited to this type of life. The hotel was located in an inner suburb of working people--wharf laborers, factory laborers, etc., and one needed to be "one of the boys." It was a hard life with plenty of work and long hours; after a year we sold out to try something else.

Our next venture was to open a china and glassware gift business, in one of the newer, outer suburbs. We took the Lease of a new shop premises and started one of the first open-style shops where customers could browse and make their own selections of merchandise. We had good advice on the area and the location, as well as the expected growth of this suburb; and the business turned out to be better than our expectations right from the opening. To add to our good fortune and planning, and hard work, it was not too long before some of the city retailers opened branches which brought more customers to the area and our business grew and prospered in accordance with the growth of the district.

Eventually we had the opportunity to purchase the premises which we did to ensure our tenancy. In the meantime, we had purchased a home in the district and also had a prime building block on which we planned to build a new home one day. We had also purchased a block of ground here where we now live on the North Shore. It was possibly an "investment," but also not beyond the realm of us having a home there some day.

One day we received a very generous offer to lease our shop property to another business, and after some consideration we decided to accept this offer and retire. But after a long rest, we were anxious to have some interest and so did some part-time relief managing for a motel chain for several years.

We then decided to build our present home here on the North Shore. We sold our first home and building block which was near the business property, and set about to incorporate ideas collected over the years into the plans for a new home. We built our present home ourselves by sub-contracting and supervising with the help of a builder foreman.

In 1959 after eight years in Australia, I had a trip to the U.S. to visit family and friends and renew acquaintances. Somehow after all those years it was not quite the same, and though I enjoyed the visit very much, I was quite anxious after four months to get back to Australia and home. When I was in

132

the U.S., my old friends thought my speech sounded very British and I suppose my accent had altered; however people here still pick me as an American, or some think perhaps I am Canadian. I have always felt accepted here and I think the greater percentage of Australians are kindly disposed to Americans. This may be to some degree contingent upon how one treats the Australians. I have at times heard Americans greatly criticized and then have been assured that it doesn't apply to me.

Still to my way of thinking, cricket does not replace baseball, nor does Australian football replace the American gridiron game. Other sports like golf, tennis, swimming, motor racing and horse racing are the same.

Anthony W

In order to understand my reasons for coming to Australia, it's necessary to go back to 1970. I received a B.S. from Illinois State University after seven years of study. While in college I worked full time at a local factory and at the time was earning $7,800 a year without overtime. This job supported me, a wife and two children.

A degree, I thought, would enable me to get a job I liked, in a location I liked, and to lead a more normal life for at least the same amount of money I was earning then. These conditions were hard to meet.

The only solid teaching offer I had was Chicago and I didn't want to live there. After a week of intensive job hunting in Denver, the best offer was driving a delivery truck for $90 a week. The university placement office had no prospects. I was feeling disappointed in America.

About this time I spied an ad in the Chicago Tribune which beckoned me to teach in the "Happy Country, Down Under." I answered the ad because of my disappointment with job hunting, but also because of a long desire to see Australia. Though the job offered included travel payments to Australia, the salary seemed very low at $4,100 per year. A lot of thoughts and discussion passed between my wife and myself. Finally, we decided to go for the following reasons:

1. the experience of a foreign school system would be valuable;
2. the salary was the same as other New South Wales teachers were living on, so it should be adequate; and
3. the personal adventure was irresistible!

As soon as that decision was made, the adventure aspect

came to the fore. My wife certainly deserves a lot of credit for her handling of the logistics of an overseas move. In between letters and phone calls, we both read everything we could about Australia, especially material about immigration. We left Los Angeles on the 31st of January, 1971, prepared for the worst that we had read about.

When we arrived on the 2nd of February in Sydney, we were pleasantly surprised. The reception was everything that was promised. Accommodations in the "Endeavour" migrant hostel reminded us of college dormitory living but was very satisfactory as we took our first close look at the country. The people were very friendly, except for one incident which to me is still more amusing than derogatory.

We were on a sightseeing trip of Sydney with friends near the entrance to the harbor. The landform at that point is a huge cliff which I later learned is a favorite spot for suicides. I decided to take a picture and to get the best possible view, I was standing on top of a three-rail fence when a car went by with a passenger shouting out the window, "Leap, you bloody North American!" How he could be certain I was an American I don't know.

As we were never city people, we were relieved to leave Sydney; though it's the nicest city we have ever seen, it's still much the same as any congested U.S. counterpart. I received an assignment to Forbes, a country town two hundred miles west of Sydney. We bought a car and drove out in order to see the countryside. With only about twelve million people (1971) in the entire country, rural scenes started appearing early. The trip certainly enabled me to become accustomed to driving in the left lane.

Rural people are even friendlier than the city dwellers. The population of Forbes is 8,000 with the nearest town twenty lonely miles away. In other directions you must travel at least sixty miles. Consequently the local people make their own entertainment, and we became more involved in the community than we ever did in America.

At first we were treated as curiosities, but within a few months that wore off and we became accepted for ourselves. Sport organizations impressed us first. Almost everyone plays sport; they don't just watch. And they don't just play relaxing sports like golf, but also those requiring more physical exertion, such as tennis, squash, soccer, field hockey and basketball. It didn't take long for an American to get involved in basketball. Another aspect to sport is the social

134

gathering at the pub afterwards. It still amazes me how these people can remain as fit as they do and drink as much as they do.

After living in the same town for four years, with excursions around the countryside, supervision of a student teacher, teacher conferences, and a wide variety of friends, the first impressions remain the same. Aussies are very sociable and friendly people.

Some criticisms of them and Australia are inevitable though, and the biggest one is the people's lack of education about their own governmental system. They are not interested enough in their own politics, but are interested in U.S. politics, especially Watergate. Television is more of a wasteland than in the U.S., mainly because they import the worst U.S. shows, and too many of their local popular shows take the form of afternoon soap operas. We have become good customers of the local library.

And lately, in the past two years, too many people seem to have given up on the work ethnic. Australian workers have never been energetic. They've always had shorter working hours and more vacations than their U.S. counterparts and didn't seem to mind the lower pay until recently. Now strikes are rampant throughout the workforce, blue and white collar workers alike. The unions, always a power, have gone berserk.

Still, it's not a bad place to live. My salary is now just over $10,000 per year. Even with inflation that is quite a rise in real income. The only reason for any return to the U.S. would be to see our parents. Here the sky is clear and our children are growing up in an environment much like the one my parents describe when talking about their childhood.

Victoria

Raymond H

My introduction to Australia was through the U.S. Army when I was a 2nd Lieutenant and my outfit was sent to a "station" (ranch or grazing property) outside Townsville, Queensland. I was there for only three weeks and had only one day in Townsville itself, but in that time had a sample of the "bush." One of our guys caught a wallaby, another caught a koala. We had hot, dry days and cool nights, not too different from Fort Bliss, Texas, which we had just left. On the day in Townsville I was taken in tow by a couple of Australian officers who showed me the town and introduced me to steak and

135

eggs, a staple dish in northern Australia cafes even in wartime, while the rest of the world was rationed in these items.

Leaving Townsville I was assigned to an outfit in New
Guinea where after two years I was granted leave to Australia.
Seeing the number of Americans on leave in Sydney, I decided
to visit Melbourne where I met Dulcie. She and her family
were extremely hospitable for the ten days I spent there and
we continued to correspond from then until our marriage later.

After a period of time spent in the Philippines and a return to the States, I once more returned to the Philippines
where I suffered an attack of appendicitis while managing a
plantation run by a man named Robbin. While recuperating, I
decided on a vacation to Australia where I renewed my acquaintance with Dulcie and we were married.

We returned to the plantation for three months; but being
ten miles from the nearest telegraph office, Robbin having sold
the plantation, and the Philippines becoming more unsettled
politically, we decided to return to Australia, this time for
me as an immigrant.

My most vivid memory of the landing at Essendon Airport
was of a hot north wind--and where did those bloody flies come
from? Any civilized fly would move if you brushed your hand
over them but not these flies; no, they merely dig deeper into
the corners of your eyes and mouth.

Like most immigrants, one expects to start at the bottom.
I did, working under a stone crusher on a hillside near Eildon
Weir to supply gravel for the village being built for the
workers at the dam site. Of course, this involved camping.
Dulcie did not like this, so after about six weeks, back to
Melbourne. By this time I had learned that the differences
between Australians and Americans was generally less than the
differences between people in various sections of America itself.

I then applied for a job as builder's laborer on a construction site not far from where we were living with Dulcie's
sister and brother-in-law, Con and Jim. What they really needed
was a foreman, so having nothing to lose I applied and got the
job. At that time most Australian tradesmen could make more
money sub-contracting; so although the project was for War Service Homes, a government entity, and the contractor was an
Australian builder, my clerk was an American and the supervisor
was a Frenchman.

136

Melbourne, like San Francisco, is subject to changes in the weather from hour to hour. But during this eighteen months I seem to remember being out of rubber boots and wind jacket for only about two weeks. We even had a snow storm, a rarity in Melbourne. Back to the tropics for me.

By this time Dulcie and I had bought a house and had a boy, Stratton, about a year old. Con and Jim took them back to live with them, and off I went to Cairns where I met some people from Mareeba, a town in the Atherton Tablelands. I got a job there with a machinery dealer and had Dulcie, her sister, and the boy up twice; but this was not Dulcie's cup of tea either, so back to Melbourne for them but I stayed on.

Tobacco prices fell and sales were not good, so I joined with another American mining tin ore at a place called Tineroo about fifteen miles from Mareeba. We got a few hundredweight of ore but did not cover expenses, so when the water ran out we went upstream about five miles and got jobs at the Tineroo dam site. A few months without Dulcie and Stratton were enough, so back to Melbourne.

This time I got a job as a country representative for a firm selling tractors. This lasted about eighteen months when we decided to take a trip home. Home to me is still the U.S.A., although I may never return. We traveled by ship, bought a car in San Francisco, drove across the States and lived in upstate New York for about nine months, then back to Melbourne.

By this time I was convinced Dulcie would be happy nowhere else, so I took a job at a hardware shop a few blocks from Con and Jim's house where we were again living. When the firm expanded and I was tranferred to a branch about ten miles away, I became tired of commuting, so we built a house in Ringwood, Victoria. In any case we now had another son, Dallas, and a daughter, Annabelle. We have lived here in Ringwood for fifteen years.

The hardware firm went into receivership, and I went into business as a floor and wall tiler at which I have made a living for the last few years. Business is brisk and in spite of inflation and unemployment, I anticipate being able to continue as long as my health holds out. After twenty-four years in Australia I am sure that any self-reliant, energetic person can have a good life here. I am still annoyed at the amount of industrial strife (strikes) the economy can stand. I am also annoyed at the benefits available to the unemployed, particularly young unmarried men. Only a thriving economy can support this.

137

Fortunately, most Australians are energetic, resourceful, intelligent, generous and not given to much pomp and ceremony, although one incident in this regard stands out in my memory. While traveling for the tractor firm, I was in Northern Victoria on the day Queen Elizabeth was to visit Shepparton, a town about a hundred miles from Melbourne. I had spent the night in a town about twenty miles north and decided to return to Melbourne that day. Practically every road leading to Shepparton was jammed with cars going there; and although it was a business day, hardly anyone was in any town for fifty miles around. Surely the Queen could not have been more popular in any of her other dominions. So much for our egalitarian-beer-drinking, football-loving, sports-minded Australian image.

Stratton is now a second-year student at Monash University. Dallas is a painter of some repute although he is only eighteen years of age. And Annabelle is about to complete her final year at high school, if she doesn't get a job at the bank. Although our children are capable academically (Dallas and Annabelle earned Commonwealth Scholarships, and Stratton was dux of the school in his second attempt at matriculation), they stand in no awe of academic qualifications and degrees.

Queensland

Neoma M

There were basically two reasons why I decided to leave the United States. First, I had been teaching. I was getting in a rut and my teaching was suffering, so I decided I needed a change. Second, I wanted to be able to live my life completely free of any complications from relatives and/or friends.

Why I chose to go to Australia requires a somewhat longer explanation. Australians speak English, and I was never good at languages. Another reason is that I had done all kinds of reading about Aussie land. The people always seemed so understanding and homely (not the ugly kind). They seemed to care about people instead of the materialism of the U.S. Also, Australia is a new country as far as development is concerned. Someone with the right ideas could do great things. Anyway, I had always wanted to travel but felt the only way to really get the flavor of the country was to live there a few years. And the last reason is that I wanted to compare the U.S. educational system with the Australian system.

My first impression of the Australians and their country was that Australians are a friendly lot--people opened their doors for me about as wide as they could.

138

It was a <u>safe</u> feeling--I didn't have to feel like I'd be mugged or raped or anything. The air even seemed cleaner and fresher (which it is).

Now, after two and half years here, I have changed just about as much as a person could possibly change. I've met very different types of people (being a Yank has let me do this--a Yank has prestige here), very rich and <u>very</u> poor. But my impressions of the Aussies and their country haven't really changed much. Australians <u>are</u> very friendly, but they like to be liked. One must never--<u>or</u> rarely--say, "At home we did it like this."

To me most Australians seem blunt and to the point--but honest. There is the smooth and sophisticated Aussie, as in any country, the big talker. A second type is the middle kind of Aussie, the hard working family man who saves his money. Then there's the crude but kind-hearted Aussie. He'd give you the shirt off his back. And there is the black Aussie; it's hard for him to adjust from his culture to the white man's culture; therefore most seem to be "no hopers."

Compared to the U.S., Australia seems lacking. For one reason, it doesn't have the numbers of people to draw from. Another thing is that the educational system still teaches facts rather than concepts, but it has improved a lot in the last year and a half. Also, what talent Australia does have moves on to England or the U.S. to make really big money.

Another thing about Australia is that the political scene is not really very good (1975). But I guess all countries are facing political unrest. The unions here are <u>very</u> strong, and the Labor government is tending more and more toward a socialistic policy.

You asked me to include any unique experiences I'd had. Well, the first day in Australia I was walking up the street and I thought, "WOW, these Australians are really with it"-- across the street on a building was a great big red flag that said "Casket," and next to it there was a sign--"Camels Cigarettes." I thought that they really get the point across that cigarettes are dangerous to your health! I later found out that caskets here are called coffins and that here "Caskets" sell magazines, cigarettes and lottery tickets (called "casket" tickets).

The last thing I guess I can add is that if an American is going to immigrate to Australia, he or she should "do as the Romans do" to some extent, and remember each American coming to

Australia is like an ambassador.

<u>Salli P</u>

My husband, Hollis, and I first came to Australia from the State University of New York at Buffalo, where we had been trying to adapt to living in the U.S. again after five years' residence abroad, mostly in Europe. We had returned to the States to settle down; but we must have had a desire to continue seeing the world, because when the company to which Hollis had been consulting earlier asked him to come to Australia for eighteen months, we had no difficulty in agreeing to come.

We had no thoughts of settling here permanently at that time; this decision was made two and a half years later when we found ourselves still in Australia. By that time my husband's work contacts in Australia had become more current than those he had in the U.S. Also, the offer of a permanent job at a university in Brisbane came along at about the time we decided we had had enough wandering. One of the attractions was the challenge of the job and the sort of life we could have in Brisbane also appealed to us. The mild climate, year-round availability of water sports, size of the city and its cultural activities were all pluses. The latter--music and theatre particularly--are much better than non-Queensland Australians think they are.

It seemed to us after a year in Melbourne and one in Canberra, and it has been proved true in Brisbane, that Australia is much more comfortable psychologically to live in than the U.S. The material standards (refrigerators, appliances, gadgetry) are lower here, but I can go to evening meetings in the city, walk through the streets at night alone, and drive, without fear of muggers.

Our arrival in Australia had a peculiarly Australian touch. We had to wait in Bangkok until there was a motel room free in Melbourne because we were competing with Australians who had come to Melbourne for Cup Day. This is an annual horse race which is considered important enough to be a state holiday. Australians seem to be confirmed gamblers. I suspect that a majority of the adult population take a punt (chance) with a casket (lottery) ticket once a week. The leagues (sports) clubs are full of people playing the pokeys (slot machines) and betting is a national sport. Another is after-work beer drinking with one's mates at the local pub. A beer shortage is a national crisis.

140

My first impressions of Melbourne were of a place which
appeared to be a combination of a movie set for an American
Western and New Orleans (there are many houses with iron lace-
work balconies), with a miniature London at its center. The
shops seemed small and understocked compared to the U.S.,
particularly the grocery stores. Later, when we were living
in Canberra, Melbourne seemed in retrospect like a mecca of
sophistication, with its museums, theatres, shopping centers
and good restaurants. Canberra has little in the way of shops,
and it shuts down in the evenings. Presumably the diplomats,
public servants and university population are revelling in
their homes. One wonders where the young people are and what
they do in this picture post-card pretty, sterile showplace.

In Melbourne we had a ready-made circle of acquaintances,
employees of the company Hollis worked with. Many became our
friends. Both there and in Canberra (where we made our own
way) we found people willing to be friendly, and more than
willing to be polite, helpful, kind and generous towards us.
They have organized sight-seeing expeditions, asked us to their
weekend cottages, taken us out in their boats, given us advice
when we asked for it and have been forbearing when we have
blundered counter to the local customs. People in Brisbane
have been even more helpful. One acquaintance of ours ordered
a car at a discount for us, rented us a riverside apartment,
stocked it with lobster, wine and fruit, met us at the airport
and settled us in. A university professor spent weeks shep-
herding my husband through the intricacies of the university
administration, and university wives made sure that I was given
a chance to choose what I'd like to do from the wide range of
women's activities.

Women in Australia are somewhat second-class citizens;
it's hard for a woman to get credit even when she is employed.
She may get less pay for the same work (differentials are published in the job ads), and at parties there is a distinct tendency for men to gather at one end of the room and women at the
other. This is slowly changing as more women go into the work
force and get recognition as professionals.

Despite their friendliness, there is an ambivalence in
Australians' attitudes toward Americans. We are admired for our
wealth, inventiveness and power. We are disliked because we
tend to give unasked-for advice and to use our wealth and power
to take over Australian resources and industry.

While I'm generalizing, I may as well try a few more. It
seems to me that a high proportion of Australians work in order
to play; that is, their jobs are a means to a beach cottage, a

141

boat or a holiday rather than an enjoyable part of their lives. Most Australians are not as compulsive as Americans about their work.

There is a myth of egalitarianism in Australia which is mostly just that. We are told that one Australian is as good as any other (in a slightly belligerent tone). However, there are clear class distinctions and Australians are upwardly mobile, moving from working class to upper middle class in one generation in many cases. They are as proud of this as they are of their equality.

Australians are just beginning to think of their land resources as limited and valuable rather than limitless and hostile. They are beginning to think of trees as desirable rather than as objects to be cleared wholesale from the land. They are considering the problems of developing mineral resources in the best way. Australians carry bumperstickers on their cars which read "Don't Rubbish Australia," and drive down the highway throwing cigarette packs and beer cans out the car windows with abandon. But they are beginning to think in terms of national interest, of the other person.

Brisbane, where we live now, has a sleepier air about it than the colder capitals. The terrain is hilly and the hills are covered with white, red tin-roofed houses set on stilts for coolness. There are always mountains in the background. Trees and bushes bloom everywhere at all seasons; it is very picturesque. Roads are winding and pitted with holes (traffic has become too heavy for the thin surfacing put on roads here). The Brisbane River meanders through the city, and is lined with parks, industries, high-rises and houses. Parks are a bit unkempt and the houses' paint is often sun-peeled. In the city-center, the old, graceful, iron-balconied hotels and columned, red sandstone law courts are disappearing under bulldozer wheels. There is frenetic building going on as the Council modernizes. The result will be a high-rise profile, softened by its mountain and green park surrounds.

Non-Queenslanders think Brisbane is very provincial. I believe this opinion is held by people who haven't been here, or at least not since a long time ago. Certainly, the politics of the State are ultra-conservative, but it is the only Australian State thus far to have free hospitalization. My husband and I can't keep up with the amount of good quality theatre and music which is offered. We couldn't get to everything we'd like to if we went out every evening. Hollis finds his work exciting and rewarding; he's having the best time of his working life. Granted, the shopping isn't as good as in Sydney or

Melbourne and not nearly as varied as in any U.S. metropolitan area. But I can find everything I need.

So we like it here and will probably stay for the next few years until Hollis retires. Insofar as I have a home now, it is here. Yet I still am and feel like an American somewhere in my core, and I will want to return eventually to the U.S. to live.

South Australia

Al S

Ten years ago my wife and I came to Australia and now live in a sparsely populated area ten miles from the center of Adelaide, South Australia. Now thirty-four years of age, I work in an electronics industry in Adelaide and am a volunteer fireman in my community.

We both were originally from Long Island in New York. I had traveled around the States and found that there were few places in which I would like to live. I didn't like the idea of having to shovel snow during the northern winters; Florida had a continual wind blowing and little geographic variety; California was packed like a can of sardines; and everywhere else decent to live had thousands of people running around. Thus we decided to take a look at Australia.

At first, we did not intend to settle permanently; however, as we learned more about the place, we found it more attractive. Three years after our arrival, we took a trip around the world and stopped in the States, but things were just as we remembered them, so away we went. In Australia there is more room to advance in several industries, because there is less competition. In other ways, though, there is less of everything--less facilities, less selection of goods, among other things. Yet there are also less people to knock you over the head, to run into you with a car, among other things.

It's hard to generalize about life in Australia, just as it would be hard to generalize about life in the States. It's simply a different way of life--to us, more pleasing and less pressured. Regarding the Australians, there are generally two types: the first type feels that if the Yanks had not fought in the Coral Sea in World War II, the Japanese would have overrun Australia, and they are thankful for American assistance; the second type feels the Yanks have taken the world for all the money they could get and these Australians want no part of the "bloody" Yanks.

143

Australians hear about all of the bazaar things and occurrences in the U.S.--18 million Americans getting food stamps (that's more Americans than there are Australians!), spectacular killings, lines of cars waiting for gasoline--on their televisions and in their newspapers; and that's why they have a distorted view of the States. There are, however, some news segments from American television which do provide a more accurate picture. But when someone comes to Australia, he realizes the United States isn't the center of the world. There's a different view from the outside looking in.

The biggest drawback about Australia for us is that we aren't near our friends and relatives in the States. Australia has changed in the past ten years, also, becoming more of a rat race with more disadvantages materialistically. There are high federal taxes, too, but one must remember that the population is spread out, yet with airline, rail and other services equivalent to those of the U.S. Moreover, there are some things in Australia which are better than in the States, like life insurance and medical fees. So, there are pros and cons to life here.

Some Americans I know from heavy industrial areas like Akron, Ohio, got tired of all the dust and filth and decided if they were going to move, they'd really move and see what it was like in the sunshine of Australia. Now they long for the material things they had in the States. They're pleased with the schools and other things here, but they want to have their cake and eat it, too. Unfortunately, it takes more hours in Australia than in the U.S. at the same type of job to be able to afford the dishwashers and other amenities they want. What happens is they come out here and try to live just like they did back in the States; they get frustrated when they can't, and want to return. What they should remember is that to be a successful migrant, one must adjust to the new way of life just like one would have to adjust if he moved from one section of the States to another.

At the present, I have no great dissatisfaction with Australia, so I see no reason to go back to the States. On the other hand, my wife would be willing to return tomorrow if the opportunity arose. She likes to have family around and can't see many advantages of living here as opposed to the U.S. I think, though, that Australia, with fewer people and abundant natural resources, has a better future than the U.S.

Bill D

    I decided to immigrate to Australia because life in sub-
urbia proved to be a tremendous bore, and my job as a plumbing
supply salesman seemed a dead end with no future for my personal development. Also, I was in a terrific auto smash,
miraculously surviving with minor injuries. I saw death coming
and all I felt was regret I didn't do differently with my life.
When I regained consciousness in the hospital, finding my injuries superficial, it was like being reborn. So my wife and I
agreed to dispose of all our goods, pack our trunks, take the
kids and go to the farthest corner of Australia as soon as
possible.

    We sailed on the P & O ship, Oriana, arriving in Fremantle,
Western Australia, January 8, 1967. At last we reached our far
corner of the world, and beginning our new life became a reality. Busselton proved just the ideal spot for our new life, so
we bought an old house and set about getting established.

    Three years after our arrival here, I owned a five-unit
apartment house, a rental house, and our family home on the
Vasse River. I must not fail to mention I owed a great deal of
mortgage money to just about every bank in Busselton. At this
time our entire family applied for and was granted Australian
citizenship. I was able to make my high mortgage payments plus
costs for reconditioning only by doing fifty-six hours per week
shift work at the nearby titanium mines, for a period of four
years. Last year I had made so much progress repaying my mortgage, and rents were up by 100 percent, that it was no longer
necessary for me to slave at the mine any longer. I obtained a
permanent position with the Busselton Post Office.

    At this time, seven and one-half years after our arrival
in Australia, I have the easiest, most enjoyable job in my life.
My properties are pretty well paid for, and rents are now sup-
plementing my income from the Post Office. Now I can look back
at my progress over the years in Busselton. The most amazing
change has taken place in myself. After a life of being a
square peg in the round hole, I have finally fit into the proper place here in Western Australia. I came here, bound and
determined to become a great success, at any cost to myself.
Indeed, I am a successful landlord; I manage business affairs
efficiently and have the ability to deal with tenants. No
stretch of the imagination, however, can make me a "Great"
success. It proved needless for me to keep my nose to the
grindstone eternally. All our needs are met by my combined

145

income, property values which continue rising astronomically, and rents which keep rising far faster than inflation.

I just turned forty; my children grow so fast, it's a pleasure being home and in control of things. Possibly one might consider me smug in my attitude, but I have this over-whelming feeling. We have financial security, social accept-ance and a good family life. I think we have it made! There's no sense in me toiling night and day anymore. All my efforts would go to the tax collector anyhow. This secure feeling and good life are really all I wanted out of my second chance at life. We have never regretted our decision to come here, or our taking Australian nationality. We look upon America as "The Old Country," much the same way as you look upon Europe. Some day we may return for a visit, but Australia is our home-land now.

Frank J

I decided to leave the U.S. because I wanted to travel as much as I could, and geographically Australia is in a good location with easy access to the Orient and Europe. With all the favourable reports of Australia, it appeared this would be a good place to settle permanently.

Upon arriving here I was impressed how friendly the Aus-tralians are, especially to the Americans. Very flattering but true. Since coming here in December, 1969, I have travelled Australia extensively. I found the southern part of Australia too cold for comfort in the winter as most homes and hotels are not heated; food and service is poor everywhere except in the larger cities.

Australians are a lazy people by nature, and this reflects on products made in Australia--overpriced, poor workmanship, and if it's mechanical, it probably won't work well. The gov-ernment owns and runs the Railway, Telephone Company, Postal Service, Electric Board--all overstaffed and inefficient. For example, in Wollongong, New South Wales, there is a new half-million dollar postal and telephone building with sixteen pub-lic telephones and at no time will more than eight of the tele-phones be serviceable.

My biggest disappointment here is the high price of land and houses--building blocks are selling for $A6,000 ($US8,500 in early 1975) and up. There is an acute housing shortage. I would like to buy a block of land and live in a house trailer, but it is not permitted in Australia, even in a remote area. It is permitted only if the trailer is placed in a licensed

146

trailer park.

Competition in business is not encouraged and most large businesses are monopolies. The liquor business is a good example--more than half of the liquor licenses are owned by the breweries.

I am inclined to liken Australia to the State of Arkansas in the U.S.--very similar--hillbilly living, especially in Queensland. I lived in Prosperine, Queensland--small farm town of 5,000 population--for three months and I'd go to the hardware store to purchase an extension cord for my toaster. They direct me to the electric shop. The butcher has no bacon--he sends me to the delicatessen. The delicatessen shop has no milk--I'm sent to the fruit store. Flashlight bulb?--I get this at the clothing store. The hardware store has a spirits license and I can purchase beer by the carton for $6.40 while the pub or bottle shop charges $9.

Australians are very sensitive to criticism and as an immigrant I'm very careful how I speak. After being here five years, I still prefer to stay here rather than the U.S. Queensland will be the only state for me, as the weather is more desirable and I find the casual living quite agreeable.

Australia is still living with the antiquated English laws and it will be a long time before any significant changes are made here. Until the migrants have a voice in the government, things will remain the same. At present, inflation and unemployment have effected the large cities. My employment in the sparsely settled northwest iron country is very good, as accommodations and food are furnished and we work seven days a week. I am making $10,000 a year gross, and can save $6,000 after taxes, which is almost $8,500 American. How much would I have to gross in the U.S. to save the same? I'd say over $20,000.

I have no regrets coming over here and all I need now is to buy a small property in Northern Queensland, and put the welcome mat out for all my friends.

L. G. M

Let me state first that I am not of that category of Americans who for various political, social, ecological or whatever reasons "ran away" from America because it was an unsatisfactory place in which to live, work and raise a family. On the contrary, I was of the opinion that all things considered, America was probably one of the best places to live. Being of a curious disposition and of a somewhat adventurous frame of mind, I

147

tend to like to live and travel overseas--around the world. This probably more than anything else prompted me and my family to make the final decision to move to Australia.

Our decision to migrate to Australia (yes, we came under the Passage Assistance Program whereby the government of Australia paid our air fares for the whole family and also paid for our household goods to be shipped) was not based on a solitary fact or reason. First of all, I was ready for a move; that is, I was just finishing my doctoral studies and had over twenty formal and complete applications out for a teaching position in a college or university setting. The family was psychologically ready as well as physically ready in the sense of having things packed up and the house being put up for sale, etc. A particular position came through and it seemed like a golden opportunity.

Another factor that influenced the decision was the fact that I was interested in Australia. For a good share of my life, I had been interested in Australia. This was one of many places that I was interested in, of course. I had heard and read of accounts of Americans who had been in Australia in World War II. Their stories and experiences all pointed to a very fine attitude on the part of the Aussies and a very friendly stance toward Americans. So in the normal channels of life and the ways that people are influenced--news of Australians, sports figures in tennis, swimming, etc.--I became interested in travelling to Australia. However, I had never felt that I would be able to "go it alone"--that is, pay my own way and take my chances when I got here. I had always looked for a "contact" before travelling to a foreign place. This lack didn't allow me to come, so I passed it up for other places that I also had an interest in but could do something about because of some relationship that enabled me to travel and be employed. I have travelled to Taiwan (eighteen months there), Guam (four years there), and places in the Mediterranean and Panama areas in the military service. Also, the family and I have circumnavigated the globe--hopping from country to country for a few days in each main city. I put this latter group of facts in to show that we have been a travelling family--looking for interesting places to go and live for a while. Also, we have travelled all over the United States.

While teaching school in Taiwan, I applied to come to Australia in 1963 but, due to having a Chinese wife, was never able to finalize that application. I had it on good authority from an Australian who came to Taiwan on a United Nations contract that I would not be able to live in Australia with a Chinese wife. However, he said, the winds of change were in the

148

offing: political biases of the older politicians were being
gradually overturned and the "white only" policy was going to
be scrapped when the new government got in. My wife is now an
American citizen and this no doubt had an effect on my being
approved this last time (1974).

We have been here in Australia for seventeen months. We
are ready to leave. We came with the idea of finally settling
down. I thought that this country was going to "develop"--
gas, oil, iron, aluminum, etc.--it seems to be well-blessed
with natural resources. However, we find that they are afraid
of developing, are jealous of what they have--don't want migrants to come and spoil it all! The present (1975) Labor
Government has practically abolished the Department of Immigration (combined it with the Department of Labor) and almost eli-
minated immigration as a means of developing and "growing."
While they should be encouraging immigration of all races,
creeds and nationalities to enrich the country and to bring
necessary skills and work potential for development, they have
actually gone full circle and are now back to the "white only"
policy and keep what is here for the Australian people and
don't share it with anyone.

Aside from the above idea, we don't like: socialization
of production and transport; very high taxes (almost double
what we would pay in the U.S.); high cost of living (all things
cost more here than they would in the U.S.; meats would be an
exception to this); backward ideas and not very modern, or up-
to-date, living standard (no heating or cooling built into the
house except for the very latest ones--and not even them in
many cases; many places still have the toilet outside the house
or attached to the back of the building)--they are about forty
to fifty years behind the U.S. Too much government control--
the government is too much in the forefront of your everyday
life. Also, there is no Bill of Rights here. I get a little
scared about that once in a while. Gangsters and crooks have
guns here but not the normal populace. I like to fire a pistol
and keep my hand in shooting--here it is made so difficult that
only the most ardent shooters even bother. Even "bb's" for a
bb-gun have to be purchased from special stores and registered
and signed for each time of purchase.

We have a lot of reasons for not liking the place. It is
much too backward in its way of life and its thinking. It is
also very racially biased, as my wife has found out on various
occasions. The people are not friendly; there are exceptions,
of course. As an example on the personal plane: only two lec-
turers here at this teacher's college where I work have seen
fit to invite my family to their home--only two out of a total

149

of eighty or ninety!

Other leanings such as a "Royalist" influence here are
not to my liking. Even the ministers of each state when they
are elected here in Australia must pledge allegiance to the
Queen of England before they can assume office. This sort of
thing galls me! They still haven't sorted out what their
national anthem is, either.* Utility bills are posted to you
every six months so this means that you have a bill for a hundred or so dollars popping up twice a year, instead of monthly
increments. Education--my field--they treat as something
mostly fit for the top 10 percent, and the rest of the population can get by with substandard schools--the old British system. Academically, my particular field is not being attended
to--reading as a major subject for college and university-level
instruction. Reading is treated as a stepchild of the elemen-
tary system. There are signs that this is changing, but the
progress is slow. It's an uphill fight to get remedial reading
trained teachers in the schools and the necessary classroom and
supplies for her to use. Another decade (it may take longer)
will see the progress made in this field of reading. I just
don't want to wait. Another main criticism we have of this
place is the "par dinkum saying," "She's right, mate," meaning
"don't worry about it; it'll get done"--like the Mexican saying
of "Manana." Australians are famous in their own land for "not
getting the job done."

Well, there you have it--much criticism. America is still
the best place in the world to live--all things considered.
Take all the racial strife, crime, pollution, etc.,--problems
that America has--and compare these with the problems of any
land. I think that you will find that most people in the world
would prefer to live in America as being the place where the
most have the best. For every problem that we have in America,
you can find the same one here plus a few more and to a greater
degree.

A final note of positiveness: Australia could be a good
place to live when comparing it to most European, African and
Asian countries, etc.; but when compared to America, it falls
far short. This is one of the big problems in Australia: its
music, its literature, its movies, its products, its "everything" is either "from" America or is "inspired by" American

----

*Author's note: "Waltzing Matilda" became Australia's
official national anthem on May 4, 1976.

know-how, techniques or money. The Aussies have developed a
feeling of insecurity of being overwhelmed by things American.
It is a problem for them, I am sure, and I can sympathize with
them. However, I can not forgive them for taking advantage of
the things that the world has to offer and not worrying about
the imaginary or real consequences of the product or the tech-
nique. This didn't seem to worry the Japanese in their endeavor to industrialize and compete on the world plane. Perhaps
the difference lies in the basic insecurity of the Australian.
The Japanese have a strong-enough culture to survive with their
own distinctly molded society. If the Australians don't have a
strong tradition, then perhaps they shouldn't worry about losing one and get into the race--they might end up with one.

Tasmania

Dashley and Nancy G

Our reasons for leaving North America are complex and varied. You might say we took stock of our stiuation in Alaska
and after considering all the relevant data we felt ripe for a
change. After five years we found ourselves in an ideal position to consider making our home elsewhere. Naturally, the
cold weather tempted us to leave but that was only one of many
factors influencing us. For instance, we had a modest house
paid for, and I, Dashley, had just finished acquiring a degree
in Education (BEd) after three years full time at the University
of Alaska. I would be needing a teaching position and would
probably have to move elsewhere to find one. We considered the
fact that we had two small children who were not caught up in a
school system yet, so they would not be affected by the move.
We miscalculated on the education bit since Australian children
begin school as much as one year earlier than North American
kids do. Another point we realized was that neither Nancy nor I
had any close ties with our relatives on either side of the family. We were one of those nuclear families with no strong bonds
with the rest of the clan. This was a major factor I think in
our case.

Now we have reviewed the nitty gritty, down-to-earth factors, so let's peek at the romantic side of the picture as we
painted it. It is probably corny to word it this way but in my
mind was a strong desire to tackle yet another of the so-called
"New Frontiers" left in the world. Australia has beckoned to me
since I was a boy growing up in Seattle. You either went north
to Alaska or across the wide Pacific. This is sort of an un-
written legacy in my way of thinking, and having had a go at
Alaska I was eager to try another country. I had done one, so
why not the other. Nancy was desirous of a sunny place to

151

settle, and all the travel brochures and Australian pamphlets filled our imaginations with warm illusions, what with our sixth Alaskan winter looming ahead. We both sought a good environment and a certain quality lifestyle to make a home and raise a family. Our research suggested Australia, particularly Tasmania, as one place that fit our blueprint for happiness. After much soul-searching and months of mulling it all over, we decided that the continent "Down Under" with its cultural similarity and apparent political and economic stability was the place for us.

Up to this point, I have presented the bulk of our reasoning and motives for immigrating as we did in 1972. If you boil it all down, what you get, I suspect, is a young couple free of debt, unencumbered by relations, deciding to move to Australia in search of opportunity, a better climate, and in my case a bit of adventure in the best spirit of the American pioneering tradition à la Daniel Boone and company. There is a bit of residue in my own memory bank that forces me to confess that I was unhappy with the fact Richard Nixon was grabbing at the Presidency and Alaska seemed destined for grim times with the impending oil boom about to strike our town of Fairbanks. We had flourished in the "Great Land" and we would never be content to move back into the urban mainstream of the U.S. of A. or of any other nation for that matter. We were sold on rural life. It seems we were destined for the other end of the earth. (We had at one time considered moving to New Zealand.)

Our initial impressions of Sydney when we docked there in November, 1972 were at first one of relief for having arrived at last. Nancy, however, became greatly disappointed soon to find things weren't lots cheaper, which she had been led to believe to some degree and had given up things she later regretted leaving. A day or two after our arrival, an overwhelming urge to flee for less hectic nonurban areas overcame us. Sydney's weather was right, but the pace and environment weren't up to par. We were pleased to reach Tasmania where we found the pace more to our liking as were the people and the scenery. It felt right to settle in Hobart then. Language was no big problem. It was and is sort of a challenge with amusing consequences. (We have noticed now, after two years here, our five-year-old, Heather, has developed a bit of an Australian accent. All of us have picked up the delightful jargon, but no others have developed accents.) We were a bit put off by the struggle to find a house to rent and the lack of job opportunities in education in southern Tasmania. But luck was with us and a private school hired me to teach third grade; and a suburban home with a lovely view of the Derwent River cropped up in the same neighborhood.

By Easter time I was stacking lumber in a Moonah furniture factory yard singing "the novice teacher blues" after losing a battle of wits with my head mistress. This board stacking paid minimum wage scale but kept me off the dole. Being an immigrant, my pride was at stake in wanting to be self-sufficient. I met many "fair dinkum" Aussies who drifted in and out of employment at the yard. It seems to have been a holding area for blokes coming and going from the Commonwealth Employment Office in Glenorchy. I enjoyed working outdoors in the shade of Mount Wellington and many earnest friendships evolved there.

Just as the job gave out, the Education Department hired me on to teach English and Social Science at Rose Bay High School, overlooking the Tasman Bridge on the eastern shore suburbs of Hobart. By the end of the year, we were fed up with the suburban scene, and the commuting life didn't agree with me. Since we could find no land in our price range, we did the practical thing and applied for a transfer to a rural school in the northern part of Tasmania. We drew Scottsdale as our assignment. We hustled up to the Northeast in our Kombi bus and checked it out. We were able to pick a house to rent and generally found the place to our liking. We stayed the year and decided to make it our home. Our third child, Holly Amber (who can have dual citizenship), our second girl, was born in December at the North Eastern Memorial Hospital in Scottsdale and about the same time we invested in ten acres of good farmland three miles outside of town. We paid $400 an acre, which is good for here!

The teaching scene still gave little satisfaction but we had found our community at last. We settled in fast, got involved in a few clubs, and I played on a local basketball team. Fortunately, our son was able to obtain his correct grade level by progressing well enough to skip a primary grade. He mastered third-grade work and gained acceptance in his new school.

At the time of this writing, we have begun building our own home after having our do-it-yourself plans approved by the local Council. Our modified log house promises to be a unique dwelling in this area, but we are confident we can construct a ten-square home to suit our needs and save on costs by utilizing our own sweat and energy in the process. Self-sufficiency is a popular word around our house and seems like the best way to prepare for the future. As immigrants, we will consider our trek to Australia a wise one if we can achieve this goal in this fine Tasmanian environment with its evergreen splendor that reminds us both so much of our old home in our native land. That's all I have to say, I guess, but Nancy will give below our impressions of the Aussies and Australia and her advice to potential migrants from the U.S.

153

We haven't changed our minds about either Australia or the
Aussies since we arrived. We respect and like, genuinely, the
easy-going, yes, even complacent, attitude of the Aussies.
They're so delightfully noncompetitive! And something I have
noticed about Australians is their strange mixture of wanting
to emulate the American way of life, and resentment for its influence!

Regarding advice to potential American migrants to Austra-
lia, I have learned a very important lesson about immigrating.
As much as I like Australia, I have discovered there is no
Utopia! In other words, I'd advise anyone thinking of coming
"Down Under" to be realistic about their expectations.

Australian Capital Territory

Robert D

The reasons why I decided to leave the United States and to
go to Australia are linked and will require some explanation.
In 1967, while at Texas Tech University, I began to ponder what
I would do and where I would go when I graduated as a civil engineer. One night at a movie, I saw a short promotional film on
Australia that really opened my eyes. I found out Australia was
a "Western" country, and I decided to look further into it. By
1968, I decided to immigrate upon graduation. Besides seeing
the film, I'd always had a sense of adventure, and figured if I
were going anywhere I'd better do it then before it was too
late (meaning married, with two kids, a mortgage and a car to
pay off). So I subscribed to the Sydney Morning-Herald for two
years till I graduated to get a good idea about life in Australia
and I also kept a card file on potential employers.

There were some secondary reasons for leaving the U.S. and
going to Australia, too. After six years at a university in a
small town (by American standards), I was sick and fed up with
small minds by that stage. By "small" I mean they were insular
and parochial people who barely knew where England was, much less
Australia, and who thought the U.S. came first in everything. On
the other hand, I found that Australians, because they inhabit a
sparsely populated land, thought in a bit bigger terms and realized there were other countries that led the world in certain
things.

In Australia, the long-term job outlook was good, and I obtained employment with the federal government in Canberra. At
present I hold an engineering, Class III position with the
National Capital Development Commission. I'm connected with the

154

Environmental Branch of the Engineering Division and have a lot
to do with noise pollution, the review and writing of environmental impact statements.

One of my hobbies is cave-exploring (spelunking), and this
had something to do with my decision to locate in Canberra (I
don't like large cities, anyway), as it's near a number of good
caving areas. I've become very active in a local caving club,
and almost every weekend I try to get away to some of the nearby caving areas. I also have become involved in some scientific
studies regarding spelunking. And once I was interviewed by the
Australian Broadcasting Commission about my spelunking activities in the U.S. and in Australia. Another hobby of mine is
traveling, and I had a real educational experience when I took a
trip around Australia. I had gotten to know already the cosmopolitan Aussie by visiting most of the state capitals; but during the trip around Australia, I got to see the countryside and
know rural Australia. I chatted with opal miners at Lightning
Ridge, New South Wales, and at Coober Pedy, South Australia;
with a professional rodeo rider in Darwin, Northern Territory;
with multimillionaire pearl farmers; and with colorful charact-
ers in the Barossa Valley, South Australia.

My opinion of the Aussies, at first, was they they were
friendly and outgoing, and that they love to go to parties. At
the drop of a hat they'd be going to a picnic or barbecue. People where I work would organize social events and invite me
along, and that was a surprise to me. I wasn't used to people
from work fraternizing so much. Where I had been in Texas, one
might have one or two close work mates, but that'd be about it.
In Australia, though, at an apartment or house party, one might
see five or six business associates, and I'm very enthusiastic
about this aspect of life in Australia. Incidentally, most
Aussies are metropolitan as well as cosmopolitan, because something like 80 percent of the people live in the capital cities.

My opinion of the Aussies is now basically the same; however, I have noticed two points which are unfavorable. In
decision-making circles, the Aussies seem to start out with good
intentions but follow up with poor execution, and once a decision has been implemented, there's a reluctance to change regardless of the consequences. I've found also that the Aussies are
fairly greedy, and I think this stems from their hedonistic outlook. They have not been so influenced by a Judeo-Christian
work ethic. Their basic attitude is "What's in it for me, mate?"

I am getting married soon and will return shortly thereafter to the U.S. for a visit. When I do, I'll be very interested to see how the U.S. has changed; however, I have a good job

and a good life (especially regarding outdoor activities) in
Australia now, and see no reason why I should return to the
U.S. to live. If I couldn't visit my family in the U.S., and
they couldn't visit me, or if I couldn't travel at all, then
that might make me consider returning to the U.S. But for the
moment, "She's (Australia) just right," and I've got nothing to
complain about here. With the exception of a few things which
might be better in the U.S. (consumer goods, for example, are
far cheaper in the U.S.), I can't see anything of real importance that would be better for me there than here in Australia.

Northern Territory

David C

When people asked me why I came to Australia, I used to
carefully explain that one of the terms of my retirement from
the Marines was free transportation to anyplace in the world I
chose to settle. So (I would say) I called MATS (Marine Air
Transport Service)--as MAC (Marine Air Command) then was--and
found that the longest free ride I could get was on a flight to
Melbourne.

I mention this story not for whatever truth there may be
in it, but as an indication that I may have been less than certain of my own reasons. When I left the service on disability
retirement on 1 April, 1963, I was unmarried and had no close
attachments. I had (and still have) my mother and a married
sister living in Michigan, but eleven years of wandering about
the rest of the world had convinced me that I was much better
suited to warmer places than that. In particular, returning to
the tropical Pacific appealed to me, both because I was attrac-
ted by the people of the region and the physical beauty of the
sea and islands, and because I was professionally interested in
the area's weather and climate. The idea of working in the Cook
Islands occurred to me and with this in mind, I began to make
inquiries.

The notion turned out to be a bust: there are no forecas-
ters stationed in the Cooks and the New Zealand government,
which administers them, is not one of the world's more attractive employers. But while I was investigating this, I chanced
to contact the Australian Bureau of Meteorology, who expressed
themselves most eager to have me join them. So I left San
Francisco for Melbourne.

With the Australian Met Service I worked in Queensland
(where I met my wife) and in Papua-New Guinea before going to
Darwin in 1966. I left the Met Service in 1969 and took up

156

full-time journalism.

During my nine years in the Northern Territory, I didn't get out of Darwin often enough to matter: twice I made the trip to Alice Springs for the Easter sports carnival and on several occasions I got into the Alligator River country east of Darwin in connection with motorcycle bush events. But for the most part, although I was living in one of the world's least populous regions, I was leading an essentially urban existence. The population of the entire vast territory was about 75,000 people and well over half of these lived in Darwin.

Darwin itself is--or was before cyclone Tracy--a remarkably cosmopolitan place. Aside from being an international port, it has a large Chinese community, whose roots go back to the early days of the settlement a century ago (Harry Chan, Mayor of Darwin until his death in 1970, was the first nonwhite Mayor of any city in Australia), and large populations of German, Greek and Italian migrants.

It is of interest that for all this assorted mob, Darwin has always enjoyed excellent race relations, while in the Alice Springs district--where a basically Anglo-Saxon community confronts aboriginals who are still tribal--race relations are about as bad as anywhere in the world.

But the point of all this is that while Darwin is certainly a uniquely Australian phenomenon, it is equally certainly a far cry from a typical Australian city. All the groups mix socially and--with the notable exception of the Greek community--even intermarry; whereas in Melbourne, for example, there are entire suburbs that are "ethnic," where the local merchants converse with their customers in the language of "the old country" and so on.

Darwin is also the center for a good deal of mineral and oil exploration--the latter mostly off-shore--which involve crews with a good many Americans in them.

Regarding my impression of the Australians, Americans and Australians seem almost interchangeable at first blush. It is only later that at awareness of real differences occurs. For example, there are two myths the Australian entertains about himself: "mateship" and resourcefulness. Both of these qualities are true, as far as they go, but both of them are also imposed on the Australian rather than being innate. The ability of a "bush mechanic" to keep a vehicle going in the Outback is a matter of survival, not playful inventiveness. And it would rarely be necessary except for the very real Australian tradi-

157

tion of "She'll be right, mate," the notion that if something works, no matter how approximately, it will be good enough to get by. A particularly characteristic Australian trait would seem to be avoidance of the supererogatory--come to think of it, I've never heard an Australian even use the word. The willingness of Americans (and others) to go out of their way to help total strangers absolutely astounds the average Australian; it is something he simply never would have thought of.

Another characteristic of the Australian is that when he is confronted with something unpleasant, he is apt to instantly consider an appeal to government on some level--federal, state or local--where an American would probably think of governmental aid as a last resort. Probably for this reason, Australians regard politics--their own and other peoples'--with a seriousness that strikes an American as slightly mad. But it is probably not they who are strange, but we.

My experience in Australia and other parts of the world is that people tend to look at their government as some sort of benevolent father figure, be it ever so weak, ineffective and inefficient. It may be doomed to disappoint them every time, but it is still there to be appealed to.

Only Americans see government as a necessary evil, intrusive and expensive (although considered from the point of view of the ability of its people to pay for it, the American federal government is probably the cheapest in the world), and I think I know why. The United States is probably the only sizeable society in the history of the world whose inhabitants shared the belief that a man could make what he liked out of his life. Whether the belief is justified or not is beside the point. The significant thing is that over a considerable part of U.S. history a majority of Americans did believe that they, as individuals, controlled their own destiny. The roots of this idea are complex but certainly involved the Puritan ethic notion of the virtuousness of hard work turned loose on the frontier where opportunity seemed almost limitless.

The upshot of all this is that an American is brought up to think of himself primarily as an individual, whereas a person anyplace else in the world is--unless he is born among the rich or those otherwise set apart--constrained almost from the cradle to think of himself as part of a group with common interests.

The difference may be subtle, but it is real and has led to a good deal of misunderstanding. It is the reason, for example, that Americans cannot understand class antagonisms as they exist in Europe; and it is why every time an American politician is

158

shot, Europeans can only see a conspiracy: political assassinations in Europe are committed by factions, not individuals.

All of this is a very long-winded way of saying that Australians, although superficially resembling Americans more than they do anyone else, continue to think like Europeans. Although they tolerate a turn of independence by Americans and others who don't know any better, an Australian who behaves similarly is immediately rewarded with the appellation "ratbag."

As for any unique experiences since I have been here, I don't suppose a major tropical cyclone like the one that hit Darwin constitutes a unique experience. In my own case, I have been through one in Florida, two in New Jersey, two in Japan, one in Okinawa and (most frightening of all) one at sea.

At two o'clock on Christmas morning (1974), when our house in Darwin started to break up, my wife and I grabbed a bottle of Vat 69, a tape deck, and a handful of Frank Sinatra cassettes and got in the car--I may as well put in a plug for it too: it's a Subaru and, although bombarded all night by flying roofing metal, it didn't let any water in. In the morning we drove around and looked at the devastation, which was just about total. The anemometer at the airport--a Dynes pressure tube--recorded a gust of 120 knots, and this wind speed was widely circulated. Later investigation, however, showed that the high gust recording was caused by the instrument being struck by some flying object and was, in fact, spurious. Extrapolation and so on gave a maximum wind of 95 to 100 knots. If this is so, Tracy was not even the strongest storm I have been through. But it was far and away the most destructive. So how come?

First, it was the gimcrack construction of most of the houses in Darwin. A friend, a retired Italian brickmaker named Ugo Priore, had built his own house with his own bricks, his own mortar, and so forth; the morning after the storm it sat without a tile out of place while everything around it was rubble. Then there was the almost total lack of meaningful preparation; on Okinawa, for example, a storm warning precipitates a big clean-up, in which even the coconuts are removed from the trees. Darwin, on the other hand, was chock full of potentially lethal missiles simply waiting to be blown around. And one loose object can, of course, put a hold in a house wall, liberating other loose objects, and so on.

The future of Darwin does not, at the moment (September, 1975), look particularly bright. Almost no rebuilding has been done, due to a combination of spiralling costs and bureaucratic foot-dragging; and while it is possible to live in Darwin in a

159

tent during the dry season, the northwest monsoon with its
rains will start in a few weeks.

For your interest though, there was one unique experience
which happened when I had been in Australia less than a year,
when I was living in Townsville and shortly after I had first
met my wife. She and I and some friends were sitting in a restaurant when we were joined by a happy individual who introduced
himself as the first mate of a Danish ship that was tied up in
the harbor. After some conversation he suggested that we come
aboard the ship "for a few drinks." The captain, he explained,
was ashore, but he could introduce us to the wonders of Danish
beer and aquavit.

So we all--about ten of us--followed him onto the ship and
into the wardroom. The only people there were a couple of cadet
officers who spoke only Danish. They remained for the party
that followed, although looking somewhat sheepish if not down-
right guilty. Our friend summoned a troop of Chinese mess stew-
ards (whom he talked to in pidgin) and we were soon neck-deep in
aquavit (which can be a very sneaky potation if you don't know
its potential). We all got roaringly drunk and ended up break-
ing crockery all over the place, in general leaving a real mess
before we staggered home to sleep it off.

It was only after the ship had sailed that we discovered
that the "first mate" was in fact a meat worker who had no connection with the ship whatsoever and had never been aboard it
before he led our merry group on our free-loading excursion.
Not one of us ever suspected a thing. It was the most masterful
con job I have ever seen and entirely worthy of the worldwide
reputation that certain Australians have enjoyed in this interesting field. I was too filled with admiration to be indignant,
but I have often wondered if the ship's real captain could say
the same thing. And I guess that's about all I have to say.

6

COMINGS, GOINGS
—AND THE FUTURE

Australia has one of the best records of any nation at keeping its migrants, between 84 and 91 percent.[1] Nevertheless, over the years anywhere from approximately 20 percent to more recently over 60 percent of those Americans who have immigrated "Down Under" have later chosen to depart, the prevailing assumption being that nearly all of them have chosen to resettle in their homeland, the United States (Table 14).[2] Why has there been such a discrepancy as 20 percent to the more recent 60 percent? The primary reason for the great increase in the departure rate has probably been the succession of the Labor Government with its liberal policies from 1972 to 1975 after the more conservative policies of the Liberal-Country coalition which were in operation from 1949 to 1972. Many of the migrants to Australia from the United States have been "conservatives" who have moved for reasons such as "for better business and investment opportunities"; therefore when the Labor Party began to initiate "liberal" reforms and when industrial strikes began to increase, a large number of these migrants lost their incentive for remaining in Australia.

Of course, there have been other motives for departure from Australia and resettlement in America, even though most migrants claim to be satisfied with life "Down Under." The motives include generalized reasons such as many Americans simply are highly mobile, as well as the more obvious reasons such as many

so-called "permanent" migrants never really intended to remain
in Australia "permanently" anyway. Businessmen sent to Australia to work for an American subsidiary for three to five years,
teachers who only intended to fulfill their two-year contracts
for tax-free salaries, and "working tourists" who never had any
intention of staying are all people who drive up the statistics
of returnees.[3]

Many Americans really do not give Australia a chance.[4]
They migrate with the intention of "seeing if things work out,"
and at the first sign of disappointment begin to consider returning "home." Actually, because of the large number of Americans who immigrate greatly uninformed about their new land, "the
miracle is not the number who return to America, . . . it's the
number who stay," in the words of a Department of Immigration
spokesman.[5] Often migrants crossed the Pacific expecting to
find a small, only slightly modified replica of the United
States, not realizing that Australia is a different land with
its own unique characteristics; and many have been unable to adjust to those differences. As one American remarked, "They were
unable, in the language of our astronauts, to attain separation
speed from their native culture."[6] The difficulty lies in the
fact that latter twentieth century American culture is one which
has bathed its citizens in comfort to such a degree that it has
spoiled its society to a considerable extent. Both an Australian and an American author, in their respective books, have
captured this characteristic and its implications for the potential failure of Americans as immigrants. In The U-Jack Society,
Ian Moffitt asserted,

> Some Americans, insulated in an air-conditioned, oil-
> heated society, lack the patience of their pioneering
> ancestors; not for them Walt Whitman's "diet hard, and
> the blanket on the ground"--they prefer quick pioneer-
> ing in comfort.[7]

And according to American television star and author Art Linkletter in his work, Linkletter Down Under,

> Americans fail in Australia, perhaps because Americans
> have been spoiled by a style of life never experienced
> by any other people in the history of the world. We've
> been conditioned to get too much too soon too often,
> and to pay for it later. We've lost the ability to
> entertain ourselves, read quietly, converse seriously,
> and stay put.[8]

Some migrants who return to the United States were unable
to find a satisfying job in Australia. Few craftsmen or trades-

men, for example, remain for very long; and executives may have difficulties as well. Robert Palioca, an executive from Falmouth, Massachusetts, attests that he was led by the Australian Government to believe that within a matter of days he could find a job paying the equivalent of $US19,000 per year, but found that he could not even obtain employment paying $A6,000 annually; thus, after losing $16,000, he and his family returned to America.[9]

For some, the United States is simply either a better place in which to live, or it is "home" even with all its flaws. After weighing the pros and cons of their situation in Australia, many judge America to be so much better as to warrant their return to the States.[10] As one of those surveyed, who felt the United States was both a better place and home, answered when asked whether he would return to the States, "I'm on my way. No matter what happens in America, it's still the strongest and the best, and it's part of me." A few who also felt the United States was better and that they might return made the very interesting comment that, in effect, only by leaving the States and living in a foreign land such as Australia had they come to really appreciate what America had to offer.

Various other reasons naturally have been offered by American migrants to Australia as to why they did, would or might resettle in the United States. A number of migrants find that Australia is too similar to America to be worth the change; while some feel that unlike life in the States, life "Down Under" is just too boring.[11] Others leave or want to depart when they do not make the quick fortune they planned on making, when their American wives begin to complain they are not happy in Australia, or when their Australian wives express a strong desire to live in the United States--at least for awhile.[12] For a few it is a case of "returning now or never," while for others it is a case of returning later to retire.[13] Then, as is regrettably always the case, there are those returnees or probable returnees who are permanent discontents and who would in all likelihood not be happy in Australia, the United States or anywhere else in the world.[14]

Unfortunately, what many who return or want to return apparently do not realize is that while they have been in Australia, the United States has changed and for the worse. Regarding increased crime, migrant Gerald Stone remarked,

> My last trip to the U.S. showed me for sure that we lead a good life here (Australia). In Columbus, Ohio (his home), old friends were afraid to let their kids go downtown to a movie. They no longer seemed to

163

know the answers to their problems. In Columbus
there's crime and fear of crime. Who needs that?[15]

Concerning greater congestion and the changing American lifestyle, another migrant commented,

> Five years after I moved to Australia, I got home-
> sick and started to return home. But I got as far
> as Hawaii and saw the freeways with their mad traf-
> fic, the big hotels, and the half-blistered, under-
> dressed tourists, and I said, "That's not for me."
> I came back (to Australia) and took out citizenship
> papers here.[16]

And in reference to the general state of American society, migrant and journalist James McCausland relates how when he returned to New York, "for the first time in his life he experienced
what must be considered culture shock." He exclaimed,

> The place was so big and ugly. What had seemed like
> vitality five years ago was exposed as tension, and
> what had looked like atmosphere was filth, and every-
> one I knew was still worried about things over which
> they had absolutely no control.[17]

All of the observances that these migrants have made have probably gone largely unnoticed by the majority of Americans living
in the United States, for the changes in American society have
been gradual for the most part. Nevertheless, these changes are
real, and they are ones which those who have immigrated to Australia should take into account when considering resettlement in
the States.

A final note might be made here about those migrants who return to America. Although it may never be proven, it is the
opinion of this writer that many of those Americans who migrate
to Australia are the least able to adapt to new conditions of
all emigrants from the United States; therefore it should not be
surprising that so many migrants to Australia return. To support this theory, if a poll could be taken of those Americans
who immigrated to Australia and then returned, and they were asked if they could have fared better as immigrants in Germany or
Brazil, for example, countries more different from America than
is Australia, it is the opinion of this writer that the majority
would answer, "No." Moreover, the percentage of those who said,
"Yes," would be far less than the percentage of those Americans
returning from Germany or Brazil who felt they could have done
better in Australia. Therefore, the relatively high percentage
of returnees from Australia should not necessarily reflect badly

on that nation alone, but should also say something about the
returnees themselves. Furthermore, before casting judgment
upon Australia and its ability to retain American migrants, one
might reflect upon the interesting and curious fact that "half
the number of Statesiders who emigrate to Hawaii come back
again."[18]

In the survey conducted by this writer, 53 percent of the
migrants indicated they either will or probably will resettle
in the United States, while 3 percent had already returned.
Predominantly more of those who specified the following motives
for emigrating from the United States and immigrating to Australia, rather than other motives listed, indicated they either
will or probably will resettle in America, or that they already
had resettled.

Motives	Percentage Who Will or Probably Will Resettle, or Who Already Resettled in the U.S.
for adventure	59.1
personal or family problems	58.1
unemployment	55.1
for better business and investment opportunities	53.8
lack of new frontiers	50.5
rise in crime rate	42.8
becoming too crowded	42.3
too much pollution	41.2
unstable, fast-changing society	37.0
pace of life too fast	36.6

In addition, predominantly more of those with the following
characteristics, than with other characteristics, indicated they
either will or probably will resettle in the United States, or
that they already had resettled.

Predominant Characteristics	Percentage Who Will or Probably Will Resettle, or Who Already Resettled in the U.S.
sex - females	58.2
occupation in the U.S. - other nonmanual workers, or	71.4

professional, technical or related workers	66.6
income in the U.S. - $8,001 to $12,000	75.0
section from which departed - South, or	60.7
Northeast	60.0
had not visited Australia before migrating	62.3
had a job set up before migrating	67.7
year of migration - 1974 (latest year of the survey)	83.3
Australian government did not financially assist passage	60.9
final place of settlement - New South Wales	64.2
occupation in Australia - other nonmanual workers, or	80.0
professional, technical or related workers	65.1
income in Australia - $12,001 to $16,000	92.3

The majority of American settlers in Australia have chosen to remain there and not return to the United States for several reasons (Tables 14 and 7). Some, for instance, have chosen to remain in Australia for the sake of their children; as one parent had cause to remark, "Here they're just kids, not sophisticated robots like they were in the U.S." While an Australian trade official has asserted that there are only two kinds of Americans who "stick" in Australia:

> the kind that has money to invest and knows how to do it, an entrepreneur, if you like. He can still make a killing. The other kind of American is the average guy that goes to Australia looking for something that can't be measured in dollars and cents.[19]

Regardless of their specific reasons for remaining in Australia, many migrants feel that the situation in the United States is going to get worse before it gets better, and they do not want to return to America until the situation is reversed "permanently."[20] In the words of one individual surveyed, "I won't return because it'll take just too long for the U.S. to overcome its present difficulties." Although they realize that Australia has problems, too, many believe that America's problems are more serious and will not be as easily solved as will Australia's.

Predominantly more of those in this writer's survey who specified the following motives for emigrating from the United States and immigrating to Australia, rather than other motives listed, indicated they either will not or probably will not resettle in America.

Motives	Percentage Who Will Not or Probably Will Not Resettle in the U.S.
impersonalized society	64.3
felt loss of freedom	61.3
poor outlook for the United States	60.9
government ineffectiveness	57.7
racial unrest	57.5
too much materialism	53.6
increased violence	52.8
high cost of living	50.0
pace of life too fast	48.8
unstable, fast-changing society	44.4

Furthermore, predominantly more of those with the following characteristics, than with other characteristics, indicated they either will not or probably will not resettle in the United States.

Predominant Characteristics	Percentage Who Will Not or Probably Will Not Resettle in the U.S.
sex - males	36.5
occupation in the U.S. - administrative, executive or managerial	61.6
income in the U.S. - less than $4,000	46.1
section from which departed - South, or	35.7
West	35.7
had visited Australia before migrating	43.7
had no job set up before migrating	38.4
year of migration - 1950 to 1964	53.4
final place of settlement - Western Australia	44.7
occupation in Australia - students	71.5
income in Australia - less than $4,000, or	36.9
$8,001 to $12,000	36.2

Finally, there are those Americans who do not know whether they will return to live in the United States (Table 7). One of these types is the person who considers Australia his present home, but who still holds out the possibility that one day in the future he or she might decide to resettle in America. For instance, Auguste Trippe from California who helps run 160,000 square miles of properties says, "My business and my home are

here. I get a kick out of bringing cattle properties into
shape. I go back to the States for visits, but I don't know if
I'll ever live there again."[21] Next, unbelievable though it
may sound, there is the American who keeps going back and forth
between both continents unable to make up his mind in which
land he will finally settle! Such is the case with William A.
Kehoe who, it has been reported,

> at last count had made twenty-seven flights across
> the Pacific, commuting back and forth between his
> business and home in California and his business
> and home in Brisbane, but still undecided as to
> which side of the ocean he would finally settle for.[22]

And lastly, there is the type of American like comedian, actor
and television personality Orson Beane, who in 1971 stated that
he had "decided not to decide where to live," when he bought a
$75,000 house in a suburb of Sydney and "applied for residence
in Australia as an alien."[23] (Perhaps it should be noted here
that Mr. Beane has since returned to and is presently living in
the United States.)

* * *

In the opposite direction of those Americans who immigrated
to Australia, and at the same time some Americans have returned
to resettle in their homeland, many Australians have immigrated
to the United States. Statistics show that between 1820 and
1974, approximately 108,750 people moved to the United States
from Australia and New Zealand, with relatively few from the
latter nation.[24] The first large wave of Australians came to
American shores with the California gold rush of the mid-nineteenth century. Among them were Edward Hammond Hargraves, who
returned to Australia in 1850 and discovered gold "Down Under,"
as well as the infamous Aussies known as the "Sydney Ducks" and
the even more notorious "Derwent Ducks" (both criminal elements
in San Francisco).[25] Later Australian rogues also came to
America, like the outlaw Frank Gardiner who came around 1900
after his release from gaol.[26] It is safe to say, however, that
the vast majority of Australians who have immigrated to the
United States have been far more desirable as migrants. Such has
been the case with the 10,000 Australian brides who came to the
States after World War II to be with their American husbands, and
the 13,000 Australians who migrated to the United States between
1965 and 1975.[27]

The contributions to American life of these Australians has
been quite notable. At least one Australian, Dr. Jill Conway, is
president of an American college, Smith College. Others have

included actors and actresses such as Errol Flynn and Merle Oberon, both of Tasmania, and Rod Taylor; singers Diana Trask and Helen Reddy, the latter now an American citizen who has stated that America is "the best country in the world"; sports figures John Newcombe, of tennis fame, and golfer Jan Stephenson; as well as the publishing magnate Rupert Murdoch and the nationally popular political cartoonist Patrick Oliphant, among numerous other Australians.

Moreover, just as American "know-how" has benefitted Australia, so too have Australian experience and expertise been of value in the United States. One Sydney firm supplied the eight 170-ton "Kangaroo" cranes used to construct the two 110-story buildings of the World Trade Center in New York City; a Melbourne company developed an American National Standards Institute "COBOL" compiler for the world's largest selling mini computer; another Melbourne firm designed the Neova Kit Hovercraft, prospects for which look very bright on the American market; Australia has assisted the American National Metric Council in preparing for the use of the metric system in the United States; and the popular TraveLodge motel chain in western American states is controlled by the TraveLodge firm in Australia.[28] There is little Australian money invested in the United States, but American firms do utilize Australian names and materials in their products--such as "Wallabees" shoes, "Dingo Boots," "Kangaroo" boys' briefs and T-shirts, and football shoes made of kangaroo hides.[29]

Why do Australians want to come to the United States? To this question there are a variety of answers. First, Australians in general like to travel. Young Australians, in particular, "think Los Angeles would be 'the' place to go," according to one American.[30] Second, many Australians come seeking greater material satisfaction via higher salaries offered in the States; and related to this financial consideration is the fact that a number of Australians are seeking to elude their nation's relatively higher tax burden upon its citizens.[31] According to Australian migrant and physician Alan Baird, who came to the United States with his family, "I was bloody tired of going cap in hand to the bank each April Fool's day for a loan to pay income tax." Describing the United States and comparing the people of the two nations, Dr. Baird remarked:

> In this area (Syracuse, New York) since I've been here,
> and in North Carolina and Texas and California, where
> I've been, we've had no trouble with drugs, no problems
> with racial conflict and we've never felt in danger.
> And if you want a difference between here and Australia,
> the people here are far more direct, they're more

assiduous, more conscientious and work harder.[32]

In the United States, Australians generally tend to act as one might expect them to act, in a rough but friendly and democratic manner.[33] In addition, they seem less arrogant and critical than Americans in Australia. Of the American people, it seems to be the general consensus of Australians who have recently arrived in the States that Americans are friendlier than are Australians. And on the whole, Americans probably do tend to be friendlier to Australian migrants than the Aussies are to American migrants.[34] What one might bear in mind, though, is that in both countries what may be taken for friendliness might actually be a temporary curiosity about a person from another land, a natural desire to be a gracious host, or a willingness to offer migrants to one's homeland at least a good first impression. This is only a qualifying observation, however, as the majority of the inhabitants of both nations are not unfriendly.

Regarding the resettlement and possible resettlement in Australia of those individuals who came to the United States, a report in 1947 indicated that "80 percent of the 10,000 Australian war brides in the United States wanted to return to their homeland with their husbands and families."[35] And available statistics tend to indicate that in fact, most Australians who have immigrated to America eventually resettled or will resettle in Australia (Table 31).

* * *

Thus far in this work, a social commentary has been written on both the United States and Australia as well as their respective peoples. This has dealt primarily with matters of the past, though, and it is with the future of the United States and Australia that many migrants have been, are and will be greatly concerned.

For the United States, the future holds a period of deceleration, as in 1950 America controlled almost 40 percent of the world's Gross National Product, but by the late 1960s this figure had dropped to 30 percent and it has continued to decline. Put in simple terms, for Americans as a whole, "the good life" could not continue or increase at the rate at which it was rising in the post-World War II period forever, especially when foreign sources had to be relied upon increasingly for certain resources and as other nations' economic demands increased.[36]

Furthermore, according to a Trend Analysis Report by The Institute of Life Insurance, the future unfortunately holds "more public frustration, worker alienation, increased potential

TABLE 31

RETURN TO AUSTRALIA OF AUSTRALIAN MIGRANTS
TO THE UNITED STATES

Australian Residents Departing:
Country of Intended Residence, U.S.A.

Year	Former Settlers Departing Permanently	Other Residents Departing Permanently	Australian Residents Departing 1 Year or More But Not Permanently	Australian Residents Returning after 1 year or More Abroad; Country of Last Residence or Where Most Time Spent, U.S.A.
1971	1,176	950	2,603	3,772
1972	1,923	994	2,868	3,775
1973	2,229	1,090	2,772	3,986
1974	1,333	949	3,781	3,311
6 months Jan-June 1975	510	456	1,856	1,432

SOURCE: Letter from the Australian Department of Immigration and Ethnic Affairs, June 16, 1976.

for productivity slowdowns, employee sabotage and job riots." The report continues that it is also a definite possibility that we will experience "defaults, bank failures, personal bankruptcies, . . . and the collapse of some major social programs and businesses."[37] Moreover, we will probably experience the same economic difficulties with inflation that we had over the last few years in the not too distant future; and presidential advisers predict that unemployment will not come down to 5 percent until 1980.

171

It is not just problems related to the economy which will
concern Americans, however, as we face serious problems concerning our energy needs and health care among other areas. What
we need most of all for the future, perhaps, is a clear sense
of purpose. In 1961, Henry Luce declared, "More than anything
else, the people of America are asking for a clear sense of
National Purpose." It seems that even though more than fifteen
years have now passed, we still have no clear sense of national
purpose and future direction. In 1975, for the first time
since polls have been taken on the subject, a majority of the
American people indicated they were pessimistic about the future
of the nation. And late in 1976, a poll by Louis Harris revealed that even though most Americans still maintained hope for the
future, they were more pessimistic than at any time in the past
regarding the fulfillment of their hopes for a decline in violence, an easing of constant tensions and a lessening of prejudice. Nevertheless, Americans have risen to meet challenges in
the past, and, as long as there is hope, we may yet overcome our
problems.

* * *

Like the future of the United States, that of Australia is
somewhat uncertain.[38] Politically, Labor will probably not remain out of power for another twenty-three years. What will
happen most likely is that Labor and the Liberal-National Country coalition will alternate control as the needs of the country
shift. For example, when inflation is finally managed because
of Liberal conservative policies, social needs will once again
become the major issue and Labor will in all likelihood then return to power.

In the realm of economics, there will be difficulties with
inflation and unemployment, but one will also see wage increases
tied to increases in productivity. In addition, there may be a
trend toward collective bargaining instead of arbitration to
solve industrial disputes. With respect to population, immigration levels will be based upon economic needs in addition to
social tolerance abilities. Quotas will possibly be established;
and integration, not assimilation, will be the primary object-
ive.[39] The total population of the nation will be almost
19,000,000 by the year 2000, with Sydney and Melbourne each having just under 5,000,000 inhabitants. And because of this
crowding, within thirty years one should see the development of
"model" cities elsewhere in Australia, fed by treated "fossil
water" from deep bore wells, and heated and cooled by solar energy for which Australia is extremely well-suited with its high
intensity of sun rays.[40]

Greater independence should also be a major characteristic of the Australian future, as one day in the not near but not distant future the nation will become a republic.[41] In this regard, Australians will become more nationalistic, turning inward and taking their national character from their own unique environment and reflecting it.[42] This is not to say that Australia will become completely independent, for it will not, at least within the next half century. It is and will remain very much dependent upon other nations such as America for its defense, and upon nations such as Japan and the United States for trade with increased relations involving China and Southeast Asia in this latter area.[43] Indeed, one will probably see the formation of a "Pacific Union," including Australia, America and Japan, among other countries, for trade and defense in the not too distant future.

The United States will soon begin to look more toward the Pacific, where most of the world's people live, as Europe begins to solidify into its own community of nations with an independent outlook and approach to its problems. American Ambassador to Australia, James W. Hargrove, has stressed the importance of the triangular trade among the United States, Australia and Japan; and on January 7, 1976, the first U.S. Congressional delegation to visit Australia in ten years arrived there. Thus, with increased interest in Australia by the United States, the former will probably also find a renewed interest in investment there on the part of the latter.

After all, as Art Linkletter has been quoted, "Australia has more potential than any other place in the world."[44] Although only approximately 30 percent of the land may be farmed at present, as 20 percent is desert and the remaining 50 percent is only suitable for raising sheep and cattle, with improved technology and irrigation techniques the situation may change in the future.[45] The mineral situation, however, is entirely different. According to former American Ambassador to Australia W. H. Crook, the staggering amount of mineral wealth there will make the nation a leading world economic force with an unprecedentedly high standard of living.[46]

Thus, although Australia will face definite problems in the future, just as the United States will, as long as Australians have hope, nearly anything is possible. In the expression of one American, "It's a country of tomorrow . . . Just knowing that Australia is out there gives a person this feeling of a good world" and makes one's heart beat young.[47] And if one believes the statement of Goodman and Johnston, who say in their book, The Australians, "In a world where so many have come to fear the beginning of the end, Australia has come only to the end of the beginning," it just may be that Australians will "point the way to a happier destiny for man throughout the centuries to come," in the words of Bertrand Russell.[48]

Besides the prognostications contained in the preceding analysis of the future of Australia, the opinions of the American migrants surveyed by this writer with respect to that future included a wide variety of comments. Predictions extended from "bleak" and "tending toward a Socialist state" on one side to "If Australia moves carefully, it'll be beautiful and great" on the other side. (Appendix XX contains additional opinions of the migrants on the future of Australia.) Regarding whether the migrants felt the future of Australia would be better than that of the United States, their opinions concerning that possibility were also quite varied. Some felt the future of Australia would most definitely be worse because the Australians would allow things to deteriorate and because there is a lack of productivity in the nation; some felt the future of the two countries would be much the same; and others felt Australia's future seemed better because the nation would be relatively uncrowded, rich in natural resources, and the pace of life would be slower. In the opinion of many, the key as to whether Australia's future would, in fact, be better is whether Australia will learn from America's mistakes. (Appendix XXI contains other opinions of the migrants pertaining to the comparative futures of both nations.)

Whether the future of Australia will be better or worse than that of the United States, it seems clear that each nation would do well to learn from and adopt certain qualities of the other. Australians might in the future develop more of Americans' diligence and originality. Americans on the other hand might fare better if they adopted the Aussies' qualities of fraternalism, skepticism (temporarily, at least), and their identity with nature as well as their senses of pleasure, fair play, family and reserve as specified by Donald Horne.[49]

*　*　*

Having thus looked at the years ahead for both countries, the future of American immigration to Australia will be the final topic of consideration. Potential migrants view the benefits of immigrating to the southwest Pacific island continent as having greatly diminished between the late 1960s and the present, and Australia no longer looks so much like the "Utopia" it once resembled to disenchanted Americans. Still, life in the antipodean continent today has many benefits which attract Americans, for even though the number and magnitude of Australia's problems have increased to a slightly greater degree than those of the United

States over the past few years, Australia's problems were significantly fewer and of a lesser magnitude to begin with in the late 1960s.

In the past there have been horror stories of American migrants who had been assured by Australian officials that they would have no trouble obtaining suitable housing and employment, only to find upon arrival in Australia that their qualifications were not acceptable and that they were placed in a quonset hut hostel with stained and dirty mattresses, and no washing or toilet facilities, refrigeration or provision for cooking. The situation in this respect has improved over the years; and now with the forthcoming increase in the level of general immigration (though the number of American migrants entering Australia in the near future will be less) announced by the government, it is even more important that Australian officials attempt to present a realistic image of their nation, especially of "urban Australia," and the difficulties which migrants might face.[50] Once in Australia, it would also be helpful if a migrant center were established in each state capital to offer counsel and advice to any migrants, whether newly arrived or not.[51]

Those types of Americans most likely to immigrate to Australia in the future will probably be young adults, adventurers eager to see the world, racists, those in search of America as it used to be with a slower pace of living, people with pioneer spirit, individuals who have no particular loyalty to the United States and who simply seek a better land in which to live, and the politically or otherwise disenchanted. Some feel that future American immigration to Australia will decline markedly because of increasing social stability in the States.[52] From a historical perspective, though, they should realize that any social stability we as a nation might now enjoy is in all likelihood only a temporary respite from the turmoil and disruption which will almost surely visit us once again in the future. Those white Americans who immigrated because of "racial unrest" in the past, for example, might very well find that they are joined in the future by other white Americans fleeing the inevitable integration of most if not all neighborhoods in the United States. As long as these latter individuals only problem regarding relations with another race is that their children are being bused to achieve a racial balance in the nation's schools, they will be "concerned" about their situation in this country, but they will not find it "intolerable." This writer ventures to predict, however, that when thousands of white Americans are confronted within their own neighborhoods with the possible reality of low-income housing projects predominantly for blacks, many of these white Americans will regrettably choose not to remain in the United States. It will be simply too great a cultural shock

175

for them as individuals to be able to adapt to the new situation.

Americans who should probably have the greatest chance of success as permanent settlers in Australia will be those who immigrate with a strong, genuine desire to pioneer, for the generally slower pace of life, and because of racial unrest in the United States.[53] They will also probably have a job lined up before they embark, a plan of where they are going, and enough funds to last them at least four months without work.[54] Furthermore, they will have come with the realization that Australia is neither "Utopia" nor a "Little America"; and they will be willing to accept Australia "for what it is" and to stay at least two years in order to really be able to determine most of the nation's positive and negative aspects. Moreover, they will be independent, able to adjust and adapt to new circumstances, have a specific goal, and not be simply trying to escape their own personal, internal problems which they will probably carry with them.[55] Regarding their dealings with the Australian people, the most successful migrants will probably be rather cautious though agreeable, at least at first, until they get to know the Australians and their idiosyncracies better.

It is important to realize, of course, that Australia is not for every American who is dissatisfied with the United States and his life in it. It would be best if most of these Americans would first look elsewhere in their own land to settle before leaving family, friends, culture and heritage to migrate to the opposite side of the planet. The primary reasons for this suggestion is that no matter what "social" motives for leaving the United States seem to be foremost in the minds of many migrants, once in Australia some do not seem to be able to adjust to living on a lower salary or wage, especially when the prices of many commodities are comparatively the same as in the land from which they came, and so they return.[56]

What then is the final verdict concerning the future of American immigration to Australia? It is that there will be fewer migrants in the near term, primarily because of the restrictions on immigration set by the Australian government, followed by a gradual and moderate increase in the long term once the problems of inflation and unemployment have been reduced and Americans can again enter in the numbers which the applicants for immigration desire. Those who do go intending to settle and remain, not those who only intend to stay a few years, however, will be better informed about their new land. Therefore, the departure rate should decrease among this category, thereby yielding an annual net increase in the ratio of arrivals to departures in the near future compared to past years. Then as America enters any future period of social dissension and turmoil, economic difficulty, high unemployment, lack of credibility in government and confidence in the political system, or energy or environmental crisis, immigration to Australia should increase once more, provided Australia is stable with no serious problems, until the situation in the United States has again stabilized. But then, only the passing of time--the future itself--will verify the validity of the prognostications offered in this work.

Footnotes - Chapter VI:

1. Hopkins, I've Had It, p. 156.

2. Ibid., pp. 156-157.

3. Department of Immigration, Survey, p. 3.

4. Ibid., p. 65.

5. Ibid., p. 58.
   Moffat and Tannen, What's It Like? p. 17.

6. Faulk and Faulk, Alternative, pp. 65-66.

7. Moffitt, U-Jack, p. 180.

8. Linkletter, Down Under, p. 212.

9. Colless, "Decline Down Under," p. 38.

10. Department of Immigration, Survey, p. 10.

11. DuBose, "New Frontier," p. 1.
    Aitchison, Americans, p. 199.

12. "Australia," Atlantic Monthly, November, 1950, p. 17.
    Faulk and Faulk, Alternative, p. 86.
    Trumbull, "Seeking Simpler Life," p. 12.

13. Hopkins, I've Had It, p. 57.

14. Simpson, The New Australia, p. 12.

15. "She'll Be Right," pp. 36-37.

16. Faulk and Faulk, Alternative, p. 166.

17. Kaye et al., "The U.S.tralians," p. 23.

18. Greenway, Last Frontier, p. 284.

19. Hopkins, I've Had It, p. 164.

20. DuBose, "Americans Who Kept on West," p. 3.

21. "'Down Under'-Souring Relations with an Old Ally," U.S.News
    & World Report, June 11, 1973, p. 72.

22. Aitchison, Americans, p. 75.

23. Elizabeth Riddell, "Goodbye, Uncle Sam," The Australian, August 2, 1971, p. 9.

24. Westerman and Bacheller, eds., Almanac, p. 222.

25. Jay Monaghan, Australians and the Gold Rush (Berkeley and Los Angeles: University of California Press, 1966), p. 121.

26. Aitchison, Americans, p. 19.

27. Ibid., p. 74.
"A 'New America'," p. 65.

28. Gunther, Australia, p. 122.

29. "A 'New America'," p. 65.

30. Faulk and Faulk, Alternative, p. 90.

31. Ibid., p. 30.

32. "'Happiness' Is Escape from Austin, Texas," The (Adelaide) News, May 14, 1975, p. 16.

33. McGregor, Profile, p. 376.

34. Riddell, "Seeking a New West," p. 11.

35. "Emigration of Americans Welcomed by Australians," New York Times, September 16, 1947, p. 28.

36. "Mood of America--'Where Do We Turn?'" U.S. News & World Report, October 6, 1975, p. 12.

37. Institute of Life Insurance, TAP Report, 12 (New York: Institute of Life Insurance, 1975), pp. 11-12.

38. "A 'New America'," p. 65.

39. Fabun, Australia 2000! p. 14.
McGregor, Profile, p. 360.

40. Fabun, Australia 2000! pp. 9, 52-53.

41. Gunther, Australia, p. 111.

42. Fabun, Australia 2000! p. 13.

43. Gunther, Australia, p. 347.

44. "What to Expect," p. 77.

45. U.S. Congress, House, Honorable Ralph Yarborough presents article on Ambassador Ed Clark in The Houston Chronicle, 89th Cong., 2nd sess., March 22, 1966, Congressional Record, CXII, Appendix, A1629.

46. U.S. Congress, House, Record of American Ambassador to Australia W. H. Crook's speech to the Australian National Press Club, 91st Cong., 1st sess., April 24, 1969, Congressional Record, CXV, 10332.

47. Helmericks, Adventure, p. 353.

48. Goodman and Johnston, The Australians, p. 285. Manning Clark, A Short History of Australia (New York: New American Library, 1963), p. 243.

49. Horne, The Lucky Country, pp. 222-223.

50. Department of Immigration, Survey, pp. 57, 59.

51. Moffitt, U-Jack, pp. 98, 99.

52. Aitken, Land of Fortune, p. 114.

53. Department of Immigration, Survey, p. 54.

54. Moffat and Tannen, What's It Like? p. 4.

55. Fabun, Australia 2000! p. 17. Hopkins, I've Had It, p. 10.

56. Aitchison, Americans, p. 200.

APPENDIXES

LIST OF APPENDIXES

181

QUESTIONNAIRE SENT TO MIGRANTS

1. How did you first become interested in Australia as a place
   to live? _____

2. Did you visit Australia before migrating? _____

3. Were you a migrant to the United States before immigrating
   to Australia? _____

4. Why did you decide to leave the United States? (Please
   check at least one.)

   too much pollution   _____
   unstable, fast-changing
     society   _____
   threat of world war   _____
   job assignment (private)   _____
   job assignment
     (government)   _____
   for health of family   _____
   rise in crime rate   _____
   high cost of labor   _____
   lack of new frontiers   _____
   racial unrest   _____
   unemployment   _____
   becoming too crowded   _____
   felt loss of freedom   _____
   government ineffectiveness   _____
   high cost of living   _____
   for better business and
     investment opportunities   _____
   increased violence   _____
   personal or family problems_____
   too much materialism   _____
   restrictive land policies   _____
   pace of life too fast   _____
   for adventure   _____
   nuclear bomb scare   _____
   high cost of land   _____

---

*The source for all appendixes will be the author's survey
unless otherwise indicated.

poor outlook for United
  States
impersonalized society   _____
other: (Please explain.)   _____

5. How did your negative impression, if any, of the U.S.
   develop (through personal experiences, news media, etc.)?

   _____

6. Was there one event that caused you finally to migrate?
   (Please explain.) _____

7. About how long (months) did it take from the time you
   first considered migrating until the time you finally decided to leave? _____

8. Why did you choose Australia instead of Canada, South
   America, etc.? _____

9. Did you have a job set up in Australia before leaving the
   United States? _____

10. In what year did you migrate? _____ At what age?__

11. Race: _____ Sex: _____

12. Income in U.S.:

    Below $4,000___ $4,001-$8,000___ $8,001-$12,000___
    $12,001-$16,000___   Above $16,000___

13. Income now:

    Below $4,000___ $4,001-$8,000___ $8,001-$12,000___
    $12,001-$16,000___   Above $16,000___

14. Single or married at the time of migration? _____

15. Did the Australian Government help pay for your migration?

    _____

16. From what city/town and state did you leave? _____
                City/town approximate population: _____

17. What was your profession in the United States? _____

18. What is your profession in Australia? _____

184

19. Where did you first settle in Australia? _____
        City/town approximate population: _____

20. Where do you live now in Australia? (City/town and
    state) _____
            City/town approximate population: _____

21. Why did you choose to settle finally where you did? ____

22. About one month after arrival, what was your feeling about
    Australia? (Please check one.) very disappointed_____
    disappointed_____ mixed feelings_____ pleased_____ very
    pleased_____.

23. What were the major difficulties that arose after your ar-
    rival (until about one year)? _____

24. What is your opinion of Australia now? (Please check one.)
    very satisfied_____ satisfied_____ mixed feelings_____
    dissatisfied_____ very dissatisfied_____

25. What is your opinion of the Aussies in general (friendly
    or not, hard-working or not, etc.)? _____

26. If any, what things in Australia dissatisfy you today?
    _____

27. What do you like particularly about Australia? _____

28. Compare the United States to Australia now. The United
    States is: (Please check one.) far worse_____ worse____
    about the same_____ better_____ far better_____

29. What do you foresee for the future (quality of life in
    Australia? _____

30. Does the future of Australia look better or worse than
    that of the United States? (Please explain.) _____

31. Do you think you may ever resettle in the United States?
    _____

ADDITIONAL COMMENTS: _____
_____
_____
_____

185

STATES INCLUDED WITHIN EACH SECTION OF THE
UNITED STATES IN SURVEY TABULATIONS
AND CROSS-TABULATIONS*

California

Northeast - Connecticut, Maine, Massachusetts, New Jersey, New
York, Pennsylvania

North Central - Illinois, Indiana, Iowa, Michigan, Minnesota,
Missouri, Nebraska, Ohio, South Dakota,
Wisconsin

West - Alaska, Arizona, Colorado, Hawaii, New Mexico, Oregon,
Utah, Washington

South - Alabama, Florida, Georgia, Louisiana, Maryland, North
Carolina, South Carolina, Texas, Virginia, District of
Columbia

Puerto Rico

---

*States not listed had no questionnaire respondents.

PREDOMINANT CHARACTERISTICS OF AMERICANS SURVEYED
WHO EMIGRATED FOR THE FOLLOWING SPECIFIC REASONS

I. Personal or Family Problems

Demographic Variables	Predominant Characteristics
sex	females
age at migration	over 40 years of age
marital status at migration	singles
occupation in U.S.	homemaker, or administrative, executive or managerial
section from which departed	Northeast
year of migration	1965 to 1969
final place of settlement in Australia	Queensland, or Western Australia
occupation in Australia	administrative, executive or managerial, or students

II. Too Much Materialism

Demographic Variables	Predominant Characteristics
sex	females
age at migration	40 to 49 years of age
marital status at migration	singles
occupation in U.S.	other nonmanual workers, or clerical workers
income in U.S.	$12,001 to $16,000
final place of settlement in Australia	Queensland, or Western Australia
occupation in Australia	clerical workers, or students

III. Unemployment

Demographic Variables	Predominant Characteristics
sex	males

187

age at migration   15 to 29 years of age
marital status at migration   marrieds
occupation in U.S.   students
income in U.S.   none, or less than $4,000
section from which departed   California, or West
year of migration   1970 to 1971
final place of settlement
   in Australia   Capital Territory
occupation in Australia   administrative, executive
                               or managerial, or profes-
                               sional, technical or
                               related workers, or manual
                               workers

IV. Impersonalized Society

Demographic Variables	Predominant Characteristics
age at migration	25 to 29 years of age
marital status at migration	singles
occupation in U.S.	clerical workers, or professional, technical or related workers, or other nonmanual workers
section from which departed	Northeast
year of migration	1970
final place of settlement in Australia	Western Australia, or Tasmania
occupation in Australia	administrative, executive or managerial, or manual workers, or students

V. Unstable, Fast-Changing Society

Demographic Variables	Predominant Characteristics
sex	males
age at migration	15 to 29 years of age
marital status at migration	singles
occupation in U.S.	other nonmanual workers, or clerical workers
section from which departed	California, or West, or North Central

final place of settlement
  in Australia   Western Australia
occupation in Australia   manual workers

VI. Government Ineffectiveness

Demographic Variables	Predominant Characteristics
age at migration	30 to 39 years of age
marital status at migration	singles
occupation in U.S.	professional, technical or related workers
income in U.S.	$4,001 to $8,000
section from which departed	California, or North Central
year of migration	1971 to 1972
final place of settlement in Australia	Victoria
occupation in Australia	professional, technical or related workers

VII. Poor Outlook for the United States

Demographic Variables	Predominant Characteristics
sex	males
age at migration	15 to 24 years of age
marital status at migration	singles
occupation in U.S.	students, or clerical workers
income in U.S.	less than $8,000
section from which departed	California, or West
year of migration	1970 to 1971
final place of settlement in Australia	Western Australia
occupation in Australia	students, or administrative, executive or managerial

ADDITIONAL MOTIVES FOR EMIGRATING FROM THE UNITED
STATES AND IMMIGRATING TO AUSTRALIA
INDICATED BY MIGRANTS SURVEYED

- age discrimination in U.S.
- aggressive ex-wife
- Americans expect too high a degree of conformity for all
  the lip service to "do your own thing" and I could
  never seem to fit in
- became engaged to or married an Aussie
- better education system in Australia
- busing of school children
- couldn't find satisfactory teaching position
- daughter and grandchildren there
- desire for a new life
- destiny
- easier to buy a cattle farm and raise and race thorough-
  bred horses in South Australia than in the U.S.
- east coast of Australia has better and less crowded surf
  than Southern California
- educational experience
- embarrassed at times by American attitude in world
  affairs and dope pushing
- family lived in Australia
- family reasons
- fear of getting married and settling down in a small
  middle class American city and living the rest of my
  life like that
- first job offered in my field was there
- free university tuition
- get away from gadget and appliance craze in America
- got Fulbright grant
- help take care of in-law
- honeymoon
- I couldn't be in Australia and see what it was like
  beforehand
- immaturity limited own prospects
- increase knowledge of and status in world
- it's simpler to exist in Australia, less needs and demands
  made on a person
- it was now or never
- Kent State and poverty
- law in the U.S. is for the rich, not the middle or poor
  class
- live with a good male companion who'd migrated

- meaningful balance of work and leisure in Australia
- middle-aged restlessness
- missionary work
- moral breakdown in the U.S.
- no medical benefits for deaf child in the U.S. and in Queensland, it's all free
- no negative reason re the U.S. but positive reasons re Australia
- no real home ties
- on a treadmill to nowhere and had to get off
- overgoverned
- parents took me
- people taught to instinctively mistrust others in the U.S.
- personal growth
- prophecy by psychic
- quick, assured, total, safe independence
- returned to native home of Australia after sixteen years in the U.S. for better education for children
- Richard Nixon and fellow government officials
- see more of world and its people, but not just as a tourist
- see wife's country
- selfish, unthinking American slobs
- semi-retirement in a then (1967) less expensive, more congenial atmosphere
- time for a change
- too many police in the U.S.
- too much compassion for the irresponsible element in the U.S.
- U.S. Air Force career adversely affected my concern for the U.S.
- U.S. government would move me for no charge
- wanted to live in a warmer climate
- weak judicial system in the U.S.

SINGLE EVENTS OR MOTIVES THAT CAUSED SOME
AMERICANS TO EMIGRATE FROM THE
UNITED STATES AND IMMIGRATE TO AUSTRALIA

- accepted for a job in Australia first
- Australian husband wanted to go home
- being nearly caught up in the Washington, D.C. racial riots
- busing of school children
- construction of a thirteen-story high-rise condominium complex in front of my house
- could no longer breathe and no longer could our children; we felt trapped and helpless
- couldn't get a job
- daughter in Australia became ill and I didn't want to commute
- death of a close personal friend
- divorced my husband of twenty-five years
- engaged to or married an Australian
- failing health of mother-in-law in Australia
- failure to expel knife- and razor-wielding students from high school because of race
- fighting the draft for seven years
- friend asked me to take over his practice of chiropractic medicine while he went on holiday
- girlfriend killed in a car accident
- got enough money for the fare
- had been tourist in Europe, the Middle East, and Asia too long and wanted to LIVE somewhere
- hated teaching English at Georgia Tech
- huge shopping center was to be built just down the road
- I quit my job and didn't know what else to do
- mining company in Australia offered to pay fare and shipping fees if I came to Australia for a year
- most favorable interview with the Australian consular agent in Los Angeles
- near fatal auto wreck
- opportunity to immigrate finally arose--graduated from school, offspring left home, became free from all business and personal obligations, paid off all debts, sold business, etc.
- opportunity to set up own business
- paid off home
- paying unjust alimony
- prophecy by psychic

192

- racial unrest in the late 1960s
- retirement from the American military
- visited Australia
- visited South Africa and found out the U.S. was not the only place on earth
- while working for the U.S. government in October, 1956, I realized how hopelessly informed the government had allowed its overseas information to deteriorate
- wounded in Vietnam and never got anything for it

REASONS GIVEN MY MIGRANTS SURVEYED FOR CHOOSING
TO IMMIGRATE TO AUSTRALIA INSTEAD OF TO
OTHER NATIONS OF THE WORLD

- accepted by school there
- Americans' praise of Australian cordiality
- Australia is family oriented
- Australia was the going thing in 1971
- Australian women have fewer "hang-ups"
- availability of educational facilities
- availability of medical facilities
- Barrier Reef and developing interest in marine science
- beautiful country with casual lifestyle and friendly
  citizenry
- beautiful trees and beaches
- better area in which to grow cotton
- better way of life
- booming prosperity there
- Canada was too cold and similar to the U.S.
- could practice profession without being licensed
- curiosity
- daughter and grandchildren live in Australia
- don't have to become a citizen
- don't know
- ease of assimilation
- engagement or marriage to an Australian
- England was too wet and crowded
- expansive land development there
- family was there
- few business and government controls
- fewer Africans
- free transportation there and guaranteed jobs for selected
  teachers
- free tuition
- friendly feeling of the Aussies for the U.S.
- friendly people in Australia
- friends were going there
- good educational standards and system
- good public transit
- good surfing
- got a Fulbright Grant
- got aid from the Australian Housing Commission
- great social benefits
- had a sponsor there
- had already immigrated to New Zealand

- had visited Australia and knew it
- hadn't been there yet
- have always been interested in Australia
- I like kangaroos (Ha!)
- influence of New Zealand relatives
- it is a young country
- it has fewer problems than the U.S.
- it is quiet
- it is the nearest thing to the way the U.S. was fifty years ago
- it is the new or last frontier
- it needs people
- it was close to Asia where I was living and to where I could return for a vacation
- less culture shock
- less emphasis on pseudo-moral judgments
- lower cost of living
- migrants and children are welcome
- my native home
- not interested in other countries
- only place I could get a good salary
- opportunity to relive the past ten years
- other places didn't want teachers
- other places were too small or isolated, or the living standards were too low
- perceived lifestyle
- progressive government policies
- prophecy by psychic
- ran out of money in India and Australia was the closest English-speaking country with jobs
- similar climate and money system as to the U.S.
- South America has corruption; it is also unsanitary and unstable there, and they don't speak English
- spouse chose Australia
- spouse's family ties were in Australia
- sunshine
- Switzerland was too close to France and Germany, and I'd had enough of big nations telling little ones what to do
- tax break as a teacher there
- to get as far away from Nixon as possible
- to go far away from the U.S. and my memories and work my way back slowly, instead of slowly working myself away from the U.S.
- unique Outback and continent
- unusual area of the world and easiest to which to adapt
- wanted to come to Australia, not to run away from the U.S.
- wanted to get the feel for my mother's country
- wanted to see the South Pacific

- wanted to see the Sydney Opera House
- was asked to do missionary work there
- white society
- would get a child endowment of $14 per month

APPENDIX VII

ASSISTED PASSAGE SCHEME UNDERTAKING
AND DECLARATION

I _____
Name

of _____
Address

_____

an applicant to enter Australia and for assisted passage to
Australia solemnly declare that if granted assisted passage it
is my intention to settle permanently in Australia and that
should I and/or any member or members of my family leave Australia before completing two years residence I will repay before
any such departure the full amount of the financial assistance
granted towards the cost of passage to Australia, pursuant to my
application, of the person or persons so departing.

I clearly understand also:

a that approval for an assisted passage granted to me (and family if any) may be cancelled by the Australian Government at any
time prior to departure and that approval of the application
does not impose any legal obligation upon the Australian Government to take me (or them) to Australia:

b that any false statement or concealment of material fact in
relation to my application may result in my being refused admission to Australia upon arrival there and further that if I
should be admitted to Australia for settlement the subsequent
discovery of a fraudulent statement or concealment in my application would be grounds for deportation under the Migration Act
1958 as amended from time to time.

Signature of applicant _____ / /19

Declared before me at _____ on this

_____ day of _____ 19

Signature of Australian Government representative _____

197

APPENDIX VIII

MAJOR DIFFICULTIES FACED AFTER ARRIVAL
BY MIGRANTS SURVEYED

- adjusting to actual distance from home in Maine
- adjusting to diminished office hours
- adjusting to life away from parents
- adjusting to season and climate changes
- adjusting to teaching kids who seemed little interested in learning
- American aggressiveness not being well received here
- American bores
- anti-Americanism
- anxiety about national events and crises in the U.S.
- arrived as the recession started
- Australians' attitude toward "Yanks"
- avoiding con-men and real estate swindlers
- bad cooking
- being an American
- being gypped on a car purchase
- being placed in a horribly isolated spot by the State educational department
- being wiped out in a flood
- change of food
- children regularly stoned and verbally abused going to and from school
- coldness
- companionship--didn't feel like I belonged
- constant ribbing for being a "Yank"
- convincing Australians I was there to settle and not to just make money and leave
- convincing my wife she could overcome loneliness
- could not find a decent Mexican food restaurant
- crazy drivers
- dealing with outdated methods
- dealing with the New South Wales Department of Education bureaucracy and the centralized educational system
- dealing with uneducated people with no class
- deciding on a business to establish
- deciding what bait to use on the fish
- deciding where to settle
- devaluation of the U.S. dollar
- different names used for the same thing (American "biscuit" is an Australian "cookie")
- expecting things to be too much like the U.S.
- feeling of "underachievement" and uselessness

- finding edible meats (sausage had mutton in it)
- furnishing home
- gaining acceptance by the Australians
- getting a loan for a car
- getting children in school
- getting first paycheck
- getting news about the U.S.
- getting permanent residency
- getting used to a less luxury-conscious culture
- getting used to driving on the left
- getting used to flies
- getting used to fresh meat to eat
- getting used to windows without screens
- had to send to the U.S. for film
- hard to find good help
- household appliances from the U.S. were no good by themselves, because Australia uses 240 volts and transform-
  ers are expensive
- housing shortage in 1951
- I did not know anyone, and it was difficult making friends
- I was on the defensive regarding occasional derogatory
  remarks about the U.S. and Americans
- idiotic, murderous traffic regulations
- illness, including mental illness due to abrupt government
  change and deceptive information given by the Australian
  government before my immigration
- isolation of children
- lack of American bartender
- lack of common heritage
- lack of consumer protection
- lack of, or slow, service
- lack of social responsibility by the Australians
- lack of understanding
- lack of well-educated or intelligent females (or males)
- learning my job
- loneliness
- lower class lifestyle
- making my accent understood
- money differences
- my eighth-grade education
- my wife was dissatisfied and she still is
- no car
- no girls (small town)
- no night life
- no other Americans were around to talk over adjustment
  problems regarding the standard of living and social
  structure
- no trade
- none, because I had been there before

- none, because we had done a good deal of research before migrating, and we decided to adapt to Australia and not expect Australia to adapt to us
- not as large a range of consumer goods available
- number of things I had to buy
- obtaining supplies necessary for business
- overcharged on rent
- pace of life in Brisbane too fast
- poor schools
- relative indifference of Australians to serious matters
- shops and services not open or available on weekends or late at night
- some American job qualifications are not accepted in Australia
- spending on a lower scale
- tax structure
- tradesmen
- traffic rules
- transition into family life after a career in a foreign country
- trying to buy a house, appliances, or imported things with a few dollars
- trying to not like the place
- trying to stop comparing things in Australia to things in the U.S.
- understanding the humor
- unhealthy amount of American influence in Australia
- unheated flats
- unseasonably rainy weather (rained daily for four months in Sydney)
- watching savings disappear
- women held subservient to men

APPENDIX IX

ADDITIONAL REASONS GIVEN BY MIGRANTS SURVEYED
FOR THE LOCATION OF THE FINAL PLACE OF
SETTLEMENT

- accommodation furnished
- availability of land and houses
- beautiful location
- Busselton was the place of my greatest expectations and fondest dreams
- cheap land
- cheaper home
- close, convenient, to big-city life
- close to family and office
- couldn't make enough on the farm, so went to the city to get some money, then will return to the farm
- couldn't pay assisted passage back and it was better than N.C.
- country way of life near the ocean, good surf, reasonably priced land, clean air and water
- economics
- educational and medical facilities
- emotional reasons
- family in-law there
- few people there
- for new experiences
- free medical benefits
- friendly church
- friends there
- Gold Coast was similar to Florida
- good boating
- got a good deal on buying a house
- greater opportunity for the future
- housing good there
- husband's job was there
- irrigation farms in the area
- it was quaint
- it was the first place I landed and the only place I knew
- it was untouched by "progress"
- lake there
- land and climate good, and water was available for our crops
- lots of couples our age were there with their kids
- mountain setting
- need for us as Baha'i missionaries
- nice people

201

- no hassles
- no pollution
- no resident chiropractor
- not settled--traveling around and haven't decided where to settle for sure
- pleasant place
- quiet suburban environment
- received a good response from the Good Neighbor Council there
- relaxed atmosphere
- scenery
- secluded area
- small, friendly town where my wife and myself get involved in community activities
- suburban area was close to the center of a large city
- wanted a rural-city environment
- wanted to live in a resort town
- wanted to live in or near a city
- went to Perth from Darwin to get back to civilization
- where I spent 1949 to 1953
- wife's home
- with my low salary and the high cost of living, I couldn't afford to move out of Sydney

APPENDIX X

MAP AND KEY OF THE MAJOR AMERICAN ENTERPRISES
IN EXPLORATION, CONSTRUCTION AND
EXPANSION IN AUSTRALIA AS OF 1964

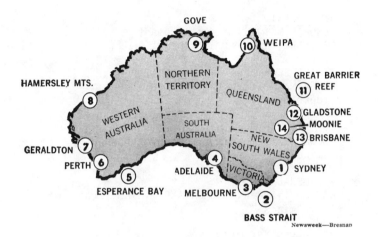

1. SYDNEY
FORD, assembly plant
GENERAL MOTORS, assembly plant
CHRYSLER, new plant
BORG-WARNER, auto transmission plant
SCHERING CORP., new drug plant
AMERICAN CYANAMID, sutures plant
MERCK & CO., new drug plant
COCA-COLA, new bottling plant
CRANE CO., new pump and valve plant
IBM, new headquarters building
GENERAL FOODS, instant-coffee plant
GOODYEAR, tire plant
STAUFFER, chemical plant

2. BASS STRAIT
STANDARD OIL OF NEW JERSEY, off-shore
    drilling

3. MELBOURNE
GENERAL MOTORS, foundry and engine
    plant, assembly plant, new technical

    center
AMERICAN CYANAMID, new chemical plant
H. J. HEINZ, food processing plant
FORD, assembly and manufacturing plant
EASTMAN KODAK, new film and camera plant
CAMPBELL SOUP, new canning plant
ALCOA, new aluminum smelter

4. ADELAIDE
GENERAL MOTORS, assembly plant
CHRYSLER, new assembly plant

5. ESPERANCE BAY
CHASE MANHATTAN, 1.4 million-acre land
    development

6. PERTH
ALCOA, new alumina refinery, and bauxite
    mines

7. GERALDTON
HANNA MINING AND HOMESTAKE MINING, iron
    ore mines

8. HAMERSLEY MTS.
KAISER STEEL, iron ore

9. GOVE
REYNOLDS METALS, proposed bauxite mining

10. WEIPA
KAISER ALUMINUM, bauxite mining

11. GREAT BARRIER REEF
GULF OIL CORP., offshore oil exploration

12. GLADSTONE
KAISER ALUMINUM, alumina refinery

13. BRISBANE
GENERAL MOTORS, assembly plant
FORD, assembly plant
AMOCO, new oil refinery

14. MOONIE
UNION OIL CALIFORNIA, oil wells and 190-
    mile pipeline to Brisbane

APPENDIX XI

REQUIREMENTS FOR ESTABLISHING A BUSINESS
IN AUSTRALIA

Each foreign company must, within one month after it establishes a place of business or commences to carry on business in a State or Territory, lodge with the Registrar of companies in that State or Territory:

1. A copy of the certificate of incorporation or a document of similar effect, certified by a registrar or assistant registrar of joint-stock companies or by an official of the Government of the country in which the company was incorporated.

2. A copy of the charter, statute, or memorandum and articles of association of the company duly certified by an official of the Government to whose custody the original is committed, by a duly certified notary public, or by statutory declaration of a director, or manager, or secretary of the company before a notary public.

3. A list of directors of the company, containing prescribed particulars listed in the above paragraph.

4. If there are local directors, a memorandum stating the power of the local directors.

5. A memorandum of appointment or a power of attorney under the seal of the company, authorizing some one or more persons resident in the State to accept, on behalf of the company, service of process and any notices required to be served on the company.

6. Notice of location of registered office and of the days and hours during which it is accessible to the public and a statutory declaration in the prescribed form by the agent of the company.

In general, when these requirements have been satisfied, a certificate will be issued proclaiming that the company has been registered under the State Companies Act. Upon receipt of this certificate, the company is granted substantially the same rights, powers, and privileges as any company incorporated in that State.

SOURCE: U.S. Department of Commerce. Economic Trends and

Their Implication for the United States-Australia. The United States Government Printing Office, September 1, 1969, p. 10.

MAP AND KEY OF NORTHERN TERRITORY U.S. OWNERS

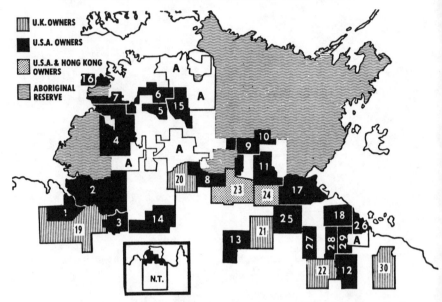

	U.K. OWNERS
	U.S.A. OWNERS
	U.S.A. & HONG KONG OWNERS
	ABORIGINAL RESERVE

1.	Bullo River	Charles Henderson, Washington, D.C.
2.	Collibah	Recently sold to a U.S. group
3.	Fitzroy	Allen Chase, Los Angeles
4.	Tipperary	Midland, Texas group
5.	Ban Ban Springs	Nelson (Bunker) Hunt
6.	Mt. Bundy	W. R. Grace and Company
7.	Stapleton	Messrs. Townsend from Florida
8.	Mataranka	Maritime Fruit Co. of NYC and Israel
9.	Mountain Valley	Dillingham Corp., Honolulu
10.	Mainoru	Forster, South Carolina
11.	Roper Valley	Recently sold to a U.S. group
12.	McArthur River	D. Howenstine, Indiana
13.	Kalala	Nelson (Bunker) Hunt
14.	Delamere	Luke Wise and Others--recently changed ownership to other U.S. interests
15.	Goodparla	U.S. group from California
16.	Finnis River	Mr. L. Rebourse
17.	St. Vidgeon	Mr. M. Howard, HAT Cattle Company
18.	Nathan River (E1/2)	Recently acquired by U.S. group, Ohio
25-29.	Unknown American Owners	

A. Vacant Crown Land to be allotted to "suitable allottees" over the next few years.

SOURCE: Ray Aitchison, Thanks to the Yanks (Melbourne: Sun Books, 1972), pp. 108-109. Copyright 1972 by Sun Books. All rights reserved. Reprinted by permission.

APPENDIX XIII

MAP AND KEY OF BIGGER AMERICAN-OWNED
AND PART-OWNED STATIONS IN
WESTERN AUSTRALIA

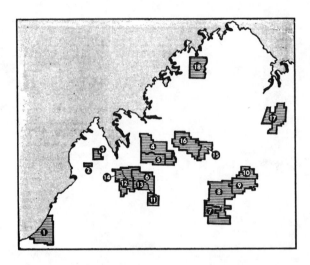

1.   Linkletter Enterprises of U.S.
2-8.   Australian Land and Cattle Company
9-13.   Kimberley Cattle Pty., Ltd.
14.   Unknown
15-16. King Ranch of U.S.
17.   W. A. Goddard of U.S.
18.   AMAX Corporation of U.S.

        SOURCE: Ray Aitchison, Thanks to
the Yanks (Melbourne: Sun Books, 1972),
pp. 108-109.

ADDITIONAL OPINIONS OF THE AUSTRALIAN
PEOPLE STATED BY MIGRANTS SURVEYED

- accustomed to people of different backgrounds
- afraid of Americanization, yet lack initiative of their own
- aloof
- authoritarian
- average people in the cities
- becoming tense in large urban areas
- believe all they read in the newspapers about how terrible the U.S. is
- bludgers
- cautious until they know you
- clanish
- close-minded
- competent
- country people can be bigoted and provincial, but are generally good-hearted
- excellent people
- "expletive"
- exploited
- generally efficient
- genuine
- good and bad
- good workers
- great differences between educated and uneducated
- higher than usual percentage of them are louts
- hospitable
- in a healthy way they ignore things that are unpleasant or threatening
- insecure
- interesting
- irresponsible
- lighthearted
- love Americans
- loving people
- loyal
- mediocre personalities
- men are not hardworking
- mix well
- narrowminded
- nationalistic
- not as industrious as a race in a colder climate
- not friendly, not gracious, not helpful, not too sincere

on a long-term basis, not used to cooperating, not very
social-reformist, and not very well-educated
- outgoing
- poorly-trained teachers
- reasonable
- resentful of Americans
- ridicule "Yank" blow-hards
- rude shop attendants
- satisfied
- skeptical of foreigners
- smug
- socially snobbish
- straightforward
- stubborn
- stupid
- too inbred
- trusting
- unassuming
- unaware their liberties are not guaranteed
- un-Christian
- uneducated Aussies are defensive toward Yanks
- very fair
- very pollution-conscious
- very superficial interest in the heart of life
- vital
- women are hardworking

-

ADDITIONAL "LIKES" ABOUT AUSTRALIA INDICATED
BY MIGRANTS SURVEYED

- ability to change jobs and travel with no problems
- abundance of local "veggies"
- after work (and often at work) the boss is just another worker
- American aggressiveness can take one a long way if used correctly
- amount of uncleared land
- architecture
- atmosphere is overwhelming
- attitude that work is a method of paying for leisure
- Aussies
- automatic national wage raises
- beautiful Perth
- "bed and breakfast" hotels
- better students as only the top 10 percent can go on to university
- better teaching conditions
- bush
- bushwalking
- cheap dental care
- cheap wool sweaters
- children and wife contented
- children's safety
- clean mountain streams in which one can swim or from which one can drink without fear
- closeness to history
- concern for the preservation of nature
- cost of living vs. income
- country towns
- don't have to be a crusader or need as much money
- enjoyment of life is more important than work
- entertainment variety
- equality of income
- "fair go" attitude
- family doctors still abound
- feeling I might live longer
- fishing
- fresh air
- friendliness of migrants and shop people
- funky old English traditions
- geography and topography
- get more out of recreation time

- good boating, bus service and taxis (public transportation), combination of old and new in the cities, and
  public transportation and plays in Melbourne
- good question??!!
- good springboard to the world
- good transcontinental trains
- grants for rural culture (plays, operas, etc.)
- Great Barrier Reef
- green cities
- gum trees
- hardly any tipping
- hardworking people
- healthy young men and women
- hearty people
- homogenous society
- horse racing
- "I don't give a damn" attitude
- inexpensive phone calls and recreation
- inflation
- innocent people
- isolated areas
- it is a person-to-person country, a vigorous nation, a
  wholesome place, a young country and it is about the
  same as the U.S.
- it has vitality
- job security
- Labor Government
- lack of "junky" cartoons on Saturday T.V., and lack of
  social tensions
- large undeveloped area
- less automation
- life in general
- little competition
- local slang
- medical system
- meeting country folk and people from many different lifestyles
- Melbourne is warmer than New York
- mixture of cultures (though minimal)
- money I'm making
- more honest people, more independent people, and more people inclined to help others
- more international orientation, and more equal distribution of wealth
- most things
- multinational corporations are being prevented from continuing the rape of Australia
- my college degree makes me a big fish in a small pond
  (just the opposite in the U.S.)

214

- naivete
- natural resources
- new immigrants and people from other countries
- news reports are less worrisome
- no blacks
- no sense of perpetual crisis
- nothing
- peacefulness
- people aren't phoney, have time to be genuine, think simply and use the many parks
- planned obsolescence not in Australia
- plastic society not yet in Australia
- prices
- privacy
- restaurant variety and quality
- ripe potential for industrial development
- safety
- sailing
- saloons
- school uniforms
- seeing the "Outback"
- sense of equality and unity
- "she'll be right" attitude
- shooting
- short pub hours
- size of Australia
- skiing
- small parks and gardens
- smaller population makes things more personal
- standard of living
- sun shines most of the time
- suburban public parks and shopping center provisions for caring for pre-school children
- Sydney Harbor and the Sydney Morning-Herald
- Sydney's scenery, variety of entertainment and recreation activities
- symphonies
- they speak English
- tolerance of eccentrics and migrants
- turning Australians on to an American accent
- very, very few billboards
- "village" atmosphere even in larger cities
- "White Australia" policy
- you can be yourself

ADDITIONAL "DISLIKES" ABOUT AUSTRALIA INDICATED
BY MIGRANTS SURVEYED

- absence in most stores of free bags in which to put one's purchase(s)
- affluence
- American Ambassador Marshall Green (now-former Ambassador)
- Americans who find fault with Australia and constantly say it's better at home
- anti-American faction among British
- anti-competition laws
- apathy toward politics
- Aussies
- Aussie men
- Aussie women
- Australia doesn't know where it wants to go or how to find out, is not progressive and still has growing pains
- Australian sports don't interest me
- Australia's American image
- avoidable flooding
- bigotry
- "boom" attitude which drives Australians to build regardless of the environmental impact
- canning techniques
- can't find a place to get a good drink, meet people and talk
- climate
- Communist-dominated unions
- complacency
- compulsory unionism and voting
- consumption of too much beer and too many pills
- crime problem
- crowded cities
- delays in getting repairs, supplies and deliveries when promised
- dependence on American military protection and political good will
- dislike of the U.S.
- driving on the left
- drug abuse, beatings and pupil drunkenness in the schools
- dull political life
- east coast becoming too crowded
- elitism

- everything
- excessive drinking
- form of government
- general lack of guts
- general working conditions
- "give way to the right" traffic rules even on main streets
- government interference in business, i.e., "fair go"
- government irresponsibility and corruption
- growing materialism
- having to commute downtown
- heat
- high incidence of gambling and pornography on newstands and T.V.
- hospital system
- hot Christmases and lack of spirit
- impossibility of communicating with Aussies
- inaction on social issues
- inconveniences
- inferiority complex of Aussies
- intolerance
- introduction of colored migrants
- irresponsibility
- isolation
- Labor Government not very encouraging toward independent business
- Labor Government policies
- lack of: ambition and aspirations, choice among consumer products, emphasis on general knowledge in the universities, facilities in some restaurants to wash one's hands before eating, "frills" (air-conditioning, frozen foods, wash and wear clothes, etc.), independence (imitation of other cultures), individuality, interesting people, involvement in life, proper teaching conditions, road courtesy, social awareness and warmth in the people
- life is not as exciting in Australia
- limited opportunities for migrants with only foreign qualifications
- little bulk food, bush gear and good quality medium-priced clothes
- living on the edge of desert wastelands
- lousy Mexican restaurants
- low pay for the working class
- low value of the American dollar
- monopoly of big business
- most Australians prefer to have someone tell them what to do
- movie theatres' commercials and paternalism
- multinational corporations are still destroying much of Australia's progress

- narrowmindedness
- no buildings built specifically for medical practitioners so starting a private practice can be expensive
- no Dr. Pepper or U.S. sports information, no girls (small town), no Hershey's syrup, no mail order houses, no police where I am, and no popcorn at theatres
- not being able to bring my dog
- not enough concern for individual rights and freedom
- old-fashioned baby clothes and English rule
- overdependence on government and other authorities
- overly quick Americanization of Australia--shallow values of materialism and consumerism, among others
- pace of life faster where I'm living than where I was from in the U.S.
- parochialism
- perpetuation of old, inherited traditions which seem grotesque
- plagiarism is a way of life
- politics
- poor food at milk bars
- postal service
- price-fixing and lack of competition at retail level
- public education
- race and age discrimination
- racism
- reactionary thinking
- relaxation of immigration laws
- reserved people
- ridiculous divorce laws
- "screw you, Jack; I'm alright" attitude
- second-class meat in the butcher shops
- short department store hours
- shortages of everything
- small thinking
- sometimes the Yankee sense of competition is frustrated
- stupid and inept politicians in both parties
- stupid liquor control laws
- suspicion by Aussies concerning intellectual development
- Sydney is too fast
- telephones (government-run, long delays in installation, expensive and poor service)
- too many British attitudes among lower classes
- too many pubs
- too much drinking, static on Voice of America transmission and too much talk and no action
- too willing acceptance of inadequacies in daily living
- transportation systems
- treatment of Aborigines
- unfriendly people

- unsafe working conditions
- untruthful workers
- urban sprawl
- weak government
- Yanks and Poms (British) own the country

APPENDIX XVII

AUSTRALIAN AND AMERICAN COMPARATIVE STATISTICS

Statistical Headings	Australia	United States
Religion	Anglican - 36% Roman Catholic - 31%	Protestant - 34% Roman Catholic - 23%
Population Distribution	urban - 85.6%	urban - 74%
Ethnic Composition	Aborigines - approx. 200,000 (including mixed-bloods)	blacks - 11%
Per Capita Income	$5,880 (1974)	$5,834 (1975)
Average Weekly Wage	adult male - $219*	factory worker - about $183.10
Vital Statistics	birth rate - 17.1/ 1000 population death rate - 9.0/ 1000 population	birth rate - 14.2/ 1000 population death rate - 9.3/ 1000 population
Life Expectancy	71 years	72 years
Health Statistics	inhabitants per hospital bed - 80 people per physician - 600	inhabitants per hospital bed - 138 people per physician - 621
Infant Mortality	16.6/1000 births	17.6/1000 births

*The average weekly Australian male earnings as of Sept. 30, 1976 was $A184.70, which in terms of the revalued exchange of Dec. 7, 1976 is equivalent to $US192.08.

SOURCE: Sylvia Westerman and Martin A. Bacheller, eds.,

The CBS News Almanac, 1977 (Maplewood, N.J.: Hammond Almanac, Inc., 1976), pp. 471, 643.

APPENDIX XVIII

MALE MIGRANT INTERVIEWEES DISSATISFIED WITH THEIR PRESENT EMPLOYMENT

Age and Marital[a] Status	Last Employment and Earnings in U.S.A. (in $US)	Present Employment and Earnings in Australia (in $A)	Comments
53M0	packaging sales mana- ger (30,000)	general manager, plastics firm (8,900)	obsolete and inefficient methods
26M2	U.S. Air Force Tech. Sargeant (7,000)	technician (3,900)	few prospects
25M0	electronic technician (8,000)	electronic technician (4,000)	low earnings
32M0	rehabilitation director (10,000)	hospital rehabilitation officer (5,400)	employ, conditions unfavourable
34M1	engineer's assistant (9,000)	stores superintendent (5,200)	low earnings and limited prospects
26S	U.S. Army	accounts clerk (3,500)	low earnings
25S	U.S. Navy (8,300)	stockbroker's clerk (4,500)	came with parents
30S	sales representative, chemicals (20,000)	advertising manager (5,000)	low earnings
26S	family's roofing business (5,100)	employee roofing worker (2,500)	low earnings
25S	U.S. Air Force N.C.O.	Telecommunications Techni- cian (3,400)	low earnings

^{a}M = married; S = single.

In the case of married persons, the following number indicates the number of dependent children.

223

APPENDIX XIX

MALE MIGRANT INTERVIEWEES SATISFIED WITH THEIR PRESENT EMPLOYMENT

Age and Marital Status[a]	Last Employment and Earnings in U.S.A. (in $US)	Present Employment and Earnings in Australia (in $A)	Comments
26M0	computer engineer (11,000)	electronic engineer (8,000)	arranged in U.S.A.
31M0	engineering draftsman (8,000)	own engineering business (7,000)	had capital
38M3	sales representative (5,000)	store manager (4,200)	
30M1	civil engineer (12,500)	civil engineer (8,000)	
25M0	bank clerk (7,200)	office clerk (3,650)	
27M0	teacher (6,000)	teacher (3,900)	fewer prospects here
35M2	air traffic controller (15,000)	restaurateur (5,200)	bought business
25M1	sales representative (9,000)	trainee computer salesman (5,000)	
43M2	bank research manager (20,000)	bank automation manager (13,000)	arranged from U.S.A.
29M0	professional actor (7,000)	youth theatre director (4,000)	1-year contract
33M1	advertising salesman (10,000)	advertising salesman (5,000)	
23M0	recent business graduate	auditor (5,000)	through L & NS

APPENDIX XIX--continued

Age and Marital Status[a]	Last Employment and Earnings in U.S.A. (in $US)	Present Employment and Earnings in Australia (in $A)	Comments
37M5	own car repair business (14,000)	manager car repair firm (7,000)	critical of local technology
29M3	construction plumber (13,500)	building plumber (4,500)	but worse prospects
40M2	toolmaker (8,500)	foreman, air conditioning firm (5,200)	inferior fringe benefits
47M5	university lecturer (16,000)	university lecturer (10,000)	applied from U.S.A.
25S	engineering student	engineering draftsman (5,400)	previous visit
22S	engineering student	production supervisor (5,500)	parents in Australia

SOURCE: Surveys Section, Department of Immigration, Survey of U.S. American Settlers, Phase Two (Canberra: Department of Immigration, 1971), p. 74.

[a]M = married; S = single.

In the case of married persons, the following number indicates the number of dependent children.

APPENDIX XX

ADDITIONAL OPINIONS REGARDING THE FUTURE OF AUSTRALIA STATED BY MIGRANTS SURVEYED

- apathy
- as the population increases, so will the problems but at a slower rate than elsewhere
- bad because of strikes, unions and socialized government
- better if they get better politicians, for the ones now are not very corrupt, but they are inept
- better once they dump England and the Queen
- can only get better
- Communism may not be far away--repeat of Cuba
- constant improvement till population pressure becomes too great
- continued high standard of living
- degeneration of society
- dependent on the U.S. (because so many American companies and dollars are in Australia)
- depends on cut in income tax rate
- depends on world economic conditions, government policies, etc.
- diminishing (like everywhere else)
- depression--like the U.S.
- dire need for pollution controls, consumer protection and other controls (littering is the worst I've experienced)
- energy crisis
- ethnic pattern changing
- "expletive"
- fairly good re safety and pollution
- forced into a welfare state
- getting better if possible
- good for family life, if not too many migrants come, or if the Australians can overcome the emphasis on government, royalty, colonial ties and conservation
- government systems here are and always will be totally un-
- able and unwilling to cope
- great potential if workers don't ruin things by asking for more money and less work
- growing
- growing middle class
- growing suburbia
- happy and peaceful society
- hard but good
- immigrants will improve Australia in two generations
- improved if avoid problems of other nations, if control

226

cost of living and inflation, if take in more migrants
or if trade unions become no more powerful and taxes
are reformed
- improved standard of living
- improvement in some areas and disintegration in others
- in ten years Sydney will be as dirty as New York or Los
Angeles
- in the last of the frontiers it will be up to the individual to succeed
- increased influence in world politics
- increased taxes
- increasing population could provide public revenues necessary for growth and improvement of public programs
- inflation
- isolation could make Australia self-sufficient
- labor will offer a socialist mess, but the Liberal-
National Country coalition will offer a chance for a
progressive, democratic, capitalistic state
- lack of general high-level education will hamper
- less productivity
- little change
- middle class will become the poor class
- moral decline
- more big business with impersonal service and attitudes
- more competition, conservation, crime and violence, open-
minded people and more self-centered
- more of the same (poverty, ignorance, exploitation, monopoly and bureaucracy)
- not promising for business
- not so good regarding economics and standard of living
- pleasant culturally and people-wise, but pressure of
American lifestyle is growing
- plenty of time to enjoy life
- poor because there is no foresight
- pretty easy and uncomplicated
- prices will continue to rise because of too-powerful
unions
- rat race coming
- really great if people expose exploitation and get tough
on criminals
- she'll be right, mate!
- shortages will get worse
- shorter work hours
- should take two, maybe three, generations to ruin
- socialism will strangle economic freedoms even more than
the present strangulation
- static
- still very roomy but accelerating pace
- super increase in population

227

- tighter money
- too many exports leaving little for Aussies
- trouble
- urban areas will face problems like the U.S. (inadequate
  public transport, pollution, poor city planning, spiral-
  ing land prices and industrial unrest)
- violent conflict like Ireland within ten years
- will avoid energy crisis and economic collapse, be a nation to reckon with, become one of the most powerful
  nations if it uses its natural resources
  populated like the U.S. considering Australia's resources, continue as a classless society which is a quality
  of life, improve because it's fairly unsettled, oust the
  Australian Labor Party from power and revert to Victori-
  anism and a nineteenth century emphasis on oligarchical
  government, rank in the top five nations re standard of
  living and will struggle within an Asian political context
- worse for urban areas, better for rural areas
- worse if productivity continues to decline

APPENDIX XXI

ADDITIONAL OPINIONS REGARDING THE COMPARATIVE
FUTURES OF THE UNITED STATES AND AUSTRALIA
STATED BY MIGRANTS SURVEYED

I.   The future of Australia will be better

- abundant agricultural production, western demand for
  Australian exports and an educated and homogeneous population
- crackdown on crime when it becomes bad, less corruption
  in government, less racial tensions, not as amoral as
  the U.S. and better opportunities for jobs for children
  when grown
- develop neutral policy with other nations
- doesn't have to act as a big brother to the rest of the
  world
- due to increased awareness of need for conservation
- excellent and varied food which is cheap, and the rich
  actually pay taxes here
- fewer people, therefore less pollution and less city crowding and resulting crime
- fresher
- government is more receptive to public pressure and population is small
- has more latitude in concentrating on social problems, and
  the remedies are easier and less costly
- hasn't had to go through all the trials the U.S. has
- if Australia will become more aware of what unplanned and
  rampant industrialization is doing to the nation and
  controls it, change from the "English" system, control
  the government's attitude toward socialism, control immigration, get better politicians because the ones they
  have are not very corrupt but are inept, get Labor out,
  get more people, give individual citizens top priority,
  keep American influence out, or overcome its insecurity
  and dependence
- in the long-term quality of life (small population, mineral
  wealth, etc.)
- less violence oriented and less violence
- materially
- medical and dental care cheaper
- moral standards, being British, are higher
- more room for expansion, while the U.S. is at its peak
- more space in which to move around
- no racial problems

229

- not a world power and doesn't want to be
- not large enough to have the responsibility of a super-power
- not so extreme--U.S. media (T.V.) is plain crazy today
- people still have faith in government
- politicians aren't corrupt
- pureness of air and uncomplicated way of life
- regarding ecology and socialism
- seems to stay incredibly beautiful
- self-sufficient in food
- smaller and slower cars, so slower pace all around
- socialist approach to national problems
- socially and recreationally
- society not so complex
- strong industrial base
- the U.S. has too many irresponsible people living on the efforts of the responsible
- though Australia has inflation, it has lower unemployment, and though Australia is not as interesting or vital as the U.S., the former will be less materialistic
- till 1976 when Australia will get a new government
- unpolluted outside the major cities
- with a low population and abundant natural resources, there will be more work available and income earned over a longer period

II. The future of the two nations will be similar

- as the U.S. goes, so goes the world
- Australia has a future which could be as good (if it lets industry develop) but never better than that of the U.S.
- Australia hasn't learned much from America's mistakes and just wants to imitate the U.S.
- Australia is following in the footsteps of the U.S.
- Australia picks the worst elements of American society to imitate rather than the conservative
- for the short term (twenty to thirty years)
- we all rise or fall together

III. The future of Australia will be worse

- Australia wants to be another U.S., but they haven't got the brains here
- can't accept new ideas
- cost of living, inflation rate and taxes higher; wages and salaries lower; Labor encourages strikes and social welfare schemes mean more repressive taxes while they take away productivity incentive
- does not learn from others' mistakes

230

- economically
- for middle and lower classes once Watergate's over and Congress gets busy
- getting materialistic and developing many problems America has (crime, pollution, etc.)
- illiterate population and easily swayed by politicians
- in the short term, socialism
- Labor has stifled private initiative
- land is too inhospitable; English form of schooling leaves one-half the population undereducated and the unions cause havoc
- poor pensions if you can qualify for one, and nationalization
- professionally
- public service is too big
- regarding cultural developments in general, human relations and "real" living or the quality of life
- school-leaving age is fifteen, so Australia is producing a bunch of functional illiterates who depend on migrants for brains and work and the migrant stream is slowing
- spiritually
- U.S. has a better type of government and maintains ideals of individual rights and freedom and steers clear of socialism
- whatever else is wrong with America, the American system always has recourse for the individual built in. The Australian system does not

IV. Other comments regarding which nation's future will be better

- Australia's future is less predictable than that of the U.S.
- hard to say

SOURCES CONSULTED*

I. Books

Aitchison, Ray. *Americans in Australia.* New York: Charles Scribner's Sons, 1972.

Aitchison, Ray. *Thanks to the Yanks.* Melbourne: Sun Books, 1972.

Aitken, Jonathan. *Australia: Land of Fortune.* New York: Atheneum Publishers, 1971.

Appleyard, R. T. *British Emigration to Australia.* Canberra: The Australian National University Press, 1964.

Arndt, H. W. *A Small Rich Industrial Country.* Melbourne: F. W. Cheshire Pty., Ltd., 1968.

The Australian Institute of Political Science. *How Many Australians? Immigration and Growth.* Sydney: Angus & Robertson, 1971.

Birch, Charles. *Confronting the Future.* Victoria, Australia: Penguin Books, 1975.

Borrie, W. D. *Immigration: Australia's Problems and Prospects.* Sydney: Angus & Robertson, 1949.

Bouscaren, A. T. *International Migration Since 1945.* New York: Frederick A. Praeger, 1963.

Casewit, Curtis. *Overseas Jobs: The Ten Best Countries.* New York: Warner Books, Inc., 1972.

Chandrasekhar, S. *Asia's Population Problems.* London: Allen & Unwin, 1967.

Clark, Anne. *Australian Adventure.* Austin: University of Texas Press, 1969.

---

*Though many additional works on Australia have been consulted by the author, only those consulted which pertained directly, at least in part, to the material covered in this book have been listed here.

232

Clark, Linda. Know Your Nutrition. New Canaan, Conn.:
    Keats Publishing, Inc., 1973.

Clark, Manning. A Short History of Australia. New York:
    New American Library, 1963.

Encel, Sol. A Changing Australia. Sydney: The Austra-
    lian Broadcasting Commission, 1971.

Europa Publications. The Far East and Australasia, 1975-
    76. London: Europa Publications Ltd., 1975.

Fabun, Don. Australia 2000! New York: The Free Press,
    1974.

Faulk, Laura, and Faulk, Odie. The Australian Alterna-
    tive. New Rochelle, New York: Arlington House Pub-
    lishers, 1975.

Gelber, H. G. The Australian-American Alliance. Glou-
    cester, Massachusetts: Peter Smith, 1968.

Goodman, Robert, and Johnston, George. The Australians.
    Adelaide: Rigby Ltd., 1966.

Greenway, John. Australia: The Last Frontier. New York:
    Dodd, Mead, & Company, 1972.

Greenwood, Gordon, and Harper, Norman, eds. Australia in
    World Affairs 1956-1960. Melbourne: F. W. Cheshire
    Pty., Ltd., 1963.

Gunther, John. Inside Australia. Completed and edited
    by William H. Forbis. New York: Harper & Row,
    Publishers, 1972.

Helmericks, Constance. Australian Adventure. Englewood
    Cliffs, New Jersey: Prentice-Hall, Inc., 1971.

The Herald & Weekly Times. Wonderful Australia in Pic-
    tures. Melbourne: Colorgravure Publishers, 1953.

Hopkins, Robert. I've Had It. New York: Holt, Rinehart &
    Winston, 1972.

Horne, Donald. The Australian People. Sydney: Angus &
    Robertson, 1972.

233

Horne, Donald. The Lucky Country: Australia Today.
Baltimore: Penguin Books, Inc., 1965.

Huxley, Elspeth. Their Shining Eldorado. New York:
William Morrow & Company, Inc., 1967.

The Immigration Reform Group. Immigration; Control or
Colour Bar? Melbourne: Melbourne University Press,
1962.

Institute of Life Insurance. TAP Report, 12. New York:
Institute of Life Insurance, 1975.

Jenkins, Thomas. We Came to Australia. London: Constable and Company, Ltd., 1969.

Jupp, James. Arrivals and Departures. Melbourne: Lansdowne Press Pty., Ltd., 1966.

Linkletter, Art. Linkletter Down Under. Englewood
Cliffs, New Jersey: Prentice-Hall, Inc., 1968.

London, Herbert. Non-White Immigration and the White
Australia Policy. New York: New York University
Press, 1970.

McGregor, Craig. Profile of Australia. Ringwood, Victoria: Penguin Books, 1968.

McKnight, Thomas. Australia's Corner of the World. Englewood Cliffs, New Jersey: Prentice-Hall, Inc., 1970.

McLaren, John, ed. Towards a New Australia. Melbourne:
Cheshire Publishing Pty., Ltd., 1972.

Millar, T. B. Australia's Foreign Policy. Sydney: Angus
and Robertson, 1968.

Miller, J. D. B. Australia. New York: Walker and Co.,
1966.

Moffat, Reggie, and Tannen, Peter. Australia. . .What's
It Really Like? Orlando, Florida: Southern Cross
Publications, 1971.

Moffitt, Ian. The U-Jack Society. Dee Why West, New
South Wales: Ure Smith Pty., Ltd., 1972.

Monaghan, Jay. Australians and the Gold Rush. Berkeley

and Los Angeles: University of California Press, 1966.

Natural Resources Defense Council. Your Dollars and
Environmental Sense. New York: Natural Resources
Defense Council, Inc., 1975.

O'Brien, Eris. The Foundation of Australia. Sydney:
Angus & Robertson, 1950.

Organization for Economic Cooperation and Development.
O.E.C.D. Economic Surveys: Australia, December, 1972.
Paris: Organization for Economic Cooperation and Dev-
elopment, 1973.

Organization for Economic Cooperation and Development.
Revenue Statistics of O.E.C.D. Member Countries, 1965-
1971. Paris: Organization for Economic Cooperation
and Development, 1973.

Pagram, Edward. Never Had It So Good. Melbourne: William Heinemann, Ltd., 1968.

Potter, David. People of Plenty. Chicago: University
of Chicago Press, 1954.

Preston, Richard, ed. Contemporary Australia. Durham,
N.C.:Duke University Press, 1969.

Price, C. A. Australian Immigration, No. 2. Canberra:
The Australian National University Press, 1970.

Reese, Trevor. Australia in the 20th Century. New York:
Praeger Publishers, 1964.

Reese, Trevor. Australia, New Zealand, and the United
States, 1941-1968. Fair Lawn, New Jersey: Oxford
University Press, 1969.

Ronaldson, K. F., and Trimble, K. R. The Economic Scene,
an Australian Perspective. New York: John Wiley &
Sons Australasia Pty., Ltd., 1969.

Shaw, A. G., and Nicholson, H. O. Australia in the Twentieth Century. Sydney: Angus & Robertson, 1968.

Shaw, A. G. L. Convicts and the Colonies. London: Faber
and Faber Ltd., 1966.

Sherman, Ray A. Australia for North Americans. Sydney:

R. A. and J. R. Sherman Pty. Ltd., 1975.

Simpson, Colin. The New Australia. Sydney: Angus &
Robertson, 1972.

Spate, O. K. Australia. New York: Praeger Publishers,
1968.

Spengler, Oswald. Decline of the West. Vol. II. New
York: Alfred A. Knopf, Inc., 1945.

Stoller, Alan. New Faces. Melbourne: F. W. Cheshire
Pty.. Ltd., 1966.

Ward, Russel. Australia. Englewood Cliffs, New Jersey:
Prentice-Hall, Inc., 1965.

Ward, Russel. Australia: a Short History. Sydney: Ure
Smith, 1975.

Westerman, Sylvia, and Bacheller, Martin A., eds. The CBS
News Almanac, 1977. Maplewood, New Jersey: Hammond
Almanac, Inc., 1976.

Williams, Henry. Australia - What Is It? Adelaide: Rigby
Limited, 1971.

Yeomans, John. The Scarce Australians. London: Longmans
Publishing Company, 1967.

Younger, R. M. Australia and the Australians. New York:
Humanities Press, Inc., 1970.

Zubrzycki, Jerzy. Immigrants in Australia. Melbourne:
Melbourne University Press, 1960.

Zubrzycki, Jerzy. Immigrants in Australia: Statistical
Supplement. Canberra: The Australian National University Press, 1960.

II. Australian Government Sources

Australian Information Service. "News in Brief: Population." Australia Bulletin, No. 1 (June 1, 1976), p. 6.

Australian News & Information Bureau. Australia, an
Economic and Investment Reference. Canberra: Australian Government Publishing Service, 1961.

236

Australian News & Information Bureau. Australian Hand-
book. Canberra: Australian Government Publishing
Service, 1970.

Australian News & Information Bureau. "Postwar Reconstruction." Australian News Release. New York:
Australian News & Information Bureau, May 30, 1945.

Committee on Social Patterns of the Immigration Advisory
Council. Inquiry into the Departure of Settlers from
Australia, Final Report. Canberra: Australian Gov-
ernment Publishing Service, 1973.

Commonwealth of Australia. The Fourth Part of the World:
An Exhibition Concerning the Discovery, Settlement and
Exploration of the Continent of Australia. Canberra:
Australian Government Publishing Service, 1976.

Commonwealth Bureau of Census & Statistics, Demography
Bulletin, No. 83. Canberra: Australian Government
Publishing Service, 1965.

Commonwealth Bureau of Census & Statistics, Demography
Bulletin, No. 85. Canberra: Australian Government
Publishing Service, 1967-1968.

Commonwealth Bureau of Census & Statistics. Official
Year Book of the Commonwealth of Australia, No. 31.
Canberra: L. F. Johnston, Commonwealth Government
Printer, 1938.

Commonwealth Bureau of Census & Statistics. Yearbook, No.
57. Canberra: Australian Government Publishing Service, 1971.

Department of Immigration. Australia and Immigration--A
Review of Migration to Australia Especially Since World
War II, revised. Canberra: Department of Immigration,
January, 1974.

Department of Immigration. Australian Immigration, Consolidated Statistics. Canberra: Australian Government
Publishing Service, 1971.

Department of Immigration. Professional Opportunities in
Australia. Canberra: Australian Government Publishing
Service, 1966.

Department of Immigration, Surveys Section. Survey of U.S.

237

U.S. American Settlers, Phase Two. Canberra:
Department of Immigration, 1971.

Department of Labor and Immigration. Australian Immigra-
tion: Quarterly Statistical Summary, III, No. 29.
Canberra: Australian Government Publishing Service,
December, 1973.

Department of Labor and Immigration. Australian Immigra-
tion: Quarterly Statistical Summary, III, No. 30.
Canberra: Australian Government Publishing Service,
June, 1974.

Government of Australia. Australia, July, 1971. Canberra: Australian Government Publishing Service, 1971.

Letters from the Department of Immigration and Ethnic
Affairs, April 28 and June 16, 1976.

III. United Nations Sources

United Nations, Demographic Yearbook. New York: United
Nations Printing Office, 1948, 1951, 1954, 1957, 1959.

IV. United States Government Sources*

U.S. Congress. Senate. Address by Australian Prime Minister, Robert Menzies. 81st Cong., 2nd sess., Aug. 1,
1950, Congressional Record, IVC, 11455-56.

U.S. Congress. House. Hon. Roy O. Woodruff's reference
to Morley Cassidy's article in the Washington Star, the
issue of January 16, 1950. 81st Cong., 2nd sess.,
January 17, 1950, Congressional Record, IVC, Appendix,
A 313-15.

U.S. Congress. House. Hon. Thomas S. Gordon's reference
to "The Australian Immigrant Aims at a Sitting Duck,"
from the Washington Daily News, article by R. C. Ruark.
81st Cong., 2nd sess., January 20, 1950, Congressional
Record, IVC, A 454.

U.S. Congress. Senate. Message by President Dwight D.
Eisenhower. 83rd Cong., 1st sess., June 3, 1953,

---

*Congressional Record sources are listed in chronological order.

238

Congressional Record, IC, 5943.

U.S. Congress. House. Address by Australian Prime Minister, Robert Menzies. 84th Cong., 1st sess., March 16, 1955, Congressional Record, CI, 3069.

U.S. Congress. Senate. Report by Senator Allen Ellender concerning U.S. Programs Abroad. 85th Cong., 1st sess., February 7, 1957, Congressional Record, CIII, 1691.

U.S. Congress. Senate. Senator Jacob Javits speaking on the occasion of a lady Australian Senator's visit to Congress. 86th Cong., 2nd sess., February 1, 1960, Congressional Record, CVI, 1667.

U.S. Congress. House. Hon. J. J. Pickle's reference to Ambassador to Australia Ed Clark's arrival speech on his return to the U.S. on January 23, 1966. 89th Cong., 2nd sess., February 9, 1966, Congressional Record, CXII, Appendix, A 642-43.

U.S. Congress. House. Hon. Ralph Yarborough presents article on Ambassador Ed Clark in The Houston Chronicle. 89th Cong., 2nd sess., March 22, 1966, Congressional Record, CXII, Appendix, A 1629.

U.S. Congress. House. Reproduction of Ambassador Ed Clark's address to the San Augustine, Texas, Lion's Club on June 2, 1966. 89th Cong., 2nd sess., June 14, 1966, Congressional Record, CXII, Appendix, A 3200.

U.S. Congress. House. Speech by Hon. Jack Brooks on June 14, 1966, referring to a speech by Ambassador Ed Clark. 89th Cong., 2nd sess., June 14, 1966, Congressional Record, CXII, Appendix, A 3204.

U.S. Congress. House. Hon. J. J. Pickle presents article by Stan Stephens. 89th Cong., 2nd sess., September 14, 1966, Congressional Record, CXII, Appendix, A 4813.

U.S. Congress. House. Hon. T. R. Kupferman remarks on "American Managers as Australians See Them." 89th Cong., 2nd sess., October 19, 1966, Congressional Record, CXII, Appendix, A 5410.

U.S. Congress. Senate. Record of Ambassador Ed Clark's address to the American-Australian Association in New York on April 25, 1967. 90th Cong., 1st sess., May 24,

1967, Congressional Record, CXIII, 13771.

U.S. Congress. Senate. Record of Ambassador Ed Clark's
address to the Young Country Party Convention at
Caloundra, Queensland, on May 14, 1967. 90th Cong.,
1st sess., August 30, 1967, Congressional Record,
CXIII, 24706.

U.S. Congress. House. Hon. J. J. Pickle presents the
address of Mrs. Ed Clark to the Australian-American
Association in Melbourne on November 21, 1967, and an
excerpt from the Sydney Daily Telegraph on November 17,
1967, regarding Ambassador Ed Clark. 90th Cong., 1st
sess., December 11, 1967, Congressional Record, CXIII,
35914-15.

U.S. Congress. House. Record of American Ambassador to
Australia W. H. Crook's speech to the Australian
National Press Club, March 28, 1969. 91st Cong., 1st
sess., April 24, 1969, Congressional Record, CXV,
10331-33.

U.S. Congress. House. Letter from Hon. W. L. Clay to a
Mr. Saul Cupp on November 5, 1969. 91st Cong., 1st
sess., November 17, 1969, Congressional Record, CXV,
34484.

U.S. Congress. House. Reproduction of an article from the
Western Livestock Reporter by C. E. Schenkenberger. 91st
Cong., 2nd sess., June 25, 1970, Congressional Record,
CXVI, 21607.

U.S. Congress. Senate. Sen. William Proxmire presents the
article, "The Australian Economy Today," by W. A. Eltis.
92nd Cong., 1st sess., November 29, 1971, Congressional
Record, CXVII, 43273-76.

U.S. Congress. Senate. Address by Hon. Sir Reginald Sholl
on "Law and Order--American or Australian Model?" to the
Philadelphia Bar Association. 92nd Cong., 2nd sess.,
January 26, 1972, Congressional Record, CXVIII, 1332.

U.S. Congress. Senate. Visit to the Senate by Senator
Lionel Murphy of Australia. 93rd Cong., 1st sess.,
January 29, 1973, Congressional Record, CXIX, 2377.

U.S. Congress. Senate. Senator J. William Fulbright presents article, "Why Hackworth Went to Australia." 93rd
Cong., 1st sess., February 22, 1973, Congressional

240

Record, CXIX, 5191

U.S. Department of Commerce. American Firms, Subsidiaries, and Affiliates in Australia. Washington, D.C.:
U.S. Government Printing Office, 1962.

U.S. Department of Commerce. Economic Trends and Their
Implications for the United States--Australia. Wash-
ington, D.C.: U.S. Government Printing Office,
September 1, 1968. 10 pp.

U.S. Department of Commerce. Economic Trends and Their
Implications for the United States--Australia. Washington, D.C.: U.S. Government Printing Office, 1969.

U.S. Department of Commerce. Investment in Australia.
Washington, D.C.: U.S. Government Printing Office,
February, 1957.

U.S. Department of Commerce. "Living Costs and Conditions
in Australia." World Trade Information Service Report.
Washington, D.C.: U.S. Government Printing Office,
November 27, 1956.

U.S. Department of Commerce, Bureau of the Census. Statistical Abstract of the United States, 1975. Washington, D.C.: U.S. Government Printing Office, 1975.

U.S. Department of Commerce, Bureau of International Commerce. Foreign Economic Trends. Washington, D.C.:
U.S. Government Printing Office, March, 1972. 11 pp.

U.S. Department of State. Indexes of Living Abroad and
Living Quarters Allowances. Washington, D.C.: U.S.
Department of Labor, Bureau of Labor Statistics, Office
of Publications, July, 1973, April, 1975.

U.S. Department of State. Labor Developments Abroad.
Washington, D.C.: U.S. Department of Labor, Bureau of
Labor Statistics, Office of Publications, July, 1967,
January, 1968, October, 1970, January, 1972.

U.S. President. A Report to The Congress by President
Richard M. Nixon. U.S. Foreign Policy for the 1970s:
A New Strategy for Peace. February 18, 1970, 160 pp.

V. Australian Booklets, Journals, Articles, Essays, Papers
and Proceedings

Australian-American News. Sydney: The Australian-American Association, September, 1972. 104 pp.

Burnett, Ron. "The Jungle Ranch." Australia Now, May,
1971, pp. 23-25.

Burnley, I. H. "Immigrants in Australian Cities." Australian Quarterly, XIIL (December, 1971):57-69.

Costigan, Peter. "Refugee from Politics." The (Melbourne)
Sun, June 17, 1974, p. 8.

DuBose, Martha. "Americans Who Kept on West." Sydney
Morning-Herald, women's supplement, July 1, 1971, p. 3.

DuBose, Martha. "In Search of the New Frontier." Sydney
Morning-Herald, women's supplement, July 1, 1971, p. 1.

Graham, John. "Frontier '72." Australia Now, August,
1972, pp. 7-9.

Grant, Bruce. "The American Image in Australia." Pacific
Orbit. Edited by Norman Harper. Melbourne: F. W.
Cheshire, 1968.

"'Happiness' Is Escape from Austin Texas." The (Adelaide)
News, May 14, 1975, p. 16.

Hopkins, Frank. "The American Image of Australia." Pacific Orbit. Edited by Norman Harper. Melbourne: F. W.
Cheshire, 1968.

Horne, Donald. "Australia and Nixon--What Now?" The
Bulletin, November 23, 1968, pp. 36-40.

Hudson, W. J. "Australia's External Relations." Australian Outlook, XXV (April, 1971):69-93.

Jenkins, Thomas. "People--Heart of the Environment."
Australia Now, August, 1971, pp. 3-5.

Kaye, Ron; Keyes, Charles; Krause, Tom; and McCausland,
James. "The U.S.tralians." The Australian, Oct. 25,
1975, p. 23.

Kilby, N. C., and Kilby, V. N. Our Changing Population.
Camberwell, Victoria: Longman Australia Pty., Ltd.,
1969. 63 pp.

McGregor, Craig. "Happiness Without Guilt." Life in
    Australia. Edited by Craig McGregor. Cladesville,
    New South Wales: Golden Press Pty., Ltd., 1971.

McQueen, Humphrey. "An End to the White Australia Pol-
    icy." Australian Quarterly, VIL (March, 1972):92-102.

McRae, Mary Milne. "Yankees from King Arthur's Court: A
    Brief Study of North American Political Prisoners
    Transported from Canada to Van Dieman's Land, 1839-40."
    Tasmanian Historical Research Association, Papers and
    Proceedings, XIX, No. 4 (December, 1972):147-61.

Miller, J. D. B. "The U.S.A. and the 1980s." Australian
    Outlook, XXV (December, 1971):285-94.

The Permanent Residents' Group, American Women's Club of
    Perth, Western Australia. "For the Bread Winner."
    Newsletter from Australia, April 1, 1971, pp. 1-2.

The Permanent Residents' Group, American Women's Club of
    Perth, Western Australia. "Housing." Newsletter from
    Australia, April 1, 1971, pp. 2-3.

The Permanent Residents' Group, American Women's Club of
    Perth, Western Australia. "Money." Newsletter from
    Australia. April 1, 1971, p. 2.

The Permanent Residents' Group, American Women's Club of
    Perth, Western Australia. "So--You're Interested in
    Sunny Western Australia!" Newsletter from Australia,
    April 1, 1971, p. 1.

Potter, Sir Ian. "American Investment in Australia."
    Pacific Orbit. Edited by Norman Harper. Melbourne:
    F. W. Cheshire, 1968.

Powis, Jon. "Americans Find No Easy Way to the Top Down
    Under." National Times, March 20-25, 1972, pp. 35-36.

Randall, Kenneth. "Immigration." Australia in the Seven-
    ties. Edited by Michael Southern. Ringwood, Victoria:
    Penguin Books Ltd., 1973.

"Re-Thinking the White Australia Policy." American Quar-
    terly, XVII (September, 1945):30.

Riddell, Elizabeth. "The Americans": Part I, "Goodbye,
    Uncle Sam." Part 2, "Seeking a New West." Part 3,

"They Came, Saw, Were Conquered." Part 4, "Land at the End of a U.S. Rainbow." The Australian, August 2, 1971, p. 9; August 3, 1971, p. 11; August 4, 1971; p. 9; August 5, 1971, p. 9.

Santamaria, B. A. "Into the Seventies." Australian Outlook, XXV (August, 1971):115-31.

Serle, G. "Austerica Unlimited?" Meanjin Quarterly, No. 110, XXVI, No. 3 (March, 1967):237-49.

Smith, Ben. "Immigration Policy: A Survey of the Issues." Australian Quarterly, VIIL (June, 1971):8-15.

Tennison, Patrick. "The Accents are American." Australia Now, May, 1971, pp. 12-13.

Twain, Mark. "Australia Is as Yet Unoccupied." Australia and the United States. Edited by Norman Harper. Melbourne: Thomas Nelson (Australia) Limited, 1971.

"When Yankee Sailors First Hit Sydney." The (Melbourne) Herald, April 10, 1976, p. 29.

VI.   British Articles

Beedham, Brian. "Second to None: A Survey of Australia." The Economist, Survey, March 27, 1976, pp. 1-42.

"Consider Australia." The Economist, May 30, 1964, pp. 961-1000.

Kroef, J. M. van der. "Back to the Billabong?" Far Eastern Economic Review, LXIII (January 9, 1969):56-59.

"Wanted: More Australians." The Economist, July 6, 1968, pp. 52-53.

VII.   Swiss Articles

Geyl, W. F., Sr. "A Brief History of Australian Immigration." International Migration, I, No. 3 (1963):157-66.

"Migration Situation in Australia." Industry and Labour, 1957, pp. 80-85.

Zubrzycki, Jerzy. "Some Aspects of Structural Assimilation of Immigrants in Australia." International Migration, VI, No. 3 (1968):102-11.

VIII. United States Articles and Essays

"A Country That's Going Places." U.S. News & World
Report, December 28, 1956, pp. 65-67.

Albinski, H. S. "Australian Society." Current History,
LXII, (March, 1972):133-37, 164.

"The American 'Invasion' of Australia." Newsweek,
August 10, 1964, pp. 53-56.

"Americans on the Move." Time, March 15, 1976, pp. 54-
64.

Appleyard, R. T. "Westward the Antipodes." The California Revolution. Edited by Carey McWilliams. New
York: Grossman Publishers, Inc., 1968.

"Australia." Atlantic Monthly, November, 1950, pp. 15-
17.

"Australia as a Place to Live: the Way It Strikes Americans." U.S. News & World Report, July 1, 1968, pp. 80-
82.

"Australia: For Many, the Goal Is to Become a 'New
America'." U.S. News & World Report, October 13, 1975,
pp. 65-66.

"Australia May Allow Some Mineral Projects to Be Foreign-
Owned." Wall Street Journal, June 4, 1976, p. 11.

"Australia: Populate or Perish." Time, August 11, 1952,
p. 36+.

"Australia Seeks DP Immigrants." New York Times, Aug. 15,
1947, p. 8.

"Australia: She'll Be Right, Mate--Maybe." Time, May 24,
1971, pp. 34-38.

"Australia: Situation Vacant." Time, July 7, 1947, p.
31.

"Australia Takes a New Look--And Turns Toward the U.S."
U.S. News & World Report, April 18, 1966, pp. 74-76.

Baker, Donald. "Australia and America." The South Atlantic Quarterly, LXXI (Spring, 1972):213-24.

Bell, C. "Asian Crisis and Australian Security." The
    World Today, February, 1967, pp. 80-88.

"The Big Rise Hits Down Under." Business Week, Dec. 21,
    1963, pp. 92-93+.

Black, D. M. "Establishing a Business in Australia."
    Overseas Business Reports, No. 70-89 (December, 1970):
    22 pp.

"Booming Australia: A Nation Coming of Age." U.S. News
    & World Report, July 20, 1970, pp. 69-71.

Borrie, W. D. "Australia." Economics of International
    Migration. Edited by Brinley Thomas. New York: The
    Macmillan Company, 1958.

Borrie, W. D. "Aspects of Australian Demography." Paci-
    fic Affairs, XX, No. 1 (March, 1947):42-52.

Boyd, Harper, Jr. "Marketing Consumer Goods in Austra-
    lia." Business Horizons, Feburary, 1968, pp. 49-58.

Colless, Malcolm. "Decline Down Under: Australia, Once
    Held a Land of Opportunity, Sees Its Bubble Burst as
    Prices Rise and Jobs Vanish." Wall Street Journal,
    March 7, 1972, p. 38.

"Crime Surge Defies All Efforts, Survey of Cities Shows."
    U.S. News & World Report, June 10, 1974, pp. 34-39.

"The Crime Wave." Time, June 30, 1975, pp. 10-24.

Davies, Lawrence. "From Old World (America) to New (Aus-
    tralia)." New York Times, September 14, 1947, sec. VI,
    pp. 13, 65-66.

"Doonesbury: Drawing and Quartering for Fun and Profit."
    Time, February 9, 1976, pp. 57-66.

"'Down Under'--Souring Relations With an Old Ally." U.S.
    News & World Report, June 11, 1973, pp. 71-72.

Eggleston, F. W. "Australia's Immigration Policy." Paci-
    fic Affairs, XXI, No. 4 (December, 1948):372-83.

Eisenstadt, S. N. "Analysis of Patterns of Immigration
    and Absorption of Immigrants." Population Studies, VII
    (1953):167-80.

246

"Emigration of Americans Welcomed by Australian." New York Times, September 16, 1947, p. 28.

"Eucalypts in Florida." Editorial, American Forests, October, 1976, p. 15.

"First U.S. Emigrants Sail for Australia." New York Times, September 3, 1947, p. 12.

Forde, Francis. "Australia Needs People." The Rotarian, March, 1946, pp. 26-28.

Frankel, C. "The Scribblers and International Relations." Foreign Affairs, VIL (October, 1965):11.

Gordon, Harry. "Americans Are Emigrating to Australia." New York Times Magazine, May 17, 1970, pp. 75+.

"Government and Politics." Senior Scholastic, Dec. 5, 1951, p. 8.

Greenway, John. "The Austramerican West." The American West, January, 1968, pp. 33-37+.

Greenwood, Gordon. "The Australian Political Scene." Pacific Affairs, XX, No. 3 (September, 1947):276-89.

Hammond, S. B. "International Attitudes." Social Structure and Personality in a City. Edited by O. A. Oeser and S. B. Hammond. New York: The Macmillan Company, 1954.

Hartley, William. "Change Down Under." Wall Street Journal, February 8, 1973, pp. 1+.

Hickey, Neil. "Does TV Violence Affect Our Society?" TV Guide, June 14, 1975, pp. 8-17.

Holt, H. E. "The New Face of Australia." The Rotarian, April, 1956, pp. 12-14+.

Horne, Donald. "Australia Looks Around." Foreign Affairs, VIL (April, 1966):446-57.

Horne, Donald. "Lucky Australia." Holiday, September, 1966, pp. 48-63+.

Horsfall, J. C. "Australian Assets, Foreign Money." Hammond Innes Introduces Australia. Edited by Clive

Turnbull. New York: McGraw-Hill Company, 1971.

"How a Yank Reacts to the Aussies." U.S. News & World Report, January 1, 1968, p. 5.

Howatt, George. "'Berg Grad Likes the Land of Kangaroos; Differences Provide Stimulating Contrasts." Reprint from Muhlenberg News, December, 1954, 4 pp.

I. D. W. T. "Meet Two Australians." Senior Scholastic, December 5, 1951, p. 4.

"Industrial Disputes 1937-1954." The International Labour Review, LXXII (July, 1955):78-91.

"Is the 'White Australia' Policy Justified?" Senior Scholastic, December 5, 1951, p. 11.

Kann, Peter. "Boom Down Under." Wall Street Journal, February 9, 1970, pp. 1+.

Keatley, Robert. "U.S. Migrants Find Australia is Fine--if You Have Money." Wall Street Journal, March 16, 1966, pp. 1, 10.

Kirstein, G. G. "Letter from Australia." The Nation, April 15, 1961, pp. 326-29.

Koestler, Arthur. "Australia." Atlantic Monthly, June, 1969, pp. 12-24.

Kolodin, Irving. "The Mix That Goes Into Australia's Melting Pot." Saturday Review, August 7, 1971, p. 32.

Laffer, Kingsley. "The Economics of Australian Migration." Pacific Affairs, XXV, No. 4 (December, 1952): 360-77.

Lamb, David. "Australia Beckons to U.S. Teachers." Washington Post, August 4, 1974, sec. H, p. 7.

Lamb, David. "Australia's Lure for . . . American Teachers." Washington Post, July 28, 1974, sec. G, pp. 10-11.

Lamb, David. "The Final Children of the Earth, Whom Knowledge Has Not Scarred." Los Angeles Times, Feb. 3, 1975, sec. II, p. 5.

Lamb, David. "Use of Drugs Grows Rapidly in Australia." Los Angeles Times, August 18, 1974, sec. 008, pp. 1-2.

Lamb, David. "Won't Deport U.S. Deserter, Australia Says." Los Angeles Times, April 8, 1974, p. 10.

"The Land and Its People." Senior Scholastic, December 5, 1951, pp. 9, 20, 27.

Lang, Eugene. "Now Is the Time." International Commerce, May 4, 1964, pp. 21-24.

Lardner, J. "John Lardner's Australia: Cities, Jimmy-grants . . ." Newsweek, July 18, 1955, pp. 78-80.

Lee, E. S. "A Theory of Migration." Demography, III, No. 1 (1966):47-57.

Matthews, John. "Australian Appeal." Letter to the editor, Wall Street Journal, May 10, 1966, p. 18.

Mayer, K. B. "Social Stratification in Two Equalitarian Societies: Australia and the United States." Social Research, XXXI, No. 4 (Winter 1964):435-65.

Meissner, Frank. "Australia's Postwar Immigrants." American Journal of Economics and Sociology, XIX, (1959-60):169-77.

Melman, Seymour. "Getting the Biggest Bang for the Buck." New York Times, December 4, 1974, p. 43.

Missionaries of St. Charles. "Australian Migration Statistics." International Migration Digest, I, No. 2 (Fall 1964):228-30.

"Mood of America--'Where Do We Turn?'" U.S. News & World Report, October 6, 1975, pp. 12-16.

Moorehead, Alan. "Letter from Australia." The New Yorker, October 10, 1964, pp. 216-28.

"Negro Unit Assails Australia's 'Snub'." New York Times, August 17, 1947, p. 28.

"Notes and Statistics." The International Migration Review, I, No. 1 (Fall 1966):44.

Peterson, W. "A General Typology of Migration." American

249

Sociological Review, XXIII (1958):256-66.

Planned Parenthood--World Population. "When 2 + 2 = 0 .
. . The Population Problem." Reprint from National
Observer article by Edwin A. Roberts, June 28, 1971.

"Postwar Reconstruction." Monthly Labor Review, LXI
(August, 1945):257-60.

"Red Skelton on TV." Morality in the Media Newsletter,
May, 1975, p. 1.

Richardson, Alan, and Taft, Ronald. "Australian Attitudes Toward Immigration: A Review of Social Survey
Findings." The International Migration Review, II, No.
3 (1967-68):46-55.

Ritter, Ann. "Australia's Labor Problems and Policies."
Monthly Labor Review, LXXIII, No. 1 (July, 1951):26-30.

Rodale, Robert. "Can You Escape Down Under?" Organic
Gardening and Farming, XXI (March, 1974):44-49.

Schubert, Kenneth. "Yank's-Eye View of Australia." Senior
Scholastic, November 5, 1945, p. 14.

Serventy, Vincent. "Wildlife: Wonder and Delight."
Hammond Innes Introduces Australia. Edited by Clive
Turnbull. New York: McGraw-Hill Company, 1971.

Slocombe, C. "Incredible Australia." Travel, June, 1953,
pp. 5-8.

Spengler, J. J. "Effects Produced in Receiving Countries
by Pre-1939 Immigration." Economics of International
Migration. Edited by Brinley Thomas. New York: The
Macmillan Company, 1958.

"Steady Gains--but New Inflation Danger." U.S. News &
World Report, October 13, 1975, p. 19.

"The Story of the Australian People." Senior Scholastic,
November 5, 1945, pp. 4-6.

"Things Stirring 'Down Under': Australia Comes of Age."
U.S. News and World Report, June 3, 1968, pp. 98-100.

Thompson, Era. "Australia: Its White Policy and the

Negro." Part 1. Ebony, July, 1966, pp. 46-50+.

Thompson, Era. "Australia: Its White Policy and the Negro." Part 2. Ebony, September, 1966, pp. 96-106.

"Tomorrow." U.S. News & World Report, October 13, 1975, pp. 11-12.

Tregaskis, Richard. "Down Under Looks Up." Saturday Review, November 12, 1960, pp. 52-55.

Trumbull, Robert. "American Negro to Be an Aussie." New York Times, December 13, 1970, p. 19.

Trumbull, Robert. "Australia Eases Racial Barriers." New York Times, February 22, 1970, p. 24.

Trumbull, Robert. "Australia Has Second Thoughts as Immigrants Swell Population." New York Times, August 2, 1970, pp. 1, 11.

Trumbull, Robert. "More Americans Go to Australia, Seeking Simpler Life." New York Times, August 15, 1959, p. 12.

"U.S. Firms Expand Down Under." Business Week, Nov. 2, 1946, pp. 101-102.

Wecter, Dixon. "The Aussie and the Yank." Atlantic Monthly, May, 1946, pp. 52-56.

"What to Expect If You Emigrate to Australia." U.S. News & World Report, July 17, 1967, pp. 76-77.

"Why Country Music Is Suddenly Big Business." U.S. News & World Report, July 29, 1974, pp. 58-60.

Woodbury, Robert. "Industrial Disputes; Rates of Time Loss, 1927-1947." The International Labour Review, LX (November, 1949):452-66.

IX. Additional Newspaper and Magazine Sources

Adelaide News, May 14, 1975.

Australia Now, V, No. 4 (1976).

The Australian, March 25, September 26, October 1, 25, 1975.

Chicago Tribune, April 30, 1975.

The (Launceston) Examiner, February 7, 1975.

Los Angeles Times, March 18, April 8, July 21, August 18,
     October 3, November 13, December 19, 1974; February 3,
     1975.

National Times, May 5-10, 1975.

National Times Magazine, November 4, 1974.

New York Times, October 19, 1945; August 15-17, 27,
     September 3, 14, 16, 23, October 5, 1947; April 14,
     1948; March 2, July 19, December 23, 1959; March 19,
     1963; December 24, 1965; August 15, 1969; February 22,
     May 17, August 2, 23, December 13, 1970; December 22,
     1975.

(Raleigh) News and Observer, 1971-1976.

The (Adelaide) Sunday Mail, August 10, 1975.

Sydney Morning-Herald, May 9, 1975.

Sydney Sun, May 7, 1975.

Wall Street Journal, November 27, 1963; April 23, 1964;
     March 16, 22, May 10, 1966; February 9, 1970; March 7,
     July 17, 1972; March 21, 23, 1973; November 4, 1974;
     December 15, 1975.

Washington Post, April 3, May 1, July 28, August 4, 1974.

X.   Personal Correspondence with the Author

Autobiographical sketches by the following questionnaire
     respondents: Deborah Brennan, David Call, Hank Davis,
     Bill Domroe, Robert Dunn, Jr., Dashley and Nancy
     Graham, Raymond Hawes, Marilyn Johnson, Frank Justice,
     Neoma McGowan, L. G. McRae, M. S. Mochel, Salli Peter,
     Al Seaman, Anthony Welan.

CBS News. "Commentary" by Eric Sevareid, September 8,
     1975.

Letter on living conditions in and general information
     about Queensland from American Families' Association
     of Queensland, September, 1971.

Letters to the author from survey respondents and from Australians, 1969-1976.

Newsletter from Planned Parenthood Federation of America, Inc., May, 1976.

THE OLD AND THE NEW

"Dinkum Damper"

Just as the "bush ballad" has remained part of Australia's literary heritage, there is also an Australian food staple which has come to the present through grassroot heritage. It is "dinkum (true) damper." The make-do recipe used by early swaggies (drifters) for this bread consisted of simply pouring a little water into a bag of flour, mixing it to a dough, wrapping the dough in gum leaves which when peeled away left a flavor all their own, and baking it in ashes of the campfire.

Many of the drovers were able to bake an upgraded damper in camp ovens. Then pioneering Outback women updated their loaves by rubbing drippings or even butter through the flour, mixing it with milk, and baking it in a kitchen stove.

Today, of course, there are many variations on the basic recipe,* sometimes with additions of cooked fruits or grated cheese. Some cooks now make damper with margarine and full-cream powdered milk, which gives the crust a nuttiness. The loaf is usually sliced or pulled apart and pieces eaten with butter, honey, jam or (especially with fruit-added recipe) Australian's ever-favorite custard.

---

*Basic recipe: Two cups s.r. flour, 1/2 tsp. salt, 1-1/2 tbs. butter or margarine, 3/4 cup mixture milk and water. Sift together flour and salt, rub butter in with your fingertips, mix to a soft dough with the liquid. Mix well with broad-bladed knife. Knead lightly on lightly floured surface. Place on greased tray. Brush lightly with milk. Bake in very hot oven 10 minutes, reduce to hot and bake 10 minutes. Reduce to moderate and bake about 10 minutes longer or until it sounds hollow when tapped. Serves 5.

An Aussie Modern Gourmet Dish

The fame of the Adelaide (South Australia) gourmet dish, the "floater," has spread not only to other Australian states but even beyond the country's shores to New Zealand. This dish requires a hearty appetite by its consumers, for it contains a large homemade pie (meat pie), topped with tomato sauce and floated in a thick green pea soup.

DATE DUE